BLOOD & HONOR

BLOOD & HONOR

*Military Service, the Law, and
the Cost of Institutional Failure*

Nick Harrison

Columbia Heights Press
Washington, DC

Copyright © 2026 by Nick Harrison
All rights reserved.

No part of this book may be used or reproduced in any form
or by any means without written permission from the publisher,
except for brief quotations in reviews or articles.

First published in 2026 by
Columbia Heights Press, Washington, DC

ISBN 979-8-9945416-0-9 (Hardcover)
ISBN 979-8-9945416-1-6 (Paperback)
ISBN 979-8-9945416-2-3 (E-Book)

Printed in the United States of America

*This book is dedicated to the servicemembers
who society never fully accepts as equals,
but who still choose to risk their lives
to defend everyone back home,
and to the friends, families, and loved ones
who stand beside them and
share the burden throughout this ordeal.*

Author's Note

This is a memoir based on my personal experience. Memory, contemporaneous notes, and the passage of time have all shaped it. I tried to present events truthfully, but this is not a documentary record. It is a story about what I saw, what I felt, and what it meant to live through it.

To protect privacy or minimize harm, I have changed or omitted some names, titles, and identifying details. I have recreated the dialogue to the best of my recollection, and I compressed, reordered, or adapted some scenes to convey the emotional reality of what happened. A few individuals are composite characters drawn from multiple people and merged for narrative purposes.

This book includes descriptions of institutional failures, including discriminatory policies and actions within the U.S. military and government agencies. I describe misconduct or mistreatment based on my personal experiences or observations. I have taken care to tell the truth, but I recognize others may remember things differently and that memory itself can be imperfect.

To those who treated me with dignity and respect, I offer my sincere thanks. I name some people here because their example shaped me. I do not name others because this book focuses on systems, cultures, and the need for change.

The primary goal of this memoir is to give a voice to those who served their country but felt invisible within its institutions.

Chapter One

If you're going to start a story about Washington, DC, begin where the city itself was born. Not in a marble building, but on a hill above it all, where the man who designed the capital now rests beneath a weathered marble table monument.

I stood at the tomb and memorial of Pierre Charles L'Enfant, just below Arlington House, high on the Virginia side of the Potomac River. The sun hadn't fully burned off the morning haze, and the city unfolded in soft, muted layers below me. The Lincoln Memorial, Washington Monument, and Capitol stretched into the distance. The view carried the weight of its design.

L'Enfant envisioned a capital that would reflect the ambition of a young republic. Grand boulevards, sweeping sightlines, and monuments that spoke to permanence. He never saw that vision completed. Political infighting pushed him aside, and he died in obscurity. More than eight decades later, the nation reburied him here, in the city he once tried to shape, giving him a final resting place with the view he imagined.

Beneath my boots, the ground sloped gently upward toward Arlington House, the plantation mansion that once belonged to Robert E. Lee. Enslaved laborers built its colonnaded front tall and white, as if shaping a Virginia myth and placing it above the capital. A house that now overlooks the seat of American power.

The man who designed the capital is buried here in modest stone. The man who rebelled against it was memorialized in marble above him. Between them, the bones of a war that nearly broke the republic.

As I climbed the path toward the house, I thought about how this land had passed from Custis to Lee, from Washington's family to the Confederacy's highest general. When Lee chose rebellion over union, the U.S. government seized the property. Union officials ordered soldiers buried just outside the kitchen door to ensure the Lees could never return. The graves made the message clear. This ground belonged to the nation Lee betrayed and to the dead who paid for it.

The rows of white headstones began just beyond the garden walls and didn't stop for miles. Each one marked a life cut short, a chapter ended, a cost incurred. The Civil War Unknowns Monument sat behind the house, a tomb filled with the commingled remains of soldiers from both sides, their names lost but their consequences permanent.

It was 2013. I had just returned from war myself. Afghanistan, Kuwait, Iraq. Now I stood in uniform again, preparing to join the DC National Guard. That morning, the cadre brought us here before paperwork and briefings. Not for ceremony but for perspective.

I stood between L'Enfant and Lee and saw exactly what they meant for us to understand.

I began my walk back down the hill, tracing a path through ambition carved in stone.

These graves spoke less of their past than their dreams. The memorials of generals, admirals, statesmen, and strategists competed even here, rising from the earth with urgent silence.

I passed bronze equestrian statues, cavalry officers mid-charge, horses rearing atop plinths so tall they cast shadows across nearby rows. The sunlight struck their sabers and the plumes on their helmets, freezing them in a war that had long since passed.

Some graves rose as Egyptian-style obelisks, narrow and towering, tapering to the sky like stone needles. Stonecutters etched palm wreaths, military crests, and lines of text into their faces. The inscriptions were fading, unread by passersby. The monuments echoed the Washington Monument in the distance, multiplied yet diminished.

There were Baroque pediments and marble scrolls, headstones flanked by carved eagles or stylized torches. Draped obelisks stood beside Celtic crosses and sorrowful angels, their wings folded in stone, their faces locked in eternal grief. Every flourish seemed designed not to comfort the dead, but to impress the living.

The most elaborate were outright mythological: allegorical figures cast in bronze or chiseled from white marble. Liberty, victory, mourning, justice, frozen in dramatic poses atop stone columns. They were declarations, monuments to self, built on the edge of memory.

And yet I recognized almost none of the names.

They had lived large lives, commanding divisions, giving speeches, shaping battles and budgets, and now they sat in silence beneath sculptures no one really looked at anymore. Their monuments had become landscape, ornate and imposing and forgotten.

As I walked downhill, the ambition thinned. The headstones grew smaller and simpler. Then came a clean break, a quiet shift into equality. Here, accountability felt absolute in a way it rarely did among the living.

I reached the part of Arlington National Cemetery where Congress had intervened, where the graves were all the same: white marble rectangles, twenty-four inches tall, thirteen wide, four thick. No angels, obelisks, or soaring eagles, just names, ranks, faith symbols, and wars.

No man outshone the next, no grave competed.

Eternity no longer belonged to generals alone.

In that quiet, those uniform rows, the concept of service gained its purest expression. There was no grandeur here, just sacrifice, lined shoulder to shoulder, and leveled by time.

But even in uniformity, some names still carried weight.

I passed the Kennedy gravesite, the Eternal Flame burning low against the stone. Nearby stood the headstones of Thurgood Marshall,

William Rehnquist, and others, leaders not of battalions, but of laws and legacies. Their markers stood quiet and unadorned, carved with nothing more than names and dates. The work had already spoken for them.

I visited memorials dedicated to pivotal moments, not persons; the USS Maine mast, recovered from Havana Harbor, now poses an unanswered question. The Challenger Memorial, the Pan Am Flight 103 stone. Monuments to collective sorrow, standing not for individuals, but for consequences.

And then I reached the bottom.

The Tomb of the Unknown Soldier stood before us, marble still and perfect. The changing of the guard had begun, one figure moving with exacting precision, rifle at the shoulder, each step measured and deliberate. There were no orders, no announcements. Just a ritual.

A devotion to duty. To the unclaimed. To the unknowable.

They say DNA gave a name to the Unknown from Vietnam, returning him home to his family. Now one crypt stands empty while the others remain. But that emptiness doesn't diminish the meaning. If anything, it reveals what the tomb always meant. That some sacrifices are so complete they exist beyond identification.

Section 60, the resting place for most post-9/11 veterans who died fighting in Afghanistan and Iraq, lay at the path's end. Here, the Global War on Terror found its most human cost.

Uniformity returned and with it, fresh grief. Fresh graves. Fresh flowers. Coins stacked on headstones. Laminated photos, folded flags, handwritten letters sealed in plastic and tucked beneath the stone. It didn't feel like a battlefield cemetery. A recent departure lingered, hinting at a soon return for quiet mourning.

We regrouped quietly and piled back into the van. No one said much.

They dropped us at the DC Armory later that afternoon. Instructions: Return tomorrow; in-processing, assignments, and paperwork await. The official start of our time in the National Guard.

But the real beginning had already happened on the hill. Where vision, ambition, contradiction, and sacrifice converged, speaking louder in stone than words ever could.

* * *

The next morning, we returned to the DC Armory to begin in-processing. It was the official start of our drill weekend. The day before had been about perspective. This one was about paperwork.

I walked into the building and felt how big and solid it was. Construction began in 1940, and the building opened in 1941, rising like a solid block of concrete. Strong, simple, and designed to endure.

Its curved roof rose above the Washington skyline like an aircraft hangar. The building's plain design matched its mission. It served both the military and the local community as a place to gather.

I stepped inside and heard more than echoes of duty and honor. I felt the steady pulse of change, growth, and human effort. The summer heat filled the air. The building's air conditioning stayed off for the weekend. Each hallway and stairwell showed the building's long history. Over time, new sections and updates turned it into a wide maze. Every corridor reflected years of change and purpose.

Many people view the military as a symbol of discipline, unity, and bravery. It seems strong, traditional, and fixed. But people build and shape those systems. Inside, I met individuals who had goals, new ideas, and the courage to question what others accepted. Some revolutions start with loud action. Others begin with quiet conversations that lead to real and lasting change.

Our morning started in a plain classroom tucked deep inside the DC Armory's winding halls. A small group of new enlistees and I had gathered to begin the onboarding process. We were officially starting our service in the DC National Guard. Chairs, tables, and a projector screen filled the otherwise plain room. We listened to in-processing briefings and filled out paperwork.

Before we dove into the paperwork, the sergeant at the front glanced down at a clipboard and cleared his throat.

"Alright, let's go around. Just say your name, where you're coming from, and what your background is. Keep it tight — we've got a lot of ground to cover."

A few soldiers rattled off names and home states. My turn came, and I sat up straight.

"Sergeant Harrison. I'm back from deployments in Kuwait and Iraq. I'm an interstate transfer from the Oklahoma National Guard."

A recruiter glanced up from the back office.

"Oklahoma? You were with the 45th?"

I nodded.

He let out a short laugh. "Yeah, we saw a lot of you downrange. Almost thought you guys were active duty the way you rotated through."

I shrugged.

"Our brigadier general chased a second star so hard, he volunteered us for every tasking before the question even landed."

Laughter rippled through the room.

The sergeant grinned. "Yeah, that tracks. Nothing says ambition like volunteering for other people."

Though routine, these tasks began our long association with the DC National Guard.

After we finished in-processing, the recruiters took us downstairs to the drill hall, the center of the DC Armory. We entered a space that felt both immense and open. It served both as a military site and a place for community events. The floor stretched wide under a tall, curved ceiling held up by strong steel beams. It didn't feel like a hangar. It felt more like an industrial-style cathedral. The design focused on function, but the size and open space still created a sense of ceremony and respect.

Even without its usual weekday activity, the drill hall felt full of energy. Light bounced off the polished floor and lit up the space. Large bathrooms along the walls showed the hall could support sizeable crowds. Closed concession stands lined the edges, reminding us of past events. Although quiet during our visit, those stands showed the DC Armory's dual purpose. It served both the military and the local community.

The building's hallways showed the story of its past. A small museum displayed the DC National Guard's history. Thomas Jefferson signed the acts authorizing the District of Columbia Militia in 1802 to defend the federal government. That mission continues today. Unlike state militias, the DC National Guard has always played a national role. Its motto is Capital Guardians. Jefferson started the force during a time of strong political division and fear of government power. He built it to rise above partisan state militias and to protect the capital from threats at home.

As I toured the DC Armory, I couldn't help but feel the weight of that mission. Fresh from deployments to Afghanistan, Kuwait, and Iraq, the transition to defending my country within the capital felt both profound and fitting. Between tours, I had worked tirelessly to complete my JD-MBA. Now, serving in the nation's capital, I felt the full arc of that journey take shape. My experiences overseas had led me here. The education I'd pursued during the respites between them had led me here.

After the museum tour, the cadre released us for a quick lunch break. Most of us scattered to local carryout spots or sat in our cars with sandwiches, trying to process everything we'd seen that morning.

* * *

When we returned, the atmosphere had shifted. A clipboard sat upfront. Names were called individually. The cadre assigned us to our new units.

The moment I stepped inside, the uniform grew heavier. Not from the fabric, but from what it represented. My Combat Infantryman Badge and Parachutist Badge marked me as a combat veteran and airborne soldier. I met Staff Sergeant Michael McCullough in the military police company's section of the building. The room felt both practical and temporary. Mismatched government-issue furniture filled the space. Tables, chairs, desks, and wall lockers from different eras. Each piece bore quiet witness to long days of service. Bare walls and shifting personnel made it clear this was a place for duty, not decoration.

Staff Sergeant McCullough brought a warm presence to the plain, practical space around us. He was an older Black man who moved with ease and spoke with kindness. His calm posture and friendly smile made the strict military setting feel more welcoming. His uniform showed years of service, but his character made the strongest impression.

"Welcome. I'm Staff Sergeant McCullough, your squad leader. Let's make you feel at home."

His ease and the way he interacted with others showed he was a respected leader and a well-loved member of the tight-knit community. Staff Sergeant McCullough seemed to know everyone in the building.

As we moved through the corridors, he greeted each passerby with warmth and familiarity. Every few steps, we ran into someone. Another soldier, a civilian employee, or a fellow newcomer. Each time, Staff Sergeant McCullough paused with a smile and introduced me.

"This is our newest addition. He has a JD-MBA under his belt."

Each introduction brought a wave of embarrassment. The spotlight followed me through the hallways, even though I didn't want it. Staff Sergeant McCullough either didn't notice my discomfort or saw it as a chance to help.

During a moment of respite, leaning against the cool concrete wall, he turned to me, his demeanor shifting to something more serious.

"Listen. Your education and background. It's not just a piece of paper. Here, it can open doors and create paths where you once saw only walls."

I nodded, the initial embarrassment from all the introductions fading into something else. Curiosity, maybe, or reflection.

"You ever considered applying for the JAG Corps?"

I hesitated, then admitted, "I did. Back in school, I went through campus interviews and got a guaranteed commission. Army Reserve or National Guard. But then I got orders. Deployment came, and the entire process fell apart."

He nodded, like he'd seen that story before. "That happens. The timing's never perfect. But the opportunity doesn't go away unless you let it."

He looked at me squarely.

"When someone who came up enlisted earns a commission, it matters. It gives people hope. Soldiers know you've stood where they stand. You've waited in lines, slept in tents, dealt with the same nonsense. That kind of perspective doesn't come from OCS. You earn it."

I said nothing at first. I just listened.

"You don't have to do it," he said. "I've served long enough to know when someone's ready. You are."

There was no pitch, no pressure. Just a quiet invitation. Not meant to flatter, but to challenge.

He didn't bring it up because I glowed with potential or gave some impressive first impression. He brought it up because I'd come up through the ranks, and that mattered. Officers plan missions and make big decisions. NCOs handle the daily grind with soldiers. But soldiers trust and respect officers who have served in the ranks. They understand the long nights, the broken gear, the hurry-up-and-wait. When one of your own crosses over, it means something. It tells soldiers someone at the table remembers what it's like to be on the line.

That was his actual message. I could do it, and it would matter to the soldiers I led.

Staff Sergeant McCullough suggested the commission to me with a conviction that seemed to brook no argument, and it struck a chord. In the maze of corridors and amidst the hum of the DC Armory life, Staff Sergeant McCullough wasn't just guiding me through the physical space. He was opening my eyes to the possibilities that lay within the realm of service, beyond the immediate confines of the building's walls.

Chapter Two

My search for belonging in the nation's capital began as soon as I arrived. I found it in the vibrant LGBTQ+ community. Dupont celebrated both its diversity and its history, with rainbow flags hanging from nearly every storefront and residence. This was the gayborhood of Northwest DC. The community took pride in its historic row houses and lively streets, a sign of the battles it had fought to claim its place in the city. While adjusting to my new role in the National Guard, I was also settling into life in DC, having reported to my unit just days earlier. I wanted to build a life that blended military and civilian paths in a city where my personal and professional goals could come together.

As I walked through the neighborhood, the buildings' charm stood out right away. Every story I heard showed that this was a lively, changing community, not one stuck in the past. On weekends, laughter and cheers filled the air at Stead Park, where young gay men played kickball. It showed the neighborhood's fun and friendly spirit. My small budget limited my housing choices, but locals gave me a simple tip: walk the side streets and alleys. Many homeowners rented rooms or small apartments directly. That advice turned my search into an exploration through hidden spots and quiet gardens tucked away in the middle of the city.

During one of those early walks, I stumbled upon Cobalt, an iconic LGBTQ+ bar and nightclub on the corner of 17th and R Street. Housed in a historic 1896 row house with a distinctive square corner turret, Cobalt stood as a three-story beacon of inclusivity. Each floor featured bars and dance areas that drew patrons into the music and the moment. It was a landmark where people shared stories, found community, and built lasting friendships. Cobalt would eventually close, but at the time, it still thrived, pulsing with energy and possibility.

Just a stone's throw from Cobalt, I wandered down a quiet side street and turned into a narrow alley. Behind the Shehan Mansion, a Victorian-style building at the corner of 16th and R Street, I discovered a hidden gem. Tucked away in the back alley sat a small carriage house apartment above a former garage. It offered the privacy and charm I had been looking for, with its own security gate and a private alley entrance. The property belonged to a distinguished gay couple. One of them, John Berry, had led the Office of Personnel Management under President Obama and was getting ready to serve as the U.S. Ambassador to Australia.

I met his husband, Curtis Yee, during an open house for the unit. A slim Asian man with sharp eyes and a calm, collected manner, he greeted each guest with the same polished professionalism. You could tell he was listening closely, taking mental notes.

We spoke briefly outside the gate after I walked through the space. The unit was private, charming, and clearly in demand.

"We're going overseas," Curtis said. "So we're hoping to find someone willing to sign a multi-year lease."

"I just started as a Presidential Management Fellow. I've been exploring the city and trying to figure out where I fit in."

"We know the program. My husband ran OPM."

"Oh," I said. "That explains a lot."

"You've got a strong resume. Let's just say this house has attracted some impressive resumes."

Others had stood in that alleyway before me, hoping to impress.

That evening, I emailed with my resume, a brief note about my background, and an offer to sign a five-year lease. It felt bold, but I wanted to show I was serious.

A few days later, my phone rang.

"Hi, this is Curtis. We checked your references, and your background check came through."

I waited.

"Several people offered two years. Only you offered more. Five isn't necessary. But three is enough."

"Yes, I'm grateful for the opportunity."

"Take care of the place. I think you'll enjoy the neighborhood."

The exchange was straightforward. A few honest lines sealed the deal. Renting from LGBTQ+ leaders who had helped shape national policy made the move feel personal.

After my conversation with Staff Sergeant McCullough, I felt more at home in DC. But my future in the military still felt uncertain. I had reached out about opportunities in the JAG office. I lined up references and kept checking for news. Each week that passed without an update made the silence feel heavier. I tried to keep my focus on settling in and starting fresh.

As I settled into my new home, every personal touch I added to the carriage house studio made it feel more alive. The space reflected who I was and what I hoped to become. The small and quiet studio gave me a peaceful place to call my own in Washington, DC.

That moment carried even more meaning when I considered my background. I spent most of my childhood in Del City, Oklahoma, far from my birthplace in New Jersey, and even farther from any kind of carefree life. Both parents started college but never finished. My father, a Vietnam veteran, worked as a forklift operator. My mother managed the home and occasionally earned extra money through freelance art.

David, my younger brother, and I shared a home that was far from a haven. It offered shelter, but little sense of safety or peace. We were a household struggling with the challenges of the working class, barely

13

above poverty. Our lives were a daily struggle against the squalor of our living conditions and the scarcity that defined our existence. The weight of physical, verbal, and emotional abuse left its marks, shaping my worldview from a very young age. After my parents separated and we began relying on food stamps to get by, my mother became our sole guardian. She struggled to adapt, cycling through different careers and setbacks. We moved near my grandmother, seeking stability. The pressure continued to mount until my mother suffered a mental breakdown. It marked one of the hardest chapters of our lives.

I turned my attention to building the future I wanted, free from the weight of the past. Life settled into a new rhythm, shaped by a welcoming and joyful community. I explored the city, met new people, and embraced its culture.

Unpacking my belongings, I reached for the bottles of Atripla and my weekly pill container, practical symbols of a routine that had become second nature. Before I moved, the Oklahoma City VA Medical Center gave me a ninety-day supply of Atripla. It was enough to carry me through until I could establish care at the VA Medical Center in Washington, DC. Those three bottles on the counter gave me a reassuring sense of continuity, a reminder that my health was stable and any transition in care would be smooth. Twice a year, I went in for blood work. My viral load had been undetectable within months of starting treatment, and my immune system remained strong. The daily regimen demanded so little attention that it often faded into the background, and I followed it without complication.

In February 2014, the PARTNER study released initial findings that marked a turning point in public understanding of HIV. It showed that once you're undetectable, you can't transmit the virus. The full report in 2016 reinforced what I had experienced firsthand: the science was sound, and the treatment worked. In Washington, DC, the first signs of that progress were beginning to appear. Early ads for PrEP started showing up around the city, encouraging people to take control of their sexual health. That emerging visibility signaled a shift. HIV was still serious, but no longer a life defined by fear.

Each morning, I opened the lid on the container. Its familiar click grounded me in routine. I filled each compartment carefully, the small act anchoring me in a world that often felt uncertain. The pill container played a vital role in keeping me accountable. Sometimes, before bed, I'd catch myself wondering if I had taken my pill or if I was recalling the act from the day before. Even if I missed a dose, I knew it wouldn't derail my health, so long as I resumed the routine the next day.

Atripla came with one unexpected effect: vivid, almost cinematic dreams. I enjoyed them. Each night became an adventure filled with vibrant images and surreal experiences. On the rare nights I missed a dose, my dull dreams served as a reminder. A quick check of the pill container the next morning confirmed it. That rhythm kept me grounded in the middle of DC's whirlwind, fitting naturally into the flow of daily challenges and opportunities.

This apartment, with its bricks and beams, housed both my daily routine and the personal changes that shaped this new chapter of my life.

* * *

At the Small Business Administration, I worked in the stark but energetic halls of the Office of Veterans Business Development. Our team reflected the country's diversity, a mix of backgrounds, experiences, and perspectives. Ramona Peyton led us with strength and insight. A seasoned Black woman, she managed the Veterans Business Outreach Centers with determination and poise. She stayed ahead of the curve, tracking news, legislation, and events to keep us prepared for anything. We respected her sharp mind and valued her deep empathy. People trusted her and looked to her for guidance.

We joined around a shared mission. When troops came home from war, they faced more than just physical wounds. They also needed to find their place in a job market that had changed during their time away. The Obama Administration saw this problem and acted. In 2009, it started the Veterans Employment Initiative. In 2011, it passed the Veterans Opportunity to Work Act. These steps led to big changes in how the military helped servicemembers prepare for civilian life. The Small Business Administration created the Boots to Business Program to help veterans use their skills and experience to build successful businesses.

I didn't plan to enter this kind of public service. Deployment schedules and missed chances led me in this direction. I sat for campus interviews with my classmates, but while they started their careers, I deployed overseas. I handled real-world duties far from recruiting events and company mixers. When I came back, I didn't have a clear career path or a job offer waiting. But my military service paid for my education. I saw the value of veterans benefits because I needed them. They didn't just cover tuition; they opened doors I couldn't reach before. That experience stayed with me and built my commitment to helping others get the same chance.

While deployed, I helped prepare soldiers to transition back to civilian life. I knew how difficult that shift could be, returning from war with no clear path forward. The Commanding General told units to teach troops how to write a resume, but that wasn't enough. I built a program that went beyond resumes. It showed soldiers how to use their veterans benefits, go back to college, network for jobs, and succeed in interviews.

I put everything into the work. But the battalion operations officer pushed back, and he complained that I was being disrespectful.

I later found out that the issue reached our battalion commander, Lieutenant Colonel Christopher Chomosh. He was a no-nonsense leader who would later command the 45th Infantry Brigade Combat Team. The operations officer, a major who felt I'd stepped out of line, brought the matter up at a command group meeting, waving around a printed copy of my email like it was Exhibit A in a court-martial.

"This is insubordinate. He's being disrespectful. He's challenging command authority."

The first sergeant took the printout and read the message aloud, steady and expressionless. When he finished, he gave a subtle shrug and glanced around the table.

"He uses 'Sir,' and he closes with 'Very Respectfully.'"

The major leaned forward. "That means nothing. Just because you say 'Very Respectfully' doesn't mean it is respectful."

Silence followed.

One of the platoon sergeants leaned in, arms crossed, voice calm. "Well, sir… I just know he cares about this stuff more than anyone else I've seen. That's not disrespect. That's initiative."

Lieutenant Colonel Chomosh nodded and pointed across the table.

"I agree with that."

That ended it. The major backed off, and resistance faded.

That moment stayed with me because it showed real leadership. NCOs backed a soldier trying to do the right thing, a commander listened, and the system worked as it should.

After that deployment, I returned to the same uncertain transition I had tried to prepare others for. I returned proud of my service, only to realize the world had moved on. Public declarations of support for veterans rarely reflect the reality they face. Too many of the jobs available to us fall short of our skills, especially for those with advanced degrees. The real challenge isn't just finding work; it's rebuilding a sense of purpose after the uniform comes off.

These programs provide important support. As part of the Veterans Employment Initiative, the Obama Administration redesigned the Transition Assistance Program to better help veterans handle the uncertainty of civilian life. This fresh approach understood that one path would not work for everyone. Some veterans chose college, others picked up a trade, and many searched for new jobs. The Transition Assistance Program gave them the tools to move forward. It helped them turn military experience into civilian language, grow their networks, and get ready for the next stage of life. This change matched the same idea I had supported, the one that led to my earlier conflict with the operations officer over the need for better career planning.

For many veterans, starting a business was their goal. The Boots to Business Program helped them turn that goal into reality by changing how they saw their future. Instead of only working on resumes and job applications, the program taught them to think like business owners. They learned how to write business plans, get funding, promote their ideas, and flourish. Just as important, they met business experts who understood how hard it can be to move from military to civilian life.

In that setting, I watched something shift. Veterans realized that their military mindset could serve as the foundation for what came next. The program taught them to build success themselves.

I joined the Boots to Business Program because helping one veteran succeed did more than change one life. It created chances for others and made the path to success wider for everyone.

The work brought me back to my own transition.

* * *

On quiet weekends away from work, I wandered through Washington, DC. The city felt like a living story, written in marble and stone. While full of modern energy, its streets and buildings echoed with the voices of the past. The monuments stood silent, but they told a powerful story. A nation striving, stumbling, and inching toward its ideals.

The Founders chose classical architecture not just because it looked beautiful, but because it sent a message. They turned away from the Gothic styles used by kings and churches. Instead, they picked the balanced shapes and columns of ancient Greece and Rome. Along Pennsylvania Avenue, the Capitol and Supreme Court rose as more than just government buildings. Their design showed a belief in civic duty, fair laws, and the power of the people. Ideas that stood against the rule of kings and the belief in divine right.

Inside the Library of Congress, I walked through halls where my footsteps echoed. Marble busts of history's most important thinkers lined the way. Two books on display outside the Reading Room caught my attention. One was an illuminated Bible. Monks had handwritten and decorated each page, turning the book into a piece of art. Across from it sat a Gutenberg Bible. It looked plain, but it changed the world. Together, they showed a turning point when knowledge became something to share, not just preserve.

Outside, the National Mall stretched out like a public gathering place. The Founders didn't build it for the elite or block it off like a royal garden. They made it open to everyone. A space where people could gather, protest, picnic, or play. This openness showed that the government belongs to the people. Monuments along the edges honored Pan-American unity. They reflected the Monroe Doctrine's goal that countries in the Western

Hemisphere would break free from colonial rule and build free republics based on liberty and self-rule.

But those ideals came with a contradiction. The capital made that conflict clear. The same people who lacked freedom helped build the nation that claimed to protect it. George Washington carefully chose the city's location between slaveholding states and near his own plantation. That decision was no accident. It showed a simple belief. The capital's leaders saw the city as a tribute to wealthy landowners. A vision built on property, social rank, and enslaved labor.

Arlington House, a former plantation house, stood high on the hill overlooking the capital. It was once the home of Robert E. Lee and now faces the graves of Union soldiers. It serves as a powerful reminder of how complex our history is. At the center of the city, the Washington Monument rises into the sky. The obelisk honors the nation's first leader, but its shape comes from ancient Egypt. Another empire built on slavery. These monuments go beyond honoring the past.

As I walked, I saw a different story come into view. One shaped by money and change instead of land and labor. In the early republic, slavery created wealth. Money flowed south to support plantations. Over time, the country followed an alternative path: one built on industry, transportation, and new ideas. The Treasury Building showed that shift. It served a useful role, but it also sent a message. Finance now sits at the heart of political power. Nearby, old lockkeeper's houses told stories of earlier dreams. Canals that once moved trade before railroads took over.

One vision rooted America in bondage. The other rooted it in liberty. They could not coexist forever. The Civil War forced a reckoning. Slavery ended, but at a staggering cost of over 600,000 lives.

Arlington National Cemetery captured that shift. The burial ground took shape around Arlington House, a former plantation that once symbolized the old social order. Headstones now covered the surrounding hills. Union soldiers filled those graves in plain view as a deliberate act of defiance. This land, once worked by enslaved labor, now honors those who fought to end slavery. The rows of graves told their own story. Officers and enlisted men, black and white, known and unknown. Gravediggers laid them to rest side by side.

Across the city, new statues rose. In almost every circle and major park, Union generals took their posts. Not just figures like Ulysses S. Grant and William Tecumseh Sherman, but names few remember today. George Thomas stands watch in Thomas Circle. James B. McPherson surveys the crowds in McPherson Square. Winfield Scott Hancock guards the entrance to the National Gallery. Congress didn't commission these monuments. Soldiers raised the money themselves and chose which men to honor.

At the far end of the National Mall, the Lincoln Memorial now towers above the reflecting pool. Its placement breaks the line of sight between the Washington Monument and Arlington House. That was intentional. It marked a new moral center. Lincoln remains silent as custodian of national conscience, not as victor. In 1963, Dr. Martin Luther King Jr. stood on those steps before a crowd of over 250,000 people. He gave voice to the unfinished work of the American Civil War.

The city itself reflected that unfinished struggle. Its monuments, buildings, and landmarks told a story of resilience and change.

Chapter Three

I felt excited to join the Boots to Business Program, but problems at the office soon undercut that optimism. The program's structure did not support its ambitious goals. Congress, despite its good intentions, created confusion from the start by using vague statutory language that allowed Small Business Development Centers and Veterans Business Outreach Centers broad discretion to launch their own veterans assistance programs.

Lawmakers failed to give it a solid legislative foundation, and the cracks were showing.

The hardest part of my job was dealing with the Associate Administrator's erratic leadership. A former military officer, he had aged into a softer frame, gaining weight and losing hair, but still carried himself like a younger man. He was loud, confident, and eager to dominate the room. He saw himself as a leader others should admire, but his behavior often undermined the respect he expected.

His leadership felt like surviving a storm. It was unpredictable and exhausting. He saw himself as a power broker, blending business with pleasure while holding court at bars near the office. I often went along as an unofficial chaperone. By late afternoon, his bravado faded into unguarded confessions, spilling office gossip and half-formed plans to manipulate his colleagues' careers.

"She was asking about you last night. Wanted your number."

"She's married."

"They're separated. Or about to be. Her husband's always gone. Travels too much to matter."

He grinned.

"She's a friend. I can hook you up if you want me to."

I didn't respond, letting the silence speak for itself.

"She's your type, right? I mean, just between us — I think you two would hit it off."

I shrugged, turned toward the bar, and tried to look distracted.

"What type of woman are you into? Or man? I don't care. No judgment. I'm just curious."

"I'm not really —"

"Come on, everybody's got a type. You've been in the office long enough. You've seen people. Who's the most attractive woman on staff?"

He waited just long enough to pretend he wanted an answer.

"The Deputy's up there, right? Hands down. Total knockout."

He kept going, like he needed me to agree with him, like the entire conversation wouldn't be complete unless I signed off on his fantasy.

"I served with her in Iraq in 2009. Same forward operating base for almost a year. We worked closely — really closely. You get to know someone in a place like that. Not just what they do, but who they are. How they think. How they carry themselves under pressure."

He spoke again before I could say anything.

"She wasn't just good. She had command presence, even then. Everyone saw it. But me? I saw more. The way she handled people. The way she looked when she was tired, but still kept going. That kind of grit stays with you."

He offered a smile, but it was off. Too proud, too certain she owed him something.

"Her husband? Doesn't deserve her. Never did. I've always said that. He doesn't get her. Not the way I do."

He shook his head, as if it offended him.

"You know I got her that job, right? Told her to apply. She wasn't sure at first, but I convinced her. Said it was time she stepped up. And when she made the cert list? Man, I was so proud. I went to every single person on the hiring committee and said, 'That's who I want.' Every one of them. I made it happen. She got it. Just like that."

He leaned back, but he didn't let go. His eyes stayed on me.

"But she's great, right? I mean — you see it, right? She's sharp. Confident. Locked in. You think she's doing a good job, don't you?"

I hesitated.

He leaned forward again.

"Come on, you've worked with her. She's doing great, right?"

I gave a small nod.

That was all he needed.

"Exactly," he said, grinning as if I'd just confirmed some sacred truth. "I knew it."

He took another sip, then pointed his glass at me.

"By the way, if you ever tell anyone about this stuff, I'll kill you."

He let out a laugh. It was loud, sharp, and a little too long.

"Dead serious."

His words slurred, and his bloated ego fueled his bravado. He sat there, overweight, flushed, middle-aged, gripping his whiskey like it made him important. I didn't take him seriously. I was a big guy. He wasn't a threat to me.

He crossed every professional line in his flirtations with a female contractor. He wasn't hostile or overtly lecherous, just careless in that familiar, oblivious way some men act around women they've known too long and assume they still understand.

She joined us for drinks sometimes. She was friendly, sharp, funny, and easy to talk to. You could tell they had history. Deployment buddies, maybe. One of those long-standing ties forged in the blur of war and memory. She gave him a hard time, teased him like an old friend, and most days seemed unbothered by the attention.

But there were moments. Small ones. The way she'd pull away just when he leaned in too close. The way her smile would tighten when a joke landed wrong. She never made a scene. She didn't need to.

One afternoon, after a team meeting, she caught me on the way out.

"I don't need you to fix anything," she said, voice low. "Just don't leave me alone with him again."

It wasn't panicked or angry. Just firm.

I froze, not sure what to say.

She looked up, eyes calm and focused.

"You were in the Army, right?"

I nodded.

"Then you get it. We don't leave people behind."

She turned and walked away as if she'd just asked me to grab her an extra stapler.

But I heard her. And I carried it.

The fallout from those evenings clung to the next day like cigarette smoke. The Deputy's mood shifted by the hour. Sometimes she'd go cold toward the contractor, her tone clipped and performative, just enough venom to be felt but never called out. Jealousy shone through her words, yet she overlooked the actual issue. No one wanted to name it. The silence calcified into routine and became part of the office's unspoken reality.

The Associate Administrator diverted funds to Syracuse University to design the Boots to Business Program curriculum, but the rollout was sloppy. Under the grant, Syracuse University agreed to produce textbooks for the program, but the funding only covered a limited number. From the start, the textbooks lacked key information about the Small

Business Administration's procurement programs. The agency refused to fund updated editions and failed to plan for supplemental materials.

The shortage disrupted the office's daily routine. To fill the gaps in the textbooks, the Associate Administrator assigned Ramona to create supplemental handouts. Each morning, she arrived hours before anyone else to print the color flyers without interruption. If someone used the printer during her run, it interrupted the queue and forced her to start over. The task demanded long hours and constant focus, but she met the challenge of ensuring every training site had what it needed. After printing, she carefully assembled the packets and prepared them for shipment.

The mandate to hire and train instructors placed on the Small Business Administration's local resource partners only deepened the dysfunction. Many of these centers operated as grassroots organizations and were dependent on limited state and local funding. They lacked the capacity to manage a task of this scale. The agency blindsided them with the sudden demand to train instructors for a program built on incomplete materials. The result was a growing storm of strained relationships and logistical failures that pushed even more pressure onto our team.

Our partnership with Syracuse University and the flawed production system left us with a narrow supply, frequently dispatched under urgent deadlines. Inadequate resources and poorly prepared training sites added to the disorder. Ramona's early-morning efforts couldn't keep up. The chaos soon pulled me in. My duties shifted from routine oversight to managing crises, negotiating with stakeholders, setting expectations, and persuading reluctant partners to support a program that felt doomed from the start. The clear role I had once imagined turned into a daily struggle to hold the operation together.

The internal chaos was only one front in the storm. Outside the agency, backlash grew. Community organizations that were angered by poor support and failed execution demanded answers. Their complaints reached Congress, and soon the threat of a Government Accountability Office investigation hung over us. Congressional committees called in the Associate Administrator, and our office turned into a battle zone.

The program once again shifted my role and pushed my legal skills to the forefront. I began responding to congressional inquiries, preparing for hearings, compiling budget reports, and drafting legislative responses as part of my daily work. The role I had imagined looked nothing like the reality I now faced.

* * *

In the maze of my burgeoning professional life, solace came through personal connections. I found warmth and acceptance in the diverse arms of the LGBTQ+ community. During a serendipitous encounter on a dating app in the spring of 2014, I stumbled upon what would become a sanctuary of sorts: Stonewall Kickball.

This league offered more than a typical sports commitment. It celebrated unity, diversity, and genuine camaraderie. My teammates' faces reflected the same excitement I felt during those first moments on the field. People from all backgrounds came together, setting aside our differences for a shared love of the game and a desire to build lasting connections. Every kick, every catch, every joke, and word of encouragement created something that reached well beyond the field.

Magic came from the surrounding people. One teammate worked as a public health analyst, shaping infectious disease policy. He cracked jokes at first base. Another had just completed her second master's degree and was researching economic development in sub-Saharan Africa. She made a perfect dive in the outfield. Our pitcher worked as a systems engineer developing satellite technology for national security. Even the person running the scoreboard had experience in nonprofit advocacy. That's DC. People with degrees and accolades tucked behind amiable smiles, doing remarkable work in quiet but essential roles. Class presidents, valedictorians, and Phi Beta Kappa graduates all left their suits and strategy memos behind to play kickball and build friendships. In that field, none of it mattered. We just wanted to win, cheer each other on, and laugh when we messed up.

Stonewall Kickball was more than a game. It was a lifeline. Many had moved to DC, leaving behind familiar homes, friends, and family. None of us knew anyone. This league was an opportunity to connect with people in a way that felt intimate. It wasn't just about playing kickball. It was about forging friendships and building a new sense of belonging. Playful flirting and deep support coexisted. I met people who would check in on me during difficult times and celebrate with me during good ones.

The team became more than just teammates. We played kickball together and lived life together. Mixers with other teams turned rivalries into rounds of drinks and shared laughter. Friendsgivings brought together those who couldn't return home for the holidays, filling apartments with friends, food, and makeshift dining tables. Over long weekends, we carpooled to Rehoboth Beach, staked out spots on the sand, built bonfires, and watched the sun sink into the ocean. These moments became milestones in forming a sense of home, belonging, and community.

Stonewall Kickball became an essential part of my life. It went beyond recreation, serving as a space to build relationships, spark meaningful conversations, and create lasting memories.

VIDA Fitness became another rite of passage. It's funny when I think about it now. The quintessential gay stereotype of joining a gym filled with guys trying to become muscle guys around other muscle guys. And yet, I did it. It's what you did here. Joining Stonewall Kickball, signing up for a VIDA gym membership. It's how you acclimate. It's how you learn to become comfortable in your own skin.

For so many of us, our communities had failed to accept us. This was the space where we settled into our identities. We exchanged anecdotes, engaged in playful banter, and supported each other's goals among the clashing weights and rhythmic footsteps. It was more than fitness. It was a community where strength wasn't just physical but emotional.

The LGBTQ+ scene in the city reached far beyond gyms and sports leagues. Local bars and restaurants served as lively centers of self-expression and solidarity. Rainbow flags marked them. Whether through the energy of Pride events, the shared joy of karaoke nights, or the artistry of drag shows, each gathering celebrated the rich, diverse culture of the LGBTQ+ community in Washington, DC. This was a city where the bartender might hold a PhD in sociology or a master's in conflict resolution. Its rhythm came from driven, brilliant people, where happy hour conversations could shift easily into debates on public policy, human rights, or global development.

Within this colorful mosaic of personalities, I connected with trailblazers who had carved paths through adversity for LGBTQ+ rights and acceptance. Their tales of resilience and undeterred advocacy inspired me in ways I hadn't expected.

* * *

While my personal life moved steadily, turmoil inside the office deepened with a new program manager. He was a Navy veteran with an MBA from Cornell and experience managing DuPont's Kevlar program. His resume looked impressive, but he carried with him an unmistakable sense of entitlement that quickly unsettled the team.

From the start, he saw himself as above the collaborative spirit that had shaped our workplace. His arrival would shift responsibilities and allow Ramona to focus on managing the Veterans Business Outreach Center program. Until then, she had led the effort to produce, print, and ship materials, bringing in others when needed to meet class deadlines. It had always been a team effort, with everyone stepping in to help.

But with his arrival, that balance shifted.

When Ramona asked him if he could help prep the training packets for the next round of classes, he didn't even pretend to consider it.

"I'm a program manager, not office support," he said.

He said it loud enough to make his position unmistakable for everyone within earshot.

Since it was his program, the responsibility for producing and shipping materials shifted to him. But he didn't do it. Instead, it all fell on me.

That Friday morning, I stood in front of the copier alone, watching the same pages spool out again and again, trying not to jam. I always wore a full suit. That's how I thought lawyers were supposed to show up. Professional, respectable, accountable. And there I was, sleeves rolled back, paper dust on my hands, clearing misfeeds and swapping toner.

By the time Ramona arrived, I was still standing there, feeding the trays one by one.

She stopped in the doorway and looked at me for a second.

"You've got to be kidding me."

I said nothing. Just kept working.

A few minutes later, the rest of the team filtered in, one by one. Some peeked around the corner to check the copier queue. Others just stared at the guy in the suit standing alone at the machine while the person actually responsible for this work sat in his office doing nothing.

Then Ramona loudly addressed the room.

"We're not doing this for the Program Manager," she said. "We're doing it for Nick."

And just like that, the silence cracked.

Someone grabbed the packet covers and started stacking them.

Another reached beneath the table, retrieved the boxes, and folded them for shipment.

By noon, we had a full assembly line running.

Ramona's leadership had always been unyielding. She led by showing up, doing the work, and reminding people what mattered. People pitched in not because they respected him, but because they respected her. And because they respected each other. It became a quiet act of solidarity, a collective decision to support me, to support one another, despite his presence. Our shared adversity brought us closer, with many voluntarily shouldering the added burden just to keep the program from falling apart.

I often wondered if all this would even matter soon. If the JAG selection board came back with good news, this would be temporary. A frustrating chapter I'd soon close. Yet, in the meantime, I struggled to navigate an office that seemed increasingly like a battlefield, weighed down by the uncertainty of what lay ahead.

The Program Manager did more than avoid responsibility. He fueled division. He had a sharp instinct for deflecting blame and used meetings to undermine or dismiss my work. When problems arose, he raised his voice, stirred up drama, and shifted attention away from his own failures. Staff quietly shared their frustrations, but the leadership ignored them. The Deputy refused to acknowledge his behavior. She didn't just overlook his actions but seemed unable to see any fault in him. She dismissed every complaint and defended him without hesitation.

The Deputy also showed obvious favoritism. She approved his leave requests perfunctorily, while she denied or closely examined those from minority employees. The disparity didn't go unnoticed. It fueled resentment across the team. Watching him avoid consequences while others faced harsher treatment fractured our unit and left frustrations that never fully faded.

Despite the Deputy's constant support, the Associate Administrator saw the Program Manager differently. He admitted the guy pissed everyone off. He rarely said it outright, but he acknowledged the Program Manager was often right. That didn't stop him from taking a twisted pleasure in provoking him. It turned into a private game of sabotage.

One afternoon, he called me into his office.

"What are you working on right now?" he asked, flipping through a folder like he was half-distracted.

"Packet prep," I said. "The Program Manager asked me to get everything assembled for next week's training cycle."

He gestured dismissively. "Set that aside. This is more important."

He slid a folder across the desk like it contained classified orders.

"Don't tell him. Just say you're working on something for me. That'll drive him crazy."

He imagined the confusion, the reaction, the chaos he could watch from a distance.

The Deputy refused to acknowledge this behavior and dismissed the growing tension. Her denial clashed with the Associate Administrator's view, turning every interaction into a quiet power struggle. Their conflict added another layer of dysfunction to an already broken office.

Navigating the dysfunction took grit. Leadership urged me to stay, reminding me that if I made it through the first year, I would qualify for a one-year developmental rotation in another federal office. That promise gave me focus, a source of hope in an otherwise turbulent environment.

Determined to see it through, I focused on one goal. Make it to the end of the year. I took on the extra workload and pushed forward. I spent my weekends traveling to events, taking comp time instead of overtime pay at leadership's request. Site visits stretched into long days and late nights, but I stayed the course, knowing each day brought me closer to that rotation.

The job demanded constant effort, but I persevered. Leadership's reminders echoed during the toughest moments. "Just bear it, and you'll be able to do your developmental rotation and come back."

* * *

The trajectory of my military career took an unexpected turn with a sudden phone call that broke through the grind of my pre-Thanksgiving workweek. I'd been pushing through the days, bearing the weight of it all and staying focused on reaching the one-year mark. The constant pressure of daily demands was unrelenting, but I kept my sights set on that milestone. Then, unexpectedly, a voice broke the silence. A representative from the JAG Corps was checking to see if I was still interested in joining their ranks. They planned a panel, inquiring interview availability over the holiday weekend.

The news sent a surge of adrenaline through me and set off a flurry of preparations. I treated every minute as valuable. I arranged each ribbon and medal on my dress uniform with care and pressed every crease to razor-sharp precision. Holiday traffic disrupted transit routes, and I struggled to navigate the schedules. Refusing to risk delay, I arrived at the National Guard Bureau in Arlington, Virginia, nearly an hour early.

It was cold and silent when I arrived, the usual hum of activity replaced by the hollow stillness of a building left vacant for the holidays. The faint echo of my footsteps followed me down the corridor, each step amplifying the surrounding emptiness. The air was stale and cool, the faint hum of dormant machinery audible in the background. Sitting alone in the reception, the weight of over a decade of service as an enlisted soldier settled on my shoulders. This wasn't just another opportunity. It was a chance to bring together everything I'd learned as a soldier and everything I'd studied while training in the law. I had witnessed what happened to soldiers when their leaders failed them. It left many capable soldiers feeling overlooked and undervalued. Serving as a JAG officer gave me the authority to intervene and the responsibility to stand in the gap.

They ushered me into a spartan conference space with three officers seated at a long table, notepads in front of them, coffee cups half-drained.

They started by going around the room with introductions. Name, rank, branch. One of them looked up and said, "I noticed your email: alaskaairborne?"

"Yeah. Fort Richardson. I was there as a paratrooper after I enlisted."

"You enlisted mid-college?"

"Yes, sir. I grew up in Oklahoma. Partway through school, my academic focus slipped, and the debt piled up too fast. The path I was on didn't feel right. I needed something harder, something real."

They nodded, prompting me to go on.

"So I enlisted in the Army. Ended up at Fort Benning, then up to Alaska. Airborne. I still remember sitting on that cargo plane with sixty-three other guys, waiting to jump. Everyone was cracking jokes one minute, dead silent the next when they opened the door. We moved like we were going to the gallows."

A couple of them chuckled.

"I would not be the one who didn't jump. I think that moment changed everything. I stopped trying to avoid fear. I leaned into it."

They were quiet for a beat, scribbling notes.

"I went back to finish college," I said. "Then I started law school, but midway through my first year, I got deployed to Afghanistan."

Their pens paused.

"Security forces mission. We were supporting embedded training teams working with the Afghan National Army. Within 48 hours of hitting the ground, I was running the tactical operations center for the entire eastern region. I just had to figure it out and make it work."

That got a raised eyebrow.

"Came back, transferred law schools, had to retake my first year. Completed a JD-MBA. Then, I almost missed my last semester because I got deployed again, this time to Kuwait. Headquarters platoon sergeant. We ran convoy security as U.S. forces pulled out of Iraq. I got back, studied for the bar, and started job hunting. The federal government was the first to hire me. Presidential Management Fellow at the Small Business Administration."

"And now here you are."

"Yes, sir."

They exchanged glances, then looked at me.

"So tell us. Why the JAG Corps?"

I paused. Not because I didn't know why, but because I had lived it.

"I've served under great officers. And I've served under some awful ones. When poor leadership happens, it's the soldiers who pay the price. I've seen good troops fall through the cracks because no one was there to step in."

They were listening now.

"I've been that soldier," I said. "And I've watched JAG officers step in. The last line of defense for people who didn't have a voice. That stuck with me. A lot of law school applicants write about drive and discipline. But for me, it's not about ambition. It's about obligation. When you serve in an infantry unit, especially an airborne unit, you learn to live by a code. Duty, honor, country. You watch people sacrifice for each other, build real trust, and carry burdens together."

I could feel the room shift.

"There's a bond that comes from knowing someone else's life might depend on you, and it doesn't fade. It has kept me in uniform."

They nodded again. One of them wrote something and looked up.

"What do you think being a JAG officer will let you do that you couldn't do in private practice?"

"I could've gone that route," I said. "Most people do. I've always believed that there must be someone to advocate for the ordinary soldier. Someone who understands the experience of being enlisted. Someone who understands what it's like to follow orders in a combat zone and to answer when things go sideways. Someone who's lived that reality."

"And that someone is you."

I met their eyes.

"Yes, sir. I know what it means to carry the weight of other people's lives. And I know what it means to be failed by leadership. I want to be the one who doesn't look away. I want to be the officer who steps in."

The officers listened closely as I spoke, their pens moving in brief bursts. Their focused expressions and steady nods showed a shift, an unspoken recognition that I had earned their respect. They had heard similar stories before, but something in my response clearly resonated.

The interview concluded with a handshake. As I stepped into the crisp air and left the building behind, relief blended with anticipation.

Chapter Four

A few weeks later, during drill weekend, I spotted a man in fatigues striding down the hallway toward my company commander's office. Confident gait, focused eyes, and a face I recognized from the board as Colonel Mark Wellman. My heart kicked up a gear. He noticed me and changed course with a slight pivot of the heel.

"Sergeant Harrison." He extended a hand with the warm smile that made you brace for news. Good or bad. "I'm glad I ran into you."

I stood a little straighter. "Sir. It's good to see you again."

"Well." He let out a quick breath. "The board met earlier this week. We unanimously recommended you for one of the JAG positions. Your name came in right at the top of the order of merit list."

I opened my mouth, then closed it again.

"You look surprised."

"I am, sir. I figured I was competitive. I didn't think I'd be at the top."

"Well, your credentials were solid. Your experience overseas stood out, and it didn't hurt that you showed up with your dress uniform squared away, even on short notice. That told us something." He let that hang for a second, then chuckled. "A few other candidates wore wrinkled, ill-fitting uniforms. Missing a ribbon here, a badge out of place. Yours stood out."

I cracked a smile. "My dry cleaner should get the credit for that."

"Well, pass along our thanks." He glanced toward my commander's office. "I'm heading in to give your company commander a heads-up. Courtesy and due diligence. I want to make sure this isn't a surprise and to hear how he talks about you in an unscripted setting, outside the formal board process."

He pulled a business card from his wallet and offered it with a nod.

"Assuming this conversation goes the way I expect, someone from the specialty branch will contact you next week to help build your application packet. We'll bring you over to our office soon after that. Get you familiar with the environment, meet the team."

I took the card, glanced down at it:

Mark Wellman, Chief of Staff, Congressman Steve Chabot (R-OH).

Of course he was. It explained the polish, the presence, the practiced subtlety. I looked back up and met his eye.

"It was a pleasure meeting you." He offered a firm shake. "And I'm looking forward to working with you soon."

Then he turned, knocked once, and stepped into Captain Jeremiah Harvey's office, leaving me standing in the hallway.

After Colonel Wellman disappeared into the office, I stood there for a beat, staring at the closed door, then at the card still in my hand.

I tucked the card into my pocket and headed back to the drill hall, trying to shake off the adrenaline. The rest of the day passed in flashes. I checked off tasks, supervised weekend details, and reviewed the training roster with a few of the junior NCOs. I kept my hands busy, but my mind kept drifting back to that hallway.

Each nod or smirk from someone passing by sparked the same questions: Did they already know? Had Captain Harvey said something? Had the news spread? I pushed the thoughts aside and forced myself to stay focused and present.

As the afternoon wore on, Captain Harvey headed into the admin room, still smiling, his walk just a little lighter than usual. There was nothing to ask. The answer was already clear. So, I just waited.

When it came time for final formation, we gathered outside in the long shadow of the DC Armory, the air dry and still. Soldiers shuffled into place, boots stomping into gravel, a few whispered conversations still hanging in the air. Captain Harvey stepped up in front of the company. A round-faced Black man with a constant grin and a voice that always carried farther than you expected. He looked energized, almost proud to be holding something back.

"All right, listen up!" Harvey called out, letting the chatter die down. "I've got an announcement to make. Something that's both personal and professional for this unit."

A beat passed.

"The board selected Sergeant Harrison for a position as a Judge Advocate General. A JAG officer. Not just selected, folks. The board unanimously recommended him. His name was at the top of the list."

Murmurs moved through the formation. A few surprised looks, but mostly smiles and nods. Hands patted me on the back. One soldier let out a quiet "hell yeah."

Harvey's grin widened.

"And because of his prior military service, education, and experience, they're commissioning him as a captain. That's right. Captain Harrison."

That stopped me.

Captain? I hadn't known. Colonel Wellman hadn't said a word about rank. I'd assumed I'd start at first lieutenant, maybe O-2E if I got lucky. But Captain? That hit like a jolt right there in front of the entire company. I tried to keep my face steady, but I felt it ripple through the formation.

That drew some actual reactions. A few lieutenants at the far end shifted, glancing sideways with raised brows and half-suppressed smiles. One leaned in, whispered something, and the other nodded, smirking.

It wasn't jealousy. It was pride with just a flicker of "Damn. That means he's going to outrank us soon."

Most had already joined me in the lunch hall, asking about the LSAT, the GMAT, or what grad school was really like. I'd earned the degrees, finished the deployments, and served long enough to know the system. How to draft an op order, spot gaps in a tasking, and keep things moving. They didn't see me as just another soldier. I was the one they texted when they needed the men to form up or struggled to write a leave memo. And now, I was about to leapfrog them on the org chart.

Harvey raised a hand.

"This is a tremendous accomplishment. It reflects what he's brought to this unit. Sergeant Harrison has been a role model in this unit for soldiers and officers alike, and he'll continue to be one in his next role."

He looked straight at me.

"We're going to miss you in this company, but you're not going far, and you're not done leading."

A pause, then applause. Scattered at first, then building as more soldiers joined in. I nodded in thanks, holding back a grin.

* * *

Even before the JAG Corps acceptance, from the moment I had set foot in my unit with the DC National Guard, there was recognition of the journey I'd embarked upon. The subdued black of my Combat Infantryman Badge was more than just a piece of metal. It was a testament to my tenure overseas and an immediate passport to nods of respect.

When news spread about my imminent transition to the JAG Corps as an officer, the dynamics shifted. The officers and senior NCOs in my military police company recognized that I would only be with them for a short time. They wanted to know how best to use that time and what I hoped to accomplish before leaving. Their questions weren't just about logistics or gaps. They carried an energy of both curiosity and respect.

One afternoon, one of the platoon sergeants pulled me aside during a lull in the day. A grizzled MP who'd been in long enough to have seen trends rise and fall twice.

"So, Harrison. You've got, what, a few drills left with us?" The platoon sergeant asked, arms crossed, tone casual.

"Give or take."

He squinted. "So what do you want to do while you're still here? Before you're off writing memos and making PowerPoint presentations?"

"Honestly, I want to drive the unit. Not literally. I've seen how some of these privates operate behind the wheel."

The platoon sergeant smirked. "No arguments here."

"But I just want to look after soldiers. That's the part I know I'm going to miss. When you're a JAG, you're useful, but it's mostly briefings, investigations, paperwork, watching someone else run the show."

The platoon sergeant gave a slow nod. "You always had a thing for taking care of people. Even before they figured out you had all those damn degrees."

"I got them for the same reason I enlisted. To be useful."

He clapped my shoulder hard enough to say he saw me.

"Well. In that case, we'll step back and let you be the platoon sergeant one last time."

Over the weeks that followed, the other senior NCOs stepped back. They didn't have to. They had every right to take charge themselves. But they knew what this meant to me. They knew I would miss the early mornings, the problem-solving, the moments of trust that came with taking care of soldiers. So they let me stand in front of the formation, handle the tough conversations, run the training calendar, and lead from the front one last time. While I handled the platoon, they handled everything else. Quiet support.

I kept mentoring the new officers, sharing lessons shaped by years in uniform. To the enlisted soldiers, I was a steady presence. Someone who balanced deployments and degrees and never forgot his roots. We traded stories late at night, covered each other when it counted, and checked in even when no one asked. The respect we built didn't come from rank. It came from showing up.

* * *

In the days that followed my renewed leadership role, my journey took another turn. It began with a phone call from First Lieutenant Nicole Ono, the specialty branch recruiter for the DC National Guard.

"Good morning, Sergeant." Her tone carried the calm confidence that puts you at ease.

After the introductions, I eased into what I knew had to be addressed.

"You can probably already see I've got a non-deployable flag, but you probably can't see why."

"That's true."

"I'm HIV+. I'm planning to complete the full application and show I meet every other standard. Then I'll request a waiver."

There was a pause, but not a heavy one.

"Thank you for telling me. I appreciate you being up front."

She didn't treat it like a showstopper. If anything, she seemed almost relieved. Like someone who'd just received a clear next step.

"Well, I can schedule your appointments. We'll go from there."

We moved forward.

What followed backed up everything she'd promised. She moved through each stage of the process with precision, coordinating documents, setting timelines, and flagging issues before they became problems. There was no drama. Steady guidance and quiet professionalism.

* * *

Our preparation led to a series of medical appointments.

Walter Reed National Military Medical Center wasn't just a hospital. It was a fully operational campus, more of a military base than a medical complex. Just outside Bethesda, Maryland, guards secured its perimeter. ID checks occurred at the gates, and a steady stream of patients, staff, and uniformed personnel moved between buildings. The air smelled of concrete, wet mulch, and old bureaucracy.

I entered through the Tower, the centerpiece of the old campus. Its limestone façade was pale and dignified, stretching twelve stories high into a sky streaked with cloud. The Tower was all clean vertical lines and quiet authority, a classic Art Deco landmark of federal permanence. Built during World War II, it had weathered into something stoic and noble. Not pretty, but enduring. The bronze doors were heavy, and they opened into a wide lobby where time moved at half-speed.

Inside, the campus unfolded in a maze of hallways, elevators, annexes, and directional arrows leading to color-coded zones. America Building, Arrowhead Building, America Zone, Comfort Zone, Heroes Zone. Names that made it all sound reassuring and soft, even as the signage pointed you toward labs, imaging suites, and surgical consults.

I had a physical scheduled across several stations. Vision, hearing, lab work, orthopedics, medical history, and immunizations. I moved from floor to floor with a manila routing sheet, each stop stamped by a tech or corpsman in blue scrubs. Some rooms felt like doctors' offices. Others felt like DMV counters. There wasn't much conversation, just the quiet rhythm of military medicine. Sit. Roll up your sleeve. Look at the light. Follow the tone. Fill out the form.

I was early to the last station, so I waited in the hallway outside Internal Medicine, binder in hand. Black, heavy, perfectly organized. Tabs for every section. LASIK procedure, tendonitis treatment, recent bloodwork, HIV treatment records, specialty consult notes, fitness reports. Everything labeled. Nothing missing.

When I handed it to the intake nurse, she raised an eyebrow.

"Well, this is something." She flipped through the first few pages. "You've got this organized like an ops manual."

"Color-coded and everything. I figured if I showed up in a mess, someone might take that as a sign."

A PA joined her at the counter, leaned over to look, and whistled.

"You're certainly the most organized applicant we've ever dealt with. You even have your dental records in chronological order."

I shrugged. "It's a force of habit. The infantry taught me to pack light, and law school taught me to label."

"Looks like you're in great shape too." She flipped to my bloodwork. "PULHES code reads 111111."

She glanced up. I nodded.

"All ones. Perfect scores. Physical capacity, upper and lower body strength, hearing, eyes, everything. Basically, I'm medically boring."

The PA laughed. "Yeah, we don't see a lot of boring around here."

They ran the tests anyway. Blood draws, vision checks, ortho evaluations. Every result indicated fit and deployable.

A few days later, I returned for the verdict. The halls sat quiet in their clinical rhythm. The medical team didn't mince words.

"Sergeant, you're in exceptional health," the physician said, scanning his notes. "Fit to serve in any capacity."

Then came the pause. The one I'd been bracing for.

"However, your HIV status is the only obstacle, and it's not medical; it's policy."

Outside the military, it would not have been a problem. Here, it was.

I took that in without flinching. Labs showed I was in peak condition. Regulation said I wasn't.

As I left Walter Reed National Medical Center that day, I remained focused, neither fired up nor frustrated. The binder was heavier now, packed with updated records, clean labs, and signed evaluations. Everything said, I was healthy, ready, and qualified.

The only thing standing in the way was policy.

* * *

As I grappled with the complexities at home in DC and waited for the JAG Corps process to proceed, my business travels served as an unexpected sanctuary. Each site visit offered veterans a brief break, highlighting our work's impact on their return to civilian life.

My inaugural field trip led me to Syracuse, New York, in the early fall of 2013. The season was in full voice. Brisk mornings, trees catching fire in shades of amber and rust, the cold that didn't bite yet, just woke you up a little. Students hurried between buildings with coffee in hand and light jackets pulled tight. The air carried both the smell of damp leaves and the distant sound of the marching band rehearsing somewhere.

Syracuse University crowned the city's hilltop like a fortress of learning. At its peak stood Crouse College, a towering Romanesque Revival structure that seemed airlifted from another century. It didn't just overlook the campus. It dominated it. The stonework was dark and commanding, its bell tower casting long shadows across the campus. When it rang, the bell made the whole place feel sacred. There was a quiet intensity to the architecture, the kind that made you straighten your posture as you passed it.

Inside, I found myself in a conference room, seated across from several faculty and staff responsible for shaping the Boots to Business curriculum. Decision-makers, not just facilitators. We traded notes on delivery models, talked through the challenges of reaching National Guard and Army Reserve units, and even floated the idea of outsourcing the printing and distribution of materials to ease the load at headquarters.

At some point, the conversation hit a lull, and I leaned in.

"Has anyone considered offering college credit for the course?"

They exchanged glances. Someone scribbled in their notebook without looking up. A man in a tweed blazer shifted in his chair.

"That's a bit more complicated than it sounds."

"How complicated?"

"Well, for starters, it would trigger a full academic review. We'd need departmental sign-off and curriculum committee approval. It would take time. And honestly, we never designed the course with that kind of framework in mind.

"But the content's already solid. You're teaching fundamentals. Market analysis, legal structures, basic finance."

"Sure," said another staffer, "but it's not like instructional hours. College credit requires rubrics, assessments, and learning outcomes."

I nodded. "Right, but you already have most of that. We could get this course into the education centers on the bases if we offered it for even one credit hour. Soldiers could enroll using tuition assistance. That would make it available much earlier in their careers, not when they're getting ready to separate."

They didn't disagree, but they didn't nod either.

"When a soldier signs up for an academic course, their commanders are more inclined to sign off. They understand education, and they'll give a soldier time for that. But transition training gets ignored. Nobody wants to give their guys time off to prepare for leaving."

A woman near the end of the table chimed in.

"You're not wrong. But once we attach academic credit, we commit to it and vouch for it permanently."

"As you should. You're already responsible for the content. If the university won't stand behind it as legitimate education, why should the military treat it like anything more than a nice workshop?"

There was silence long enough to let the point land.

"We built this program for something else," someone said. "It's outreach, not a degree pathway."

"But starting a business isn't outreach. It's a grind. It takes knowledge, structure, and training. If we want this program to matter, we can't treat it like a handout at the end of someone's service. We need to meet them earlier, when they still have a paycheck, stability, a chain of command."

I let that hang.

"Otherwise, we're just patting them on the back and saying, 'Good luck out there.'"

The energy shifted. They were polite, but they were ready to move on.

We discussed schedules and contractors, yet I remember that moment vividly. Not because they disagreed, but because they seemed afraid to agree out loud.

They weren't just sidestepping bureaucracy. They were refusing to back their own program with the weight of their institution. And that told me something.

Chapter Five

The chill of the East Coast autumn soon yielded to the mild winter of Southern California, ushering in my next expedition.

It had been just a few weeks since the disappointment at Syracuse University, where hopes of college credit had evaporated into bureaucratic indifference. Still, the mission moved forward. Headquarters booked my flight to California for another round of site visits. Just me this time. The others wouldn't arrive until later in the week for the conference. But I'd asked to fly in early. I wanted to see it with my own eyes. The training being delivered to real servicemembers.

The descent into San Diego was beautiful in the way only Southern California can be. That blend of rugged coastline and ordered sprawl, the ocean casting silver light across the wing as we banked toward the airport. Heat settled gently on my skin as I stepped out of the terminal. Not the kind that scorches, but the kind that moves in without resistance. The breeze was gentle, and for a moment, it felt like the entire world was on vacation. Palms lined the curb outside baggage claim. I tossed my bag into the rental car, rolled down the windows, and started the drive north toward Camp Pendleton.

The highway stretched ahead. Navy blue ocean to the west, sun-bleached hills to the east, the road slicing right through it. It wasn't long before the signs for Pendleton appeared, plain green markers posted on the side of the 5 like any other freeway exit. They gave no hint of the scale or history of the place they were pointing toward.

I passed through the gate at Pendleton. The base was sprawling, like a city that never stopped training. Mountains loomed in the distance, ranges stretched across the valley floor, and the smell of salt air mixed with diesel. Rows of beige buildings punctuated the hills, their numbers stenciled on walls like silent coordinates. Area 21, Area 41, Horno, Margarita, San Mateo. Marines jogged along the side of the road in formation, rifles slung, boots striking in rhythm with cadence calls that echoed through the morning air.

I found the training site tucked into one of the administration complexes near Mainside. The signage was minimal, just a laminated printout taped beside a conference room door. Inside, about two dozen servicemembers sat in rows of folding chairs. Most in uniform, some leaning forward with curiosity, others reserved, arms crossed, but listening. The PowerPoint slides flicked across the screen, delivering the content we had spent months fighting to get funded, written, reviewed, and now implemented.

Watching them absorb it, I felt a mix of relief and disbelief. It was working. All the uphill battles with headquarters, the version control nightmares, the internal squabbles over how to define entrepreneurship or what counted as "military-friendly" had led to this. Actual troops in an actual room, learning about how to start a business when they get out. I stood near the back, trying not to interrupt the flow, letting the room fill in the silence between past frustration and present impact.

We stepped outside during the mid-morning break, into the sun that Southern California seemed to specialize in. Warm but forgiving, lighting up the pavement and filtering through the eucalyptus trees that lined the walkways near the admin building. You could hear the low rumble of military life in the distance. Diesel engines, cadence calls, and helicopters somewhere overhead. But here, on the side of the building, it was quiet. Just the hum of fluorescent lights behind the glass, and the distant pop of live fire from the range.

That's where I met Albert Renteria.

He was standing a few feet from the doorway, coffee cup in hand, eyes scanning the horizon like he was watching something only he could see. Latin guy, maybe mid-fifties with a stocky build in civilian clothes. A navy polo shirt tucked into khakis, sunglasses perched on his head. His beard was thick, salt-and-pepper. It looked like it had started out as a joke or a bet, but somewhere along the way, it had become part of him.

He turned to me as I stepped out.

"First time seeing it delivered?" he asked, nodding to the classroom.

"Yeah," I said. "It's strange. After months of fighting over the curriculum, all the drafts and the edits, the conference calls and the bureaucratic nonsense, it's happening. They're sitting in there listening to it."

Albert gave a low, satisfied chuckle and took a sip of his coffee. "That's what matters. All the meetings, memos, metrics, none of that matters if it doesn't reach the troops."

There was an energy to him. Not overbearing, but constant. He was always moving, even when standing still. His voice carried a rhythm. Like he was halfway between telling a story and giving a mission brief.

"I'm Albert, by the way," he said, offering his hand. "Retired Marine Chief Warrant Officer, Logistics. Now I run the Southwest Veterans Business Resource Center. Have you heard of it?"

I nodded. "I think I saw the name in one of the program materials."

"That's me. I built it. I didn't wait around for grants or favors. I paid for it myself. I had skin in the game."

He said it like it meant something sacred. And to him, it did.

"That's what small business is all about," he continued, gesturing with the hand holding his coffee. "You put your own money in, your name on the paperwork, your soul in the product. Skin in the game. These kids coming out of uniform, they need to know what that feels like. They need to stop thinking in terms of ranks and start thinking in terms of ownership."

I nodded. There was something sincere about the way he spoke. Urgent, but not performative. This wasn't a pitch. It was a philosophy. A calling.

He looked at me for a moment, studying my expression.

"What about you?" he asked. "You a veteran, or just one of those guys they bring in to write slides?"

I laughed at the jab. "No, I'm in the Army National Guard. Enlisted for a long time in the infantry. Then went back to school. Got a JD-MBA. Got deployed midway through law school. I'm assigned to the National Guard in DC now."

Albert raised his eyebrows. "So you have skin in the game."

"Yeah," I said. "You could say that."

We kept talking. He asked where I was from originally, and when I told him I was from Oklahoma, he grimaced, like he'd spent too much time stationed there.

"Why'd you leave?"

I hesitated, then told him the truth.

"It was after my last deployment. I was still overseas when the governor, Mary Fallin, announced that Oklahoma wouldn't recognize same-sex couples for marriage benefits. The Obama administration had extended those rights to servicemembers, but she refused. Ordered the state to stop processing any marriage benefits. Straight or gay."

Albert's face hardened. "That's messed up."

"It was a betrayal," I said, voice tightening. "The implicit promise when you go overseas is that the country will look after your family while you're gone. She didn't just break that promise. She used it to send a message. I came home knowing that no matter what I did, they would never accept me there. I could come back with a Congressional Medal of Honor, and it wouldn't be enough."

Albert nodded slowly, his gaze heavy. "So you decided to leave."

"Yeah. When I got back, I scheduled my Yellow Ribbon training out here in Southern California. The events alternated between Anaheim and Los Angeles. It was beautiful, warm, and laid-back. We wore civilian clothes. They brought in filmmakers, celebrities, and people who wanted to thank us for our service. They gave people time off to go to Disneyland with their families while they were going through the sessions. It felt like it was about us, about healing."

"Meanwhile, I remember seeing my old unit doing their Yellow Ribbon back in Oklahoma. They were in uniform, locked down on base. Word was that a couple of guys had gotten into fights or some kind of trouble, so leadership cracked down. No one was going anywhere. It looked miserable."

Albert let out a breath. "It's supposed to be a soft landing."

"A bridge back to your family, your life, your next step. Not more punishment or rigidity."

The compound stretched out before me. Marines in tight formation, the ocean breeze threading through the eucalyptus leaves. "I'd already decided I wasn't going back. But moments like that reminded me I'd made the right call. I tried looking for a job out here. But unless you already live here, no one takes you seriously. You tell them you're moving, they assume you're not. Doesn't matter what your resume says."

"Yeah," Albert said. "They'll hire you to stand at a gate with a security badge. But they won't put you behind a desk unless you've got someone inside pushing for you."

"I missed the on-campus job interviews when I deployed," I said. "And that window only comes around once. I looked around for months.

The first offer I got was from the federal government. Veterans preference. So I took it. Moved to DC."

Albert nodded, looking at me like he'd just filed away a missing puzzle piece.

"I like your story," he said. "You've seen the whole arc. Service, sacrifice, disillusionment, reinvention. That's what most of these folks don't get. Transition isn't a process. It's a fight. And it's personal."

We stood in silence for a moment.

"You should come speak at one of our events," he said. "Tell this story. It's powerful. Real. Most of the suits talking about transition never lived it. You did."

I wasn't sure what to say.

"You ever want to build something out here," he added, "you let me know. I know the terrain. And I've already bled for it."

He finished his coffee, tossed the cup in a bin, and gave me a long look. Like he'd already decided something about me.

Before we headed back inside, he looked at me and said, "You're doing good work. Don't let the institution wear you down."

I nodded, feeling the weight of the words even if I didn't quite know why yet.

That moment, standing outside a nondescript building at Camp Pendleton, sun high, slides paused, the Marines inside sipping terrible coffee. It was the first actual proof that what we were building mattered.

* * *

I left Camp Pendleton early, headed north with no actual destination except the coastline itself. The Pacific Coast Highway pulled me along like a song I hadn't heard in a long time, but somehow still knew by heart. The road curved in rhythm with the land. Tight bends carved into rocky cliffs, long stretches that hugged the ocean like an old friend.

Not far outside La Jolla, I pulled off near Black's Beach. The descent down the cliff-side trail was steep and almost hidden, like a secret that didn't want to be found. At the bottom, the beach stretched out, raw and beautiful. Wide sand, whitewater crashing against dark rocks. The ocean wind smelled like salt and eucalyptus.

Black's Beach was a place with a reputation. Raw and a little wild, a hidden haven known to surfers and gay men alike. No judgment, no pretense, just freedom. A patch of sand where bodies were sun-kissed and unapologetic, and where the cliffs loomed behind you like sentinels watching over something sacred. I stood there for a while, toes digging into the cool sand, breathing in that endless sky. If California were a dream, this was one of its untouched corners.

Back in the car, I kept driving. North, always north. Past Laguna, past Newport, past lives I never lived. I turned off in Anaheim, not because I had to, but because I always did. Disneyland.

As I pulled off the freeway and followed the familiar signs, a wave of anticipation settled in. Light, warm, and grounding. Every time I came out to Southern California, I made it a point to stop here. It had become a ritual. Repetition with purpose. I hadn't gone as a kid. My family couldn't afford it, couldn't make it work, but now, as an adult, I have given myself that joy. And every time I came through the gates, I felt like I was borrowing back a piece of childhood that I never got to claim.

I got through security, scanned my ticket, and stepped onto Main Street, U.S.A., where the air smelled like dreams and caramel. And then it hit me. That unmistakable scent of Disneyland corn dogs.

Just to the left of the entrance, I saw the line already forming near the little red cart tucked beside the Plaza Inn. I didn't even hesitate. That corn dog was always my first stop. Thick golden batter, fried to a perfect crunch, wrapped around a hot dog that somehow tasted like more than it was. It was served with a side of chips and wrapped in wax paper. A ridiculous indulgence and completely worth it. I stood near the curb, watching horse-drawn trolleys roll past, biting into something so simple and perfect that it felt like a reward for surviving the week, the year, the last two decades.

Corn dog in hand, I made my way toward New Orleans Square, where the line for Pirates of the Caribbean wound through faux iron gates and flickering lanterns. That ride had always spoken to me. Not just because of the movie, though I admired the swagger of Jack Sparrow and the strange dignity of the pirates. It was because of what it symbolized. Adventure, empire, rebellion. The East India Company, looming in the background like a stand-in for every bureaucracy I'd ever battled, their sails full of rules and conquest. And then there were the outlaws. Messy, flawed, wild. The map of the world was being filled in, edge by edge, as people chased treasure or freedom or both.

After that, I crossed over to the Haunted Mansion. The line moved slowly, and I didn't mind. I loved everything about it. The eerie music, the moss-covered tombstones, the elegance of the ghosts inside. They weren't frightening. They were poetic. Doomed, maybe, but flamboyant in their fate. It felt like a nod to everyone who'd been told they didn't belong and haunted the halls anyway.

Wandering past Fantasyland, where costumed performers posed for pictures with wide-eyed kids, I paused near the Disney Princes. Chiseled jaws, perfect posture, cloaks flowing in the breeze as if they'd just come off horseback. Kids looked up at them like they were real, and the Princes played along without a hint of sarcasm. Standing tall, smiling gently, dropping to one knee to greet them. It made me smile without

Irony or cynicism. Just aspiration. Everyone there was trying to believe in something beautiful.

And then, as always, I ended up in front of the castle.

You first see it framed by trees, banners fluttering, the pale blue roof catching the light, and it doesn't matter how old you are. You stop, because you're not just looking at a building. You're looking at the place where the story begins.

Just outside, near the bridge, I waited for the crowd to thin enough to get a clear shot. My phone went to a friendly tourist couple, and I asked them to take a photo. Standing tall, corn dog long gone, sunglasses tucked into my collar, hands relaxed at my sides. I smiled without thinking about it.

Later, when I posted the photo on Facebook, a friend commented:

"You look like a giant outside the castle."

Another said:

"That poor kingdom does not know what's coming."

I laughed out loud reading it. But part of me felt something deeper. Because they weren't wrong. I felt like a giant. Not because of my height, but because I had carried so much for so long. War, identity, rejection, responsibility. Here I was, standing near something whimsical. Smiling.

After snapping the photo in front of the castle, I lingered for a while in the park, just watching the crowds. Families huddled around maps, kids tugged at their parents' hands, and couples leaned into each other as staff announced the fireworks schedule. There was something disarming about it all. The permission to feel wonder again. The rare luxury of joy without explanation.

I drifted back to the car, pulled out of the Disneyland parking structure, and merged back onto the highway.

As I made my way into Los Angeles, the late afternoon sun dipped low on the horizon, casting that golden wash across everything. The light that makes the city feel eternal, cinematic, and possible. I passed under signs for Hollywood, the traffic thickening just enough to make me slow down and look. The Hollywood Sign appeared in the distance, letters cut clean against the hills like ambition itself had etched them into the earth. It was smaller than people expected. But more enduring than they gave it credit for.

Driving through Hollywood, I passed the old Paramount lot. The arched gates flanked by palm trees, just like in the movies. The façades were faded, but the illusion still held. Massive soundstages loomed behind tall fences, their silence thicker than it should be. The streets inside were replicas. Small-town squares, city corners, slices of somewhere else. This was where America was dreamed up. Not as it was, but as it wanted to be. Framed, lit, and rehearsed until the fiction felt like truth.

I kept driving until I hit the entrance to Griffith Park, winding my way up through the long, curved roads that lead to the Observatory. The switchbacks narrowed as the city fell away behind me. The park itself is sprawling, one of the largest urban parks in the country. Trails veined through chaparral and dry grass, dotted with dog walkers, hikers, lovers with arms around shoulders, and time to spare. It didn't feel like a city. It felt like a vantage point from another world.

And then the Observatory came into view.

Griffith Observatory sat like a temple at the edge of the known world. Pale, domed, stoic. There was something almost sacred about it. Its columns, its rotunda, its enduring presence in a city built on reinvention. I parked and walked the last stretch on foot, letting the hum of the crowd fade into the rustle of wind through the trees. From the terrace, the city stretched out in every direction. Grid lines of streets, the shimmer of the Pacific in the far distance, mountains folding into mist.

It wasn't just the view. It was the idea behind the place. Griffith J. Griffith, eccentric and controversial, had donated the land and the funds to build it with one clear purpose. So that everyone, regardless of wealth or education, could look through a telescope and see the stars. He gave it to the public. No entrance fee, membership, or velvet rope. A monument to access. To wonder.

In Oklahoma, people chipped in for things and wanted their names carved somewhere visible. When they raised money for the State Capitol dome, every oil company and wealthy family that contributed expected their name to be etched around the perimeter and got it. You look up at that dome today and see a roll call of donors wrapped around the thing like credits on a movie poster.

But Griffith gave the whole observatory. The land, the building, the endowment, everything. And they almost turned him down. Different world entirely. Not people buying their names engraved in stone, but someone handing over a gift so people could look up at the stars.

I walked through the exhibits. Models of the solar system, the giant Foucault pendulum ticking away at time, people clustered around displays that showed how the universe expands. In the next room, the Tesla coil sat behind thick glass, silent at first, then suddenly crackling to life. Lightning arcing through the air, filling the space with the raw, humming energy of discovery. You could feel the quiet awe in the room. Kids asked questions. Couples leaned in close. Tourists whispered in languages I didn't know. And everyone was looking outward. At galaxies, at time, at what lies beyond our own orbit.

It made me feel small in the best possible way.

As dusk fell, the sky turned a smoky lavender. The city below glittered, lights coming on one by one like someone dimming the room before the feature presentation. I stayed until the first stars broke through the haze. Then I made my way back down.

By the time I hit West Hollywood, the night had taken hold. The sidewalks were alive. Joggers in tight shirts and designer sneakers, couples weaving between sidewalk cafes, laughter spilling out of rooftop bars like music. There's a casual glamor to it all. Everyone looks like they're about to be discovered, or are pretending they already have been.

I walked for a while down Santa Monica Boulevard, passing juice bars, boutique gyms, and storefronts offering everything from skincare to crystal alignment. It was easy to lose time here under the string lights, among the beautiful people, surrounded by a world that pretended it would last forever.

I made my way to The Abbey.

It's more than a bar. It's a cathedral of queer joy. Inside, the air pulsed with movement. Chandeliers swayed overhead, heat rising from the crush of bodies as they moved in rhythm with the music. Bartenders poured cocktails with the precision of performers. Someone danced shirtless on a raised platform while drag queens held court at the far end of the patio. It was chaotic, curated, and completely alive.

And the men looked like Greek gods. Sculpted, radiant, sun-kissed. Chests carved by hours in the gym, perfect skin, confident posture, and they wore clothes that looked tailored to their bodies. You could feel it in the way they moved. Like they belonged, like they expected to be wanted, like they had already arrived. It should have been intimidating. But it wasn't, because here, you didn't need to match it to exist among it. That was the magic. The door was already open.

I found a spot near the bar and ordered something citrusy and sweet. A gin drink with lavender notes and a kick like a soft rebellion. I leaned back against the polished edge, sipped, and watched the room move around me. No one was hiding. No one was apologizing. Not for who they loved, or how they dressed, or what they wanted from the night.

That was the difference. In Oklahoma, I'd had to fight for air. Here, I was inhaling freely.

I leaned back in my seat, letting the night settle around me. For the first time in a long time, I felt like I wasn't chasing the dream. I was inside it. Living it. Even if just for the night.

And I realized I kept coming back here, not because it was beautiful.

I came back because it believed in people like me. That was all. And it was enough.

Chapter Six

By the time the conference kicked off in Long Beach, I had already been in California for a few days. The Associate Administrator, the Deputy, and the Syracuse University team flew in that morning, just in time for the walk-through and opening remarks.

This was the first Veteran Women Igniting the Spirit of Entrepreneurship conference that Syracuse University had ever held, only for women veterans. From the start, it was clear they hadn't grasped the conference's necessity.

It wasn't indifference. It was disbelief. A blind spot. The assumption was that entrepreneurship was gender-neutral. The same approach used with male-dominated groups would work here, too. Someone even said it outright in an earlier meeting: "Isn't this just the Boots to Business Program with a different logo?"

But the women in the room didn't need to be convinced. They already knew the difference.

They began coming up during breaks. Some came casually, others with quiet urgency. Not to ask questions about business plans or pitch decks, but just to say thank you. One woman said she almost didn't register because she assumed it would be like every other veterans event. Male-dominated, performative, vaguely hostile. Another told us:

"This is the first time I've ever felt safe in a veterans space."

That sentence stuck. The military had shaped their lives. Yet, it had left them with so few spaces where they could let their guard down. Too many of them had stories that went unspoken. Harassment, assault, retaliation, betrayal. According to the VA, more than one in three women veterans has experienced military sexual trauma. For many, it's the reason they left.

This conference wasn't a cure, but it was a pause. A pocket of relief. Here, they didn't have to perform toughness or swallow their own stories to fit in. No one was being asked to prove they belonged.

Laughter came easily. Ideas flowed. Conversations turned to the businesses they wanted to build. For meaning, for healing, and for control, not just for money. One woman said she wanted to open a gym for women veterans who didn't feel safe in civilian spaces. Another talked about a child care business for families of deployed servicemembers.

And for a few people in the room, something shifted. These were the ones who had questioned the need for this event. You could see it in their posture, in the way they stopped glancing at their phones and started listening. The data points were gone. The lived experience was right in front of them.

One of the Syracuse University staffers stood at the back of the ballroom. He was arms crossed, silent for most of the day. During one panel with a woman talking about how her business was a way to reclaim agency after leaving the service, he leaned over to no one in particular:

"I think I get it now."

He was late to the realization, but at least he arrived.

* * *

As the season changed, my approach changed too. I had just returned from Walter Reed National Medical Center, and I had assembled my waiver packet, but I knew I was heading into unfamiliar territory. Waiting for the system to move on its own no longer seemed viable. I needed to know if anyone had ever tried to do what I was attempting and what they had run into.

So I reached out to OutServe-SLDN. During Don't Ask, Don't Tell, these had been two separate organizations. SLDN provided legal defense for LGBTQ+ servicemembers facing discharge. OutServe operated as an underground support network for LGBTQ+ troops serving in silence.

I'd found OutServe while deployed in Kuwait, after Obama mentioned it during a State of the Union speech. It had been a lifeline then, connecting gay and lesbian servicemembers who had no other safe way to find community. After the repeal of Don't Ask, Don't Tell, the two organizations merged.

I figured if anyone could help navigate uncharted territory like mine, they could. I sent a brief message explaining my background, my status, and my plan to submit a direct commission packet as an HIV+ soldier. I asked for advice or a point of contact.

A woman replied a few days later. She didn't have an answer, but she understood the situation and connected me with someone who might know more. Another HIV+ servicemember active in the OutServe-SLDN Facebook group. Her response was direct and supportive. It made me feel like I wasn't just sending emails into a void.

The other servicemember got in touch not long after. He greeted me like an old colleague and didn't hesitate to share his own experience. His tone was candid and grounded.

"I wish you luck with the commission. I've never heard of anyone getting it, not with the service obligation that comes with a direct commission. I haven't seen it happen, but that doesn't mean it hasn't."

He offered to connect me with others and asked if I wanted to join the HIV+ forum. He never assumed, always left space.

We kept talking in the days that followed. Our exchanges were unstructured but meaningful. Two servicemembers comparing notes about life inside a system not built for people like us. There was no sugarcoating, but no discouragement either. He understood the fight from experience.

That connection led to others. Soon, I found myself in conversations across the OutServe-SLDN Facebook group, where a dozen different stories emerged. Each was different, but the tone was similar. It gave me a clearer sense of the road ahead. No one promised success. But they offered perspective, context, and community.

* * *

Things became more complicated as First Lieutenant Ono and I worked to assemble the waiver packet. We were trying to build a strong case, a clear, well-documented request for an exception to Army policy. But we still weren't certain who could approve it. So I reached out to the Office of the Surgeon General.

The email was straightforward. I explained I was HIV+, preparing a direct commission packet for a legal position with the DC National Guard, and looking for guidance on where a waiver request should go. I referenced AR 600-110 and AR 40-501 and asked whether their office had any role.

The next day, a response arrived, and after a follow-up call, someone connected me with a senior officer in the office.

"Sergeant Harrison, I reviewed your inquiry. I want to be upfront. Our office isn't the one responsible for this regulation."

According to her, their office oversees AR 40-501. That covers the medical fitness standards. If asked, they could provide a professional opinion on my condition, but the policy governing HIV and commissioning wasn't theirs.

"That falls under AR 600-110. And the proponent for that regulation is the Army G-1."

"So the Surgeon General's office can't approve a waiver?"

"No. We're not the policy owner. We can't start or approve anything related to HIV and commissioning. If the G-1 wants our input, we'll provide a medical opinion, but the decision belongs to them."

Her tone had no defensiveness, just clarity. The Surgeon General's office could evaluate my medical records, but only if the G-1 asked them to. And the G-1, not the Army's medical leadership, was in charge of whether someone like me could commission. No one was saying the science was wrong. They were saying it wasn't theirs to act on.

That distinction stuck with me. I didn't grasp the implications yet, but I was understanding the disconnect. The Army's policy on HIV wasn't being shaped by doctors. It was owned and managed by personnel officers. People with no involvement in treatment or clinical outcomes.

* * *

The Washington DC VA Medical Center isn't fast. It's not sleek or modern. You'll wait in line, sometimes for a while. The building is institutional, and a little worn, with fluorescent lights that buzz and tile floors that reflect years of traffic. Yet, it has a gravity to it. A rhythm. A purpose that's easy to overlook if you're just passing through.

I've never been a long-term patient here. Not retired, not fully disabled, not someone who uses all the services. But I've come often enough to understand why people return. Why they choose this place even when they have other options.

A crowd already fills the entryway most mornings by the time I arrive. Veterans are being dropped off by shuttle or city van. Some alone, some helping one another down the ramp. You see people navigating the hallways with the coordination that comes from long practice. A cane in one hand, a folder in the other, a knowing glance to a nurse passing by. The check-in kiosks hum quietly. The TV in the waiting room is always a little too loud.

It's not just a medical facility. It's something closer to a meeting ground. You can see it in the small things. The way people greet each other, the conversations that start in the pharmacy line, and the cafeteria tables where no one eats alone. People linger here. Not because they have nowhere else to be, but because this place still feels connected to something they were once part of.

There's a kind of unspoken order to the building, a system that makes sense once you stop expecting it to resemble a civilian clinic. There's a bulletin board near the elevators, covered with flyers for group therapy times, service officer hours, town hall notices, and low-cost dental clinics. The canteen sells shaving kits and toothpaste, socks and snacks, all at prices that reflect how many here live on fixed incomes. The cafeteria, tucked in the basement, smells like institutional coffee and reheated eggs. Still, it draws people in. There's always someone to talk to there.

I'm not one of the old-timers who've been coming here for years, but I respect the space. I get why people come back. Not just for treatment, but for a kind of familiarity they don't find anywhere else. No one has to explain why they're here. There's relief in that. In not having to translate your experience to be understood.

That morning, I made my way past the front desk and nodded at a man I'd seen before. He nodded back, a quiet acknowledgment, nothing more. But that's part of what defines the place. No need for introductions, just a shared understanding.

My conversation began with one of the nurse practitioners known for her steady presence and her way of listening without interruption. She was an older woman who had seen a lot. Not hardened by it, but softened in a way that made her especially good at her job. At the VA, nurse practitioners often handled most of the patient interaction when the doctors were away, so I had gotten to know her well. She was always friendly, always empathetic, with a quiet warmth that made you feel heard even before you spoke. I told her about my aspirations to commission as a JAG officer and the need for a medical endorsement. She didn't flinch. She just listened.

"We're no strangers to these requests."

A smile spread across her face, easing the weight I hadn't realized I was carrying.

"We've composed similar letters for individuals going into law enforcement and the foreign service."

She paused.

"Consider it a shared journey. We're here to support these transitions."

Her words grounded me. I wasn't alone. My goals weren't unreasonable. And there were professionals who understood how to help make them real.

A few minutes later, Dr. Maggie Czarnogorski stepped in. She was poised, kind, and deeply informed, as always. Before joining the VA, she had worked in the White House Office of National AIDS Policy. Like many of the physicians at the Washington DC VA Medical Center, she had shaped federal programs and national health policy but needed to maintain her clinical credentials somewhere. She did that here.

After we exchanged greetings, I explained the details of my case and what I hoped to accomplish.

She nodded as I spoke, already tracking the nuances.

"The wheels are already turning on policy changes. There's a broad recognition that military regulations around HIV need to evolve."

A momentary pause.

"It's not a question of if, but when."

She leaned forward.

"Changing regulations is arduous and slow, but the understanding and the will for change are there."

Before I could ask, she offered what I had hoped for all along.

"I'll draft the letter. You're more than capable of serving, and I'll make that clear."

That was it. No ceremony. No dramatic pause. Just someone doing their job, and doing it well.

* * *

As I neared the end of my first year at the Small Business Administration, they assigned me a capstone project: leading a national evaluation of the Boots to Business Program. I was to travel across the country, conduct a series of listening sessions, and produce a report on what was working and what wasn't. It was supposed to cap off my year before beginning a developmental rotation at another agency. But the work became a lesson in navigating dysfunction.

A low-grade power struggle gripped the office, simmering beneath every conversation between the Program Manager and the field operations liaison. The liaison was a tall, broad-shouldered former naval aviator in his fifties, with bright blue eyes, neatly combed silver hair, and an easy, amiable smile that rarely left his face. He was always friendly and affable. He carried himself with the calm confidence that made people want to follow his lead. But that didn't stop the tension. From the start, clipped emails marked their relationship, side-eye in meetings, and a tone of mutual resentment that never quite turned explosive, but always threatened to. They argued over everything. Control of site visit agendas, slide presentation order, and even event introductions.

The disagreements weren't loud, just grinding, repetitive, and petty. The Program Manager accused Field Operations of overstepping, with the liaison inserting himself where he didn't belong. In response, he saw the Program Manager as territorial and ungrateful for the field's support. Every time I thought the tension had cooled, another minor argument flared over logo placement on a flyer, access to an email list, or the version of the talking points in circulation.

At one point, the liaison suggested we bring donuts to each site visit. "It's a small thing, but it matters. A way to say thanks. These folks are doing this on top of their day jobs." I thought it was a good idea, so I paid for half. The Program Manager bristled and said it was "a waste of government funds." He added that it "sent the wrong message." The donuts weren't government-funded, but that didn't matter to him. The argument dragged on for days. In the office, in the van, over dinner in Dallas. The liaison stopped asking. He just bought the donuts.

Caught in the middle, I tried to keep the peace without taking sides. Of course, that was impossible. Cooperation from Field Operations was still essential, so I kept communication open. I included the liaison in calls, reviewed logistics with him, and treated him like a partner because he was. He was the only one who went to every single site with me. The only one sitting in those rooms, hearing what people were saying. But every time I gave him that courtesy, I got disdainful looks from the Program Manager. More than once, he pulled me aside after a meeting. "You know he doesn't speak for the agency, right?"

The dysfunction wasn't just inconvenient; it was corrosive. We were supposed to be gathering feedback and building trust across the network. Yet, I was playing mediator between two people who saw each other as threats. There was no hiding it. At one session, the liaison mentioned that Field Operations had sent out a survey the previous year. The Program Manager interjected without even looking up. "Not that it was useful." You could feel the temperature in the room drop.

This wasn't about professional disagreement anymore. It had become personal. I was stuck trying to keep the project and my working relationships from going down with it.

The liaison and I traveled together to every stop on the tour. Columbia, Dallas, Denver, Louisville, Tampa, and Phoenix. The Program Manager joined only two of the visits, and when he did, he flew in late. Hours after we had already landed and begun prep, his texts would start arriving from the plane or the airport hotel:

Status? How's the room? Do you have a feel for the crowd yet?

They weren't questions. They were signals. Reminders that he expected to be informed and deferred to, even when he wasn't on the ground.

At the sessions themselves, he radiated discomfort. He'd introduce himself without bothering to stand. During one event, I was trying to draw out a response from an instructor who had agreed to take part with no additional compensation. As the man described driving hours each weekend to deliver the program, the Program Manager began tapping the agenda with his pen, pressing me to move on. The tapping got louder. The district director turned and stared at him. No one said anything, but the room felt tight.

All of this tension came to a head in Florida. At the Tampa session, the Small Business Development Center pushed back on the mandate.

They explained that most of their funding came from state and local sources, and those funders didn't see the value in supporting a program aimed at servicemembers who might leave Florida the moment they separated. They didn't say they wouldn't do it, just that it stretched their resources thin.

Back at headquarters, the tension boiled over.

We had just returned from the Tampa site visit. Me, the field operations liaison, and the Associate Administrator, who had flown down for part of it. The Program Manager hadn't joined us on the ground, but now that we were back, he made a point of being in the room.

It should have been a routine debrief. Instead, it became a showdown.

The field operations liaison described what we saw in Florida: the Small Business Development Center staff faced overwhelming demands. State and local sources funded them, and they resisted committing more time and energy to a federal mandate because they lacked resources.

"They're providing more hours of entrepreneurship training to servicemembers than they offer anyone else. They're doing it with no dedicated funding. It's not that they don't care. They're at their limit."

The Associate Administrator leaned back in his chair, eyes narrowing.

"They took federal money. They knew what they signed up for."

The Program Manager jumped in, eager to nod along, echoing the appointee's frustration. "Exactly. We can't let them drag their feet. If they're not stepping up, then maybe someone else should get the grant."

That was the wrong thing to say.

The liaison didn't raise his voice, but his response cut through the room. "They're not dragging their feet. These folks are burning out and still showing up, still delivering, week after week. They keep going because they believe in the mission. But at some point, if we keep piling it on, we're going to lose them."

The Associate Administrator exploded. He struck the table with his palm. "Fine. If Florida doesn't want to do it, I'll take the damn grant and give it to someone else."

The room went quiet.

I sat there, stuck between them. The liaison held his ground. The Program Manager stared down, saying nothing now. No one moved.

That moment didn't just expose the politics behind the program. It underscored the disconnect between headquarters and the field, between the people giving the orders and the ones doing the work.

* * *

By the time we landed in Phoenix, I was dragging. We'd just wrapped a site visit in Denver less than 36 hours earlier. Altitude, tight timelines, delayed flights. I hadn't recovered. My clothes still smelled faintly like the last hotel room. And stepping off the plane in Arizona felt like walking into a blast furnace.

The heat in Phoenix wasn't just oppressive; it was disorienting. It radiated up from the pavement in thick, visible waves, distorting the horizon and scorching everything in sight. The sidewalks were empty. No one lingered outside unless they had to. Every movement felt slow, deliberate, the way you move when your body's trying to conserve energy just to function.

It was just the two of us on this leg. Me and the field operations liaison. Tired, sunburned, and running on too little sleep, we made our way to the rental car and drove straight to the district office. But first, we stopped for donuts, an unspoken ritual by now. He believed in the small things, in gestures that set a welcoming tone. I didn't argue. It was one of the few steady things we carried from stop to stop. After the last few tense meetings in Florida, we needed a win.

The Phoenix district office sat low and wide against the desert light, built to endure long summers. Inside, the air smelled like paper, recycled air, and cheap coffee. No one rushed. Phones stayed in pockets. Conversations began without being forced. There was no scrambling here. Everyone showed up. Everyone was ready.

This was a site that worked.

The team submitted every report on time. The instructors covered every class. There were no compliance issues, no last-minute rescheduling, no behind-the-scenes panic. The district director ran a tight ship, and it showed.

We set up the room, laid out the donuts, and waited.

The focus group started with calm voices and thoughtful responses. No one bristled at the questions or tried to steer the conversation. These were instructors and program staff who had figured out how to make it work. The bureaucratic obstacles hadn't stopped them. They weren't looking for credit. They were here to be helpful.

Then one instructor, a sun-creased man with a quiet voice and a deeply lined face, told us how he spent his weekends.

"Every Friday, I load up my little RV, kiss my wife goodbye, and drive a few hours across the state to the base. I camp nearby, teach the class all weekend, then drive back Sunday night."

No fanfare, no complaints. Just quiet, steady commitment.

I asked if the school helped cover his costs. He shrugged and said that when he first brought it up, he sat down with the college president.

"Told him what we were trying to do. Who it was for."

He paused.

"'The college president looked me right in the eye and said, 'Do whatever you have to do to make it happen. We'll figure out the money. This is too important not to do.'"

That moment stayed with me.

We'd spent weeks traveling the country, and at every stop, we saw people juggling federal expectations with local realities. Yet, in Arizona, there was no extra funding, no fanfare, no drama. They were just doing it. Because they believed in it. Because someone up the chain had given them permission to care.

As we packed up, stepping back into the sweltering afternoon, I realized how rare that was. The professionalism, the clarity of purpose. The willingness to carry the mission on their backs, even if it meant driving an RV across the desert to do it.

That evening, the field operations liaison and I loaded back into the rental car and drove up the winding road toward Dobbins Lookout. The session had wrapped, and the last handshake had faded into the dry heat. It was our last site visit together. The last leg in a stretch that had taken us from Columbia to Dallas, Denver to Louisville, Tampa to Phoenix.

The car climbed slowly. The engine strained against the steep incline. The heat outside was still punishing, even as the sun dipped toward the horizon. Long orange slashes stretched across the desert floor. When we reached the top, we got out and stood in silence, staring out over the grid of Phoenix. The flat sprawl shimmered below us like a mirage.

He broke the silence first.

"This was a good idea, nice to end on a high note."

I nodded. "Yeah. It's a good place to catch our breath."

He stood with his arms folded, not facing me. Just watching the sun drop behind the mountains, washing the valley in amber.

"I know it hasn't been easy. Back at the office. I know how hard it's been dealing with the Program Manager, and I appreciate you sticking with this and with me through all of it."

He let out a dry laugh.

"Yeah, well, we've both put up with our share of bullshit this summer. But this trip was worth it."

The valley stretched below, the city turning golden and silent in the fading light.

"What we saw today, that's what I want the report to reflect. What we saw today was instructors going way beyond what's expected, university leadership stepping up, no grant dollars, no extra staff, just a sense of duty. That's what this is."

He nodded, still facing the city.

"They're not doing it for the money, they're doing it because it matters. Because these guys coming home deserve more than a slideshow and a checklist."

I could feel the fatigue in my bones. Not just from the heat, or the miles, or the work. It was deeper. The exhaustion that comes from holding things together for too long. Mediating fights, absorbing frustration, pushing against indifference.

The wind picked up, finally cool, brushing across our faces.

"You think they'll listen to any of it?"

I stayed quiet at first.

"I don't know, but I'm going to make sure they have to read it."

Chapter Seven

By May, I could see the finish line.

It had been a year since I took the job at the Small Business Administration, and I'd been drilling with my military police company the entire time. The days bled together with constant travel, late nights, and pressure from every direction. The pace stretched me thin, but I kept going in my civilian job and in the National Guard. One mission after another with no room to fall apart and no one to hand it off to.

Now, the end was in sight. A developmental rotation after the summer, a chance to breathe, to rest, and to recover. For the first time in a long time, I let myself believe it might get easier.

But first, we had the July 4th mission. This drill weekend in June was where it all came together.

The focus was on weapons qualification. We were getting ready for range operations, reviewing rosters, checking equipment, and making sure everyone was on track. If we didn't get it done now, it would be that much harder later.

Captain Harvey had left, and First Lieutenant Namataka Heru had stepped into command. He was tall and athletic, with a professional bearing. His uniform was always crisp, his voice steady and direct. He didn't bark orders or put on a show, but people listened. When he laid out expectations, there was no confusion, and when he gave an order, people moved.

They assigned me to oversee the ammunition point. We were working out of a corrugated metal shed that was simple and boxy, hot inside. It looked like someone had dropped a storage container in the middle of the range and called it an office. The air hung heavy with the smell of gun oil, canvas, and sweat. I had a small team with me. Junior enlisted and a couple of cadets, all of them competent and opinionated.

Before we tarted, First Lieutenant Heru came by with instructions.

"Each soldier gets three magazines," he said. "Two loaded with ten rounds each, one with twenty. I want them in standard bandoliers, alternating direction. Keep them clean. Keep them labeled."

He waited a beat, then nodded and walked off to deal with the next fire somewhere else on the range.

It didn't take long before the grumbling started.

"Sergeant, I'm not trying to be difficult, but why don't we just load all the magazines with twenty? It's way faster, and that's how we'll actually shoot in real life."

"Yeah, and it saves ammo cans. Less waste and less hassle."

"Feels like we're making this harder than it needs to be."

They weren't wrong. From a practical standpoint, it was, but that wasn't the point.

"I hear you, and you can make that case to First Lieutenant Heru if you want to propose an alternative. But I'll tell you now, he was clear about how he wants this done. That's his call to make."

They exchanged looks.

"You think he'll listen?"

"If you make a professional case, maybe. Until then, he's the commander. That means it's his prerogative, and it's our job to carry it out completely. That's what following orders looks like."

The conversation quieted, and they got back to work. A little less enthusiastic, but more focused. I didn't blame them. It's hard to explain to a young soldier that the chain of command isn't just about obedience but about trust. About doing your part so everything doesn't fall apart.

Later that day, the weather turned. I'd moved up to the tower, calling out commands over the PA as soldiers cycled through the firing lanes. My voice carried steadily across the range. One sergeant smirked and said I sounded like I was narrating for NPR.

"Relaxing as hell, Sergeant — almost forgot I was holding a rifle."

There was some laughter, a little teasing, but we'd found a rhythm. For a few hours, the range ran like a machine.

By the time we rolled out the .50-cal machine guns, the air turned electric. Clouds piled thick and low. We had stripped the guns of oil, hoping to make post-range cleaning easier. But that made them vulnerable. Exposed steel waiting to rust.

Then the storm broke.

Rain sheeted from the sky like it had a vendetta. In seconds, the gravel turned to soup. Soldiers scattered beneath ponchos and the overhangs of Humvees. They clutched MREs and rifles, eyes wide and unsure.

"Let's go! We need to get the guns covered, now!"

No one moved.

"Come on! We can't leave these out here!"

I leapt onto the hood of the nearest Humvee and grabbed the .50-cal, throwing my weight into it. That did it.

"Shit — go, go, go!"

"Careful, Sergeant! You're going to slip!"

"Let us get it — we've got you!"

They hadn't been stalling. They'd just needed a spark. A clear direction. And maybe, in that chaos, a reason to move that wasn't just fear of messing up but a desire to protect one of their own.

Within seconds, we were moving as a team. We pulled tarps, unmounted weapons, and worked with hands slick and boots sliding. The rain didn't let up, but it didn't matter. We secured the guns.

Later, soaked and breathless, I collapsed into the driver's seat of one of the Humvees. The roof ticked with rain, steady and soft now. Inside, the cab was quiet with the sound of damp gear shifting and heavy breaths.

From the backseat, a young private spoke. Not loudly, or for effect. "You're such a soldier!"

There was no sarcasm in her voice. No punchline, just something simple and sincere, a little awed, almost reverent. Like she'd seen something, something she couldn't quite name, but recognized all the same.

I met her eyes, and she meant it.

* * *

The change came quietly with no big announcement, just a shift in responsibilities. They moved me from the Program Manager's supervision to the office's procurement analyst. The analyst had his own priorities and left me to work independently. A welcome change from the chaos I'd grown used to.

Then the Deputy left for her two weeks of annual training with the Air Force Reserve, and everything shifted.

The Associate Administrator named Ramona as the acting deputy while she was away. For the first time in months, it felt like the place might run the way it was supposed to.

I loved Ramona in charge. Every time she came into the room with a plan or a directive, I couldn't help breaking into a broad grin and saying, "Yes, ma'am."

She let out a short, surprised laugh and shook her head.

"You are getting way too much pleasure out of this."

"Maybe, but you can't deny the morale boost."

We both knew what I meant. Ramona didn't let things slide or shrug off dysfunction. No excuses for the Program Manager's disorganization. She paid attention, asked smart questions, and held people accountable.

I threw myself into the work. I had two major assignments on my plate. The focus group report and the process flowchart for the new course materials system. I wanted both to land with clarity and weight.

The report captured what I'd seen in the field. State and local economic development partners are doing everything they can to hold the program together, improvising around gaps left by headquarters. They weren't resisting oversight. They were compensating for it, stretching themselves thin because they believed they owed it to returning servicemembers. I mapped the pressure points, broke down what was working and what wasn't, and backed it up with clean data, field notes, and a set of direct, practical recommendations.

The flowchart was something else entirely. A sprawling, color-coded diagram with three swim lanes that tracked how requests moved through the new system. I had to be together three or four sheets just to fit the whole thing. It looked absurd on my desk, but it showed exactly where the process broke down and why everyone was frustrated.

The legal white paper was separate. A brief addendum to the report outlining the violations in our data collection practices. No OMB clearance, no control numbers, no Privacy Act statements. It included the citations. The statutory language. Everything they needed to understand the risk and address it, without politicizing the rest of the report.

When I turned everything in, Ramona didn't just skim it. She sat with it, reading line by line, flipping pages, making notes.

"This is excellent work. You laid it all out. And this part about the forms. That's serious."

"OMB has not cleared the intake forms we were using in the field. There's no control number, no compliance with the Paperwork Reduction Act. There's no Privacy Act statement. What we're doing is illegal."

"You put that in writing?"

"I triple-checked the statute before I wrote it. I also ran the whole thing by the field operations liaison and made sure it wasn't just me seeing red flags."

"You know, it's refreshing to have someone around who isn't afraid to just say it."

"Thank you. That means a lot."

"I don't know how the Program Manager keeps getting away with this stuff. But this is solid work. Really impressive."

"I also shared the report with the senior policy advisor. She thanked me for calling out the data collection issue. Said she raised the same concern a year ago and got ignored."

"Of course she did."

"She said it was validating to see it in writing, like someone else finally noticed."

"Well, I noticed. The Deputy will be back next week, but I'm glad this landed on my desk first. Great job."

For the first time in months, I didn't just feel competent. I felt seen, not for finishing the work, but for the way I'd carried it.

* * *

I hadn't expected it to feel like a pattern, but it was starting to.

A few days after Ramona read the report, I stood on 17th Street, waiting for the Capital Pride parade to begin. and there it was again. That sense of being seen, not in part, but whole.

I'd been to Pride events before, in smaller cities and quieter spaces with rainbow flags and drag performers, corporate booths and cautious smiles. But this was something else. The city felt alive. LGBTQ+ organizations, schools, hospitals, businesses, unions. Every corner of society was there. And so many churches. Not picketing, not preaching, but marching with collars and cassocks, signs that read "God is love" and "We welcome everyone."

Then came the moment that stopped me cold.

A military color guard.

Real, uniformed servicemembers marching in formation, carrying the American flag.

It was the first time in history that a military color guard could march in a Pride parade. The President had approved it himself, just a few years after the repeal of Don't Ask, Don't Tell. And there they were, marching for all of us who had served in silence. And I didn't feel like I had to carry it alone anymore.

I felt a lump rise in my throat.

I'd spent years serving quietly, calculating how much of myself I could show. Every drill, every deployment, every casual conversation was a negotiation. Can I say this or can I be that? Will this be the moment it all comes crashing down?

It wasn't just the color guard. It was the totality of it. Companies with their full leadership teams walking in step, community groups waving from floats, schools and libraries, sports teams and unions, churches and synagogues, bars and bookstores. They weren't performing acceptance. They were living it.

The message was everywhere, unspoken but undeniable. All of you belong here.

And I finally believed it.

The tension I'd been holding in my shoulders, the armor I'd learned to wear, loosened. The years I'd spent trying to reconcile who I was with the uniform I wore felt a little lighter.

That day changed something in me.

Nothing split me in two. There was no need to hide. I was proud to be queer and to wear the uniform, both at the same time.

* * *

I'd taken a few days for Pride. Time to breathe, to feel like myself, to just exist without explanation. The parade had been a revelation. A military color guard, churches and congregations, companies and crowds. For the first time in a long time, I felt proud not just to wear the uniform, but to exist fully without having to edit or manage myself.

That Monday, with the day still off, I heard the Small Business Administration was hosting an internal LGBTQ+ event for employees in the headquarters building. Something small, meant to mark the month and show that the agency supported its workforce.

Didn't have to go, but I showed up anyway.

Jeans and a plain button-down. Still riding the energy of the weekend, still holding onto that clarity, that sense of belonging I'd felt just a day earlier.

When I stepped into the auditorium, the atmosphere shifted. A few heads turned. Someone smiled a little too quickly. Others blinked in surprise. I spotted two of the event organizers by the refreshments table. Both were mid-level program staff I'd worked with before, always professional, always friendly.

One of them caught my eye and waved me over.

"You came in on your day off? I think this is the first time I've seen you not in a suit."

"Yeah, well — Pride felt like something worth showing up for."

They exchanged a look that mixed appreciation with curiosity.

"Well, we're glad you did."

We talked for another moment or two. Pleasantries, thanks, and a quick run-down of the agenda. I could still feel the quiet ripple my presence caused. Not disruptive, not hostile, just noticed.

A few rows ahead, the Associate Administrator and the Deputy stood off to the side, whispering to each other. Both glanced in my direction, then looked away.

I found a seat near the back and listened as the event began. One speaker, someone from HR maybe, opened with a line meant to sound bold but landed more like a slogan.

"At the Small Business Administration, we don't just tolerate diversity — we embrace it."

There were remarks about how far the agency had come. About allyship. About representation. Someone talked about "bringing your entire self to work," and I wondered how many people in the room actually felt like they could.

The words were well-meaning. Yet, as I sat there, I could feel the distance between what was being said and what was being seen. I was now part of the category being celebrated.

The warmth I'd felt at the parade, that open-armed embrace from churches, companies, the military itself, wasn't here. Certainly not in that room and not in the way my office leadership looked at me now.

They might have felt awkward. It could have made them rethink some situations they'd put me in. Maybe they just didn't know what to say, but something shifted that day. Not in policy or procedure, but in how they saw me.

When the event ended, I thanked the organizers and slipped out.

There was no speech. No statement. Just me, showing up.

Chapter Eight

Returning from the Pride events, I stepped back into the Small Business Administration office, but something felt off. The sense of joy and belonging I'd carried from the weekend didn't follow me inside. I'd shown up at the LGBTQ+ employee event in casual clothes, on my day off. After that, people saw me differently. They were polite and quiet.

The Associate Administrator had once joked about setting me up with one of his female friends. Now he no longer made small talk. The Deputy stopped lingering in the hallway after meetings. Everything became business-only. The air had changed, and I felt it in the way people looked at me and in what they no longer said.

I'd just submitted my focus group report, the one meant to inform our upcoming program brief for Congress. It summarized what I saw during site visits: dedicated field staff trying to hold the program together, pushing themselves past their limits without genuine support. It offered clear recommendations, backed by data and practical insight.

I kept the more serious legal issue separate.

The intake forms being used in the field weren't compliant. They were missing Privacy Act statements, lacking an OMB control number, and without Paperwork Reduction Act clearance. This wasn't something I buried, nor did I mix it into the main report. Instead, I drafted a separate memo that was precise, cited, and clear, and submitted it alongside the report so leadership could act discreetly, if they chose to.

The assumption was that they'd want to fix it, but they didn't.

That Friday, they called me in for a performance discussion. We met in the Associate Administrator's office, around a small circular conference table. He and the Deputy sat at the table when I walked in. The report was already laid out, the memo beside it.

The Associate Administrator barely glanced at the pages. He flipped through them with flat disinterest.

The Deputy had her pen in hand. She looked more thoughtful. Her eyes paused on the legal memo.

"So, this separate document — you are saying the intake forms violate the Privacy Act?"

"And the Paperwork Reduction Act. OMB has not cleared them, and there's no control number. That means we're collecting sensitive data without required disclosures. I cited both statutes."

The Associate Administrator leaned back in his chair, unimpressed.

"We are preparing to report outcomes to Congress. We need those numbers, and you want to discard them because of a missing disclosure?"

"No. I want us to collect data legally. What we're doing now puts us at risk. If someone outside the agency notices or if a veteran complains, we're exposed."

The Deputy looked at us. "You're sure about this?"

"I triple-checked the statute, and it's not a gray area."

The Associate Administrator gave a short exhale — something between a laugh and a scoff.

"Well, now you've said it, and we've heard you. So drop it. Whether we act on it — that's our decision."

He picked up the memo, held it by one corner, and let it fall to the floor beside his chair.

"Appreciate the effort, but give us things we can use."

The Deputy broke in, her tone quieter, less pointed. "Take the weekend to absorb all this. Think about how you want to proceed. Come back Monday and let us know."

She said it like she was offering space, but I knew what they wanted.

They weren't inviting a conversation. They were telling me to shut up and making it clear they had no intention of fixing anything.

I nodded, collected my folder, and walked out.

Now I had the weekend.

* * *

By the time I left the conference room, the building was already emptying. It had that quiet, drained stillness. Fluorescent lights buzzed in half-vacant hallways, doors already half-closed.

I didn't go straight back to my desk. I took the elevator down, walked just around the corner from the building, and slipped into the Starbucks tucked beside the lobby entrance. It was one of those cramped city locations, a little too bright, a little too cold. A long line of commuters still in work clothes stretched ahead of me.

The smell hit me right away. Burnt coffee, steamed milk, something sugary. It was comforting and familiar, a break from the office tension still clinging to my skin.

I ordered a mocha frappuccino. Cold, thick, and sweet. More milkshake than coffee, topped with a swirl of whipped cream and a drizzle of syrup.

The barista handed it to me with a tired smile. "Have a good weekend."

I stepped aside and stood by the window for a minute, the condensation already slick against my hand. Outside, people were laughing. A couple walked their dog, a group of interns already dressed for a rooftop happy hour. I felt detached from it, still processing the performance review, still replaying when my memo hit the floor.

Their instructions weren't a request. They were a warning, wrapped in civility, but unmistakable. They weren't debating the issue. They were telling me to drop it. The legal memo was separate, and they wanted to keep it that way as something they could ignore.

Already, it was clear what they wanted. What wasn't clear yet was what I was going to do.

Instead of heading straight back upstairs, I got off on the second floor and turned down the corridor toward the ethics office.

I remembered the line from orientation, months ago, sitting through those endless onboarding briefings: If you ever have an ethics question, come talk to us.

This felt like a question.

A woman sat at the front desk, typing with one finger. She looked up as I approached. Late sixties, maybe, with long gray curls pulled back in a loose twist. She perched her glasses low on her nose and looked at me like she'd been expecting me all day.

"Hi. I was hoping to talk to someone in the ethics office."

She gave a small smile. "That's me. Come on in."

I followed her into a side office. Small, windowless, quiet. A few framed posters with old federal ethics slogans on the wall. A government-issued desk, a dusty filing cabinet, and a half-dead plant in the corner. She gestured for me to sit.

"I work in the Office of Veterans Business Development, and I've got something I'm not sure what to do with."

She folded her hands and waited.

"I submitted a report this week. It included findings about how we've been collecting participant data. I didn't include the issue in the report itself. I wrote a separate memo. The intake forms we've been using don't have Privacy Act statements. OMB never cleared them. No control number. That violates the Privacy Act and the Paperwork Reduction Act. It's not a policy issue. It's a legal one."

I paused. "They told me to drop it."

She leaned forward like I'd confirmed something she'd suspected.

"That place is a cesspool, isn't it?"

I let out a quick breath. "Yeah. That's feeling accurate."

There was a pause. "As a lawyer, doesn't that come with a separate obligation? I remember there were post-Enron requirements for attorneys. We're not supposed to just let this stuff go."

She tilted her head. "I don't remember the specifics for attorneys, but you're right. You have a duty to report as a federal employee. Especially when you've identified a legal violation or a risk to a federal program. That's not optional."

I nodded.

"If you want, I can look into who that report would go to. We might escalate it, even anonymously, if that's important."

"Thank you. Let me think about it over the weekend, and I'll get back to you on Monday."

She gave me a steady look. Someone who'd seen this play out before.

"Take your time."

I stood, thanked her again, and stepped back into the hallway.

The mocha frappuccino in my hand was gone. Just a swirl of melted foam and syrup at the bottom of the cup. Dropped into the trash as I passed, it landed with a hollow thud, louder than it should have been in the quiet corridor.

Rather than heading straight back upstairs, I wandered the building for a few minutes. Moving slowly, letting the fluorescent light and institutional air settle over me like a weight. Not looking for anything, just trying to understand what had just happened.

No one told me I was wrong.

There were no questions, no requests for clarification, and no alternative offered.

They acknowledged what I found and just as clearly dismissed it. They expected me to go along with that. Not explicitly, not with threats or demands. Just with that same measured civility that masks so much in government.

Maybe that's what haunted me most. The way they had already factored my silence into their plan.

* * *

Sunday night was restless.

Sleep didn't come. I tossed. Paced. Lay still, staring at the ceiling like it might offer an answer. The conversation kept repeating itself, every phrase, every look, the way the memo hit the floor like it didn't matter.

I knew what they wanted, what they expected.

By morning, I knew what I had to do.

When I walked in on Monday, the office was quiet. The silence made everything feel sharper, more exposed. I'd just dropped my bag by my chair when the Deputy appeared in the doorway.

"Can you come with me?"

I followed her down the hallway. No pleasantries or eye contact. Just the rhythmic click of her heels echoing against the linoleum. We passed closed doors and silent cubicles until we reached the Associate Administrator's office.

The Associate Administrator was already seated at the round conference table, arms crossed, a folder in front of him. He didn't look up.

We sat, and no one offered a greeting.

I met her gaze, steady. "I did some research over the weekend. And I realized that as a federal employee, I have a duty to report legal and ethical violations."

Her expression didn't change.

"I'm not trying to be adversarial. I want to fix this. I can help develop a plan, work with the field, and figure out a path to compliance. But we can't ignore it, and I can't pretend I didn't see it."

The Associate Administrator shifted in his chair, still not meeting my eyes. He exhaled once, not loud, but audible.

"I've brought it to you for action, but I can't drop it."

The Deputy gave the briefest nod, then turned to him.

They exchanged a glance. Unreadable, but unmistakable.

And just like that, it was over.

"Okay." She closed the folder without opening it. "Thank you."

There were no questions, no follow-up, no acknowledgment.

I stood and walked out.

I'd made my decision, and now they had to make theirs.

About an hour later, a meeting invite popped up in my inbox. No details or agenda. Just a room and a time.

The Deputy sat waiting. The HR representative sat beside her, a folder open on the table with my name printed across the tab. They had staged it, prepared for it, and decided on the outcome days ago.

"It was a tough decision. But I've let you go."

There was no lead-in, no justification, just the cool detachment of bureaucratic language, spoken by someone who'd rehearsed it.

I didn't answer immediately because I was too busy trying to push down the wave of disbelief rising in my chest.

The July 4th mission started at the end of the week. Military orders were already in hand. They knew that. And when I came back, a developmental rotation was supposed to start, something they'd dangled for months like a promise, like a light at the end of everything they'd put me through.

My termination came just days before my reporting date. They were denying my military leave, canceling the rotation, wiping their hands of me, not because they had to, but because they could.

And it wasn't just any office. This was the Office of Veterans Business Development. The one place in the agency that was supposed to understand what military service meant, to value it, and to protect it.

Instead, they were using it against me.

The Deputy had just come back from her two weeks of annual training, supported and accommodated, and now she was sitting across the table from me, ending my job to make sure I didn't get the same.

The betrayal hit like a gut punch. It was personal.

The HR rep opened the folder and began reading from a script. Last paycheck, COBRA coverage, and return of government property. He didn't look at me when he spoke. He could've been listing office supplies.

Then, before he finished, the Deputy raised her hand.

"Before we continue, I just want to make sure you say anything you want to say."

Anything?

How could she sit there and talk about "difficult decisions" while cutting loose a veteran on the eve of military duty? Every late night, every weekend sacrificed, every ounce of goodwill poured into an office that couldn't even offer the dignity of honesty. None of it mattered. The comp time they made me take instead of paying overtime? Now they took that back, too.

Did any of it ever matter?

But I already knew the answer.

"There's nothing else to say," I said.

She gave a small nod. The HR rep resumed his script.

They asked if I wanted to go back to my desk and pack up, or if I preferred someone else to do it for me.

"I'd rather just leave," I said.

I stood, and I walked out of the room, down the hallway, and out of the building.

That was the end.

* * *

I didn't head home right away.

After I left the building, I just kept walking past the guards, the concrete barriers, the badge scanners. Past the rows of idling motorcades and the polished glass of federal office windows. The Capitol rose ahead of me, still and white against the gray sky, its dome wrapped in scaffolding for repairs.

I turned west, past the Library of Congress and down toward the National Mall, letting the sidewalks guide me. It rained, a quiet, soaking kind of rain that crept into your collar and sleeves. The kind that made you feel you were dissolving into the city.

There weren't many people out. A few joggers, a lone school group huddled under ponchos, a man selling hot dogs from under a dripping umbrella. The day made everything feel distant, even the monuments.

When I reached the World War II Memorial, I stepped inside the circle without thinking. It was quiet, not just from the weather, but in a deeper way. A kind of hush that held the space together.

Workers completed the memorial only a few years earlier. I remembered the news coverage, the speeches, the flag-waving dedication on the National Mall. Veterans organizations had been organizing Freedom Flights, chartering planes to bring aging World War II veterans to Washington to see it before they passed. For a while, it had been full of cameras, wheelchairs, salutes, and emotion.

But not that night.

It was evening by the time I arrived. The sky hung overcast, rain falling steadily. Crowds had cleared, and the plaza stood empty.

Stone glistened. Fountains ran. A wide bronze wreath hung on each state's pillar, rain sliding down like tears. Beneath it all, the field of stars shimmered under the surface of the wall. 4,048 of them, each one representing 100 American lives.

I stood there, staring at them. Each perfect little gold star, neat and measured, meant to stand in for a hundred dead bodies. I couldn't stop thinking about who decided that was enough. That this was how we'd remember them, not by name or by story, but through elegant symmetry and quiet math. A design that lets you say we remember you without having to feel the weight of it.

Rain kept falling. Wreaths hung heavy on the pillars. Water spilled into the stone basin.

All those stars just shimmered, like that was supposed to be enough.

I plodded through it, one wet footstep at a time.

The memorial's design was broad and symmetrical, with no names carved into its stone. That made it feel both grand and impersonal. A tribute not just to individuals, but to the idea of sacrifice itself. That made it heavier somehow. The silence pressed in.

Stopped in front of the pillar for "Oklahoma," then for "California," then for "District of Columbia." Said nothing, just stood there and let the weight settle. The weight of service, of memory, of what gets honored and what gets forgotten.

Just north of the World War II Memorial, Constitution Gardens sat half-forgotten. I crossed the street and followed a quiet path through the trees, slipping into a pocket of green that felt removed from everything else, from the monuments, the tourists, the city itself.

The rain had settled into a fine mist, soft and steady. It hung in the air like a veil, catching the light and making everything seem hushed, reverent. The pond curved in on itself, its surface dimpling with every drop. Overgrown grass softened the edges of the walkway, and long, heavy willows leaned low over the water, their branches trailing like fingers in mourning.

A few ducks floated aimlessly, drifting through the gray as if they belonged to another world. Everything here felt still, not stagnant, but suspended. Like time had loosened its grip on the place.

I found a bench tucked beneath a tree and sat, letting the rain soak into my clothes. I didn't care. The quiet wrapped around me, soft and complete. The only sounds were the faint hiss of rain through leaves and the occasional ripple of wings skimming the water.

For the first time that day, I was alone. Not in the logistical sense, but in the emotional one. There was nothing to manage, no one to perform for. Just me, the weight of what had just happened, and the ache of something I couldn't name yet. Part betrayal, part grief.

I sat there for a long time, watching the rain slide off the branches and into the pond, disappearing without ceremony.

I thought about how fast it had all fallen apart and how silent the ending had been.

Eventually, I rose and kept walking past the Ellipse, up to the north side of the White House. It stood pale behind its fence, floodlit even in the afternoon gloom. No one was there. Just the low hum of security systems and a few silent figures in uniform.

Across the street, the Old Executive Office Building loomed, massive and elaborate, like something half-forgotten from another empire. It stopped me mid-step. For a moment, it pulled my focus away from everything else.

The building stretched the length of the block, a sprawling monument to a different age of government. Rising from the sidewalk like a fortress carved from smoke and shadow. Built in the late 1800s to house the State, War, and Navy Departments, it was one of the first federal buildings to break from neoclassical tradition. People hated it when it went up, thought it was too ornate, too French, too dark. Mark Twain called it a "grand and gloomy pile." Congress nearly demolished it more than once, but it endured.

Tiers of gray granite and slate pressed upward into mansard roofs, dormer windows, and wrought-iron balconies. Stone columns marched along the façade in row after row, each one framed by flourishes that bordered on Gothic. Out front, a pair of cast-iron cannons sat on either side of the steps, relics of 19th-century war, their barrels slick with rain, mouths pointed downward like they were tired of all of it.

I stopped and stared for a long moment. The building looked cold, impassive, but not empty. Places like that are never empty. There's always someone watching, some silent hand moving behind the scenes.

I don't know what made me stop and take it in. Maybe it was the scale. Maybe it was the silence. Or maybe I just needed something solid to stare at, something older and heavier than I felt in that moment. The building didn't care what had happened to me. It had outlasted secretaries, scandals, and wars. It had held its ground while everything shifted.

Eventually, I turned and kept walking, but the image stayed with me. That dark, brooding stone, those silent cannons, and the way it all seemed to say: you are not the first to be forgotten here.

From there, I walked north through wet streets and neighborhoods that blurred together, familiar but cold. Up past Farragut, past the circle, past places I used to think felt solid.

By the time I reached Dupont, the rain had soaked me through. My jacket stuck to my arms, and my shoes left trails of water behind me, but I didn't care because I wasn't rushing anymore.

That walk fixed nothing. But it gave me something to hold on to. Space, clarity, the chance to feel the weight of what had happened, with no one telling me to let it go.

Chapter Nine

In government, most exits come with ceremony: a farewell email, a handshake, a hallway send-off. Mine came with silence.

The aftermath began with confusion, not clarity. No one in the office had been told. I reported to the procurement analyst, and even he did not know. For days, he went around asking, "Where's Nick?" "What happened to Nick?" He cornered the Associate Administrator in his office, pressing for answers. The response was vague: I had "pushed the Deputy too hard on something." That was it.

But silence rarely holds when people still believe in decency.

The truth filtered out through sideways glances and half-whispered conversations. When people learned I'd been let go, some of them responded in ways I'll never forget.

The senior policy analyst showed up at my apartment with a grocery bag and a bundle of things she'd been storing at an old rental. A strange, mismatched set of items that somehow said what I needed to hear: I've got you. No lecture, no pity, just a quiet act of care from someone who understood what it meant to lose your footing.

Ramona Peyton went one step further.

She retrieved everything from my desk before the facilities team could get to it, wrapping each item in newspaper herself, piece by piece, because she'd seen what happened when the building staff handled things. Careless, impersonal, broken. She would not let that happen to me, not to my things.

And then she left the agency.

"I thought you were part of the 'in' group. But seeing what they did to you, one of their own, made me realize what they could do to me and the other minorities in the office. So, I got out of there as quickly as I could."

It wasn't just about that moment. Ramona had been holding that office together for years.

She came from the Office of Congressional and Legislative Affairs, assigned to help Bill Elmore, the first Associate Administrator of Veterans Business Development and the man who helped write the bill that created the office. When administrations changed and the new leadership distrusted her, Elmore requested her assignment to his office and she never stopped working.

Ramona was brilliant and relentless. She was a senior GS-14, the civilian equivalent of a Lieutenant Colonel. Yet when she went out to military bases for site visits during the launch of the Boots to Business Program, base commanders mistook her for a secretary. One housed her in the enlisted barracks until he realized who she was, then begged her to return, promising better conditions. She didn't.

When the program ran out of printed instructional materials and couldn't afford to replace them, Ramona saved it. She contacted the Veterans Business Outreach Centers and pulled in enough surplus materials to keep things going until they could print more. When procurement flyers needed to go out and no one else took responsibility, she came in early and ran them off herself. She never asked for credit. She just made sure the mission didn't fail.

Ramona was everything the agency claimed to value but failed to reward. Competence, commitment, and institutional knowledge.

Ramona should have been the deputy. When the Associate Administrator left, she should have been his successor, but those in charge overlooked her, just as they overlooked so many other Black women in the federal workforce with long records of competence and impact.

That's the part that still stays with me.

These hidden figures are everywhere in government, never complaining, never making a fuss. Just serving quietly and consistently, driven by a belief in the mission even when the institution doesn't believe in them. Ramona was one of the best public servants I've ever worked with, and the agency lost something irreplaceable when she walked away. Veterans lost something too.

She also wasn't the only one who left the office.

The silence around my firing didn't last. The agency's attempt to shroud my exit collapsed under the pressure of growing questions, not just about me, but about the culture inside.

That was the moment I stopped grieving.

When I reached back out to the ethics office, the woman who'd helped me there didn't hesitate. "So, you told them what they were doing was illegal, and they fired you," she said. "You need to sing like a canary."

So I filed a complaint with the Office of Special Counsel. The preliminary findings supported me, and they recommended my reinstatement. But the agency refused, and the Special Counsel, still recovering from a high-profile loss in another case, chose not to press the issue further. That left me stranded in the backlog of the Merit Systems Protection Board, a body that lacked enough appointed members to form a quorum and couldn't hear appeals. By 2022, over 3,500 cases had piled up before officials restored a quorum. My case was one of them, buried beneath thousands of others. It would take ten years to resolve my case.

They even tried to block my unemployment benefits, claiming misconduct, but the DC Office of Unemployment Compensation saw through it. They ruled in my favor. A small win that acknowledged the truth, but didn't take away the sting.

The deeper truth was this: every step after my firing seemed designed not just to remove me, but to erase me. Strip away the opportunities I'd earned, undermine my record, and make sure nothing followed me out of that building.

And for a while, I thought they might succeed.

But they didn't.

* * *

In the weeks that followed my sudden exit from the Small Business Administration, everything blurred. Part disbelief, part exhaustion. I polished my resume, refreshed my LinkedIn, sent out applications, and took meetings that went nowhere. Every polite email that ended in "we've moved in another direction" felt like a slow unraveling of not just a job search, but of an identity. I wasn't just trying to get rehired. I was trying to piece together a version of myself that still made sense after being cast aside by the very institution I'd fought to uphold.

Then the phone rang.

It was Billy Jenkins.

Billy had once served as the deputy in the Office of Veterans Business Development. A steady presence who knew how to navigate both the politics and the purpose of the job. These days, he runs a small consulting firm in Alexandria and works with the American Legion on veteran entrepreneurship. We'd worked side by side during the rollout of the Boots to Business Program, part of the Obama Administration's broader push to support veterans transitioning to civilian life.

"Hey." His voice came slowly, cautiously, like someone already bracing for confirmation. "I heard you left the Small Business Administration."

"Yeah, a surprise exit."

"I figured. That place, let's just say I've seen it chew up good people."

He let the silence sit for a moment, then pressed on.

"So what's next? You got anything lined up?"

"Not yet."

"You working any leads?"

"A few. Nothing solid."

Another pause. Then a familiar edge of purpose crept into his voice. "Alright. I'm going to make a call."

Fifteen or twenty minutes later, my phone rang again. Joe Sharpe.

Joe was the Director of the Veterans Employment and Education Division at the American Legion. A longtime advocate who helped veterans find jobs, explore career paths, and figure out their next steps after coming home. I'd worked with him, too, back when we were building out the national framework for the Boots to Business Program. Like Billy, he was one of the few who understood how much this work meant and what it cost.

"Billy filled me in," he said. "That whole situation, man, I'm sorry. You deserved better."

I said nothing.

"I want you to come to Charlotte to the American Legion National Convention. It's a big one this year. Job fair, panels, networking events. We've got companies hiring, agencies recruiting. It's a place to reset."

I shifted in my chair.

"Joe, I appreciate it, but I don't want to show up looking like someone who needs a handout."

"You're not. You're showing up like someone who served, who built something real, and who's still got more to give. This isn't charity. It's a community."

He let that hang for a moment.

"If you can get yourself there, we'll cover your room. You won't be on your own."

That landed harder than I expected, not just because of the offer, but because of what it touched in me. Pride, fear, the quiet question that had taken root in the back of my mind: Was all of it for nothing?

"Alright," I said.

"Good," Joe said. "Because this isn't the end. It's just a pivot, and we've got your back."

Their offer wasn't charity. It was the veterans community doing what it does best, stepping up for one of its own.

My employer had just fired me from a job that was supposed to help others transition. Now it was fellow veterans reaching out to help me, not because they had to, but because they believed in the work I'd done and weren't about to let me fall through the cracks.

That's what made it matter. They didn't ask for an explanation.

* * *

A humid July dawn rolled in over Washington, DC, and the city stirred with that anticipation that only comes once a year. Independence Day. The streets were still quiet, but the energy was rising. You could feel it building in the stillness, like the pause before a drum line.

They activated our unit for the holiday weekend. The mission was straightforward in theory: support the city, maintain security, and help manage the crowds expected to flood the National Mall.

Inside the DC Armory, the day began like most others. No speeches, no flag-waving. Just soldiers doing the work. I sat with the lieutenants, walking them through the convoy plan. My voice was steady, focused. I wasn't trying to impress anyone, just making sure every piece was where it needed to be. Ours was the responsibility that doesn't draw attention until something goes wrong. The Army and Air Force both had pieces in play, but holding it all together fell to us. The military police.

We rolled out across the city, our convoy cutting through streets I knew well. The marble monuments and the clean sightlines of the National Mall passed by in flashes. Silent, orderly, waiting for the chaos to arrive.

We pulled up to our staging area and stopped short.

A woman sat on the curb in front of the lead vehicle. One hand rested on the frame of her bicycle. She wasn't moving.

Behind me, one lieutenant asked, "Is she serious?"

"I've got it."

The metal stairwell clanged beneath my boots as I stepped out into the morning air. The engines behind me idled low, like a held breath.

"Ma'am, we need to clear this area. For everyone's safety."

She glanced up but didn't move.

"Been here since six, just wanted a spot in the shade."

"I understand, but this isn't a spectator area. It's a tactical lane. Vehicles will pass through here all day."

She looked past me at the convoy, then back.

"So, where am I supposed to go?"

"There's a designated viewing area just across the lawn. It'll give you the same view, and you won't have to worry about getting run over."

She let out a breath. Not defiant, just tired.

"Fine," she said, rising and brushing off her shorts. "Didn't think it'd be an entire production."

"It's not. Just making sure everyone gets through the day."

She wheeled her bike away, saying something I didn't catch.

"Happy Fourth."

She gave a small wave without turning around.

Applause rose from the back of the bus as I climbed back on board.

"She give you hell?" someone asked.

"She gave me a moment. Let's form up."

The soldiers filed off the bus and into position, their boots hitting the pavement in rhythm. A quiet cadence that nobody in the crowd would hear, but one that held the whole day together.

There was something steadying about it. A shared, unspoken sense of duty beneath the holiday noise. We weren't part of the spectacle. We were there to make sure it could happen.

The mission itself was short. We kept watch over the crowd as the sun climbed and the National Mall filled with families, tourists, and celebration. By nightfall, the fireworks began. Bright declarations of independence streaking across the sky.

I wasn't thinking about recognition. I was just doing the job the way I always had.

But a few weeks later, one lieutenant handed me a small box.

The Air Force Achievement Medal.

It turned out that members of the Air National Guard had noted how I'd handled myself that day. The planning, the briefing, the way I de-escalated tension before it ever built up. I hadn't even realized they were watching.

A flush rose to my face as I turned the medal over in my hand.

Not the agency that cast me out, not the institution that looked the other way. But people who understood.

From the people I served beside. People who knew what it meant to show up, hold the line, and do the work, even when no one's watching.

***

Not long after the holiday, First Lieutenant Nicole Ono submitted my request for a medical waiver. A few days later, my phone rang. Her voice was quiet, uncertain. I hadn't heard that tone from her before.

"This is ridiculous. I filed your waiver, and someone from the National Guard Bureau called me. A contractor who lit into me."

I sat up straighter.

"What do you mean?"

"He said it was a waste of time. They're downsizing and the National Guard doesn't approve waivers, especially not for anyone with HIV."

She paused. I could hear her trying to keep her composure.

"It wasn't just what he said. It was how he said it. Like I should've known better than to even try, like I was out of line for submitting it."

I let the silence sit for a beat, then spoke as calmly as I could. I'd had practice holding the line when people tried to make me feel small.

"You did the right thing, ma'am. He was out of line, and you don't answer to him. But we need it in writing. Can you call him back and ask for a formal denial?"

She was silent for a bit. I could hear her breathing, tight at first, then slower, more measured. When she spoke again, something in her tone had shifted.

"Okay, I'll call him back."

She called again later that afternoon. Her tone was different now. Clear, focused.

"I told him his response wasn't good enough. Said we needed it in writing for official review. He didn't like it, but he didn't push back."

"Thank you, ma'am."

"We're in this together. And I will not let some contractor scare me off doing what's right."

It wasn't a victory. Just someone else choosing to stand their ground.

* * *

After the stress and turmoil of the past few weeks, the idea of driving down to Charlotte felt like a chance to clear my head. Before I even set out, I started looking for somewhere along the route that might offer a break. Someplace quiet, different, that didn't look or feel anything like Washington. Asheville kept coming up. The pictures, the descriptions, the mountains. It struck me as a place that might give me a little space before I reached Charlotte. So I decided to stop there first. I packed a bag, got in the car, and headed south.

The drive eased itself into a rhythm. The city thinned behind me, the interstate stretched wider, and the scenery opened into long runs of farmland and small towns. By the time the road began climbing into the Blue Ridge, the landscape had shifted completely. Ridges rose in layers of blue and green, folding into one another like slow breaths. Light filtered through the trees in narrow beams, catching the curves of the road. There wasn't anything dramatic about it. Just a steady, quiet sense of being somewhere else.

Asheville had an energy all its own. A mix of Southern and unconventional that didn't apologize for the combination. Murals spilled over brick walls, rainbow flags hung from windows beside Appalachian quilts, and old churches sat across from coffee shops full of people with books and laptops. I spent a day wandering around town, letting myself drift from bookstore to café to side street without thinking about anything.

Then I drove out to the Biltmore.

The light turned to soft gold by the time I reached the estate. A long lawn stretched out before a stone mansion that looked like a French chateau parked in the North Carolina hills. Steep slate roofs and tall chimneys stood against the sky. Gables, turrets, and sculpted pinnacles crowded the silhouette. The façade showed windows in rows and carved stonework that felt ornate by intention, not accident.

I walked up the sweeping approach, past clipped lawns, reflecting pools, and rows of hardy plantings that framed the house without softening its presence. The place did not ask you to slow down or quiet your mind. It pulled your gaze outward and held it there.

Inside, the momentum continued. A great hall opened before me with dark wood paneling polished smooth. Ceilings rose high with carved beams. Rooms off to the sides held walls hung with tapestries and portraits that filled every inch of visible space. A stair rose in graceful loops beneath a chandelier of iron and glass that seemed too large to be anything but necessary.

The house did not calm me. It took over my sight and my thoughts, crowding out everything that came before. For a moment, I stayed in its pulse, watching light shift across stone and wood, letting the details fill up my mind so nothing else could find room.

The detour did not change what waited ahead. It gave me a momentary distraction shaped by sheer scale and visual force. When I turned back toward the drive, the people who had kept me steady remained close in thought, steady and present as I moved on.

* * *

After the stop in Asheville, I got back on the highway and continued the drive down to Charlotte. The miles went by easily. Long stretches of interstate, familiar exits, the kind of quiet where you can hear your thoughts but don't have to wrestle with them. By the time I reached the city limits, I felt steady enough to face whatever waited at the convention. I didn't know what the week would bring, but it felt important to show up. To stand among other veterans and remind myself that I was still part of this community, that I hadn't vanished just because an agency tried to erase my exit

The American Legion's national convention was what you'd expect. Rows of men in polos and Legion caps, white hair and deep creases, ribbons from wars fought long ago. The demographic leaned old and white, and that wasn't subtle. Here and there were younger faces. Women and veterans of color, pockets of change trying to push through an institution built for a different time.

I saw a few familiar ones near the registration line. Former colleagues from the Office of Veterans Business Development. Their expressions shifted when they saw me. Surprise first, then something warmer.

"Nick? I didn't expect to see you here."

"Joe Sharpe made the pitch, and I couldn't say no."

We found a spot off to the side, out of the current of passing bodies.

"They said nothing. Just that you were gone. No memo, no goodbye."

"I'm not surprised," I said. "Clean exits make things harder to bury."

There was a pause. Someone lowered their voice.

"You did a good job. We all knew that. We noticed it."

I nodded, grateful and a little hollow.

Later that afternoon, the buzz shifted. People started making their way toward the ballroom. President Obama was to speak. Word was he'd be announcing reforms to the VA and discussing transition support.

But before the speech, something odd started happening near the stage. Event staff, volunteers in suits and lanyards, began encouraging veterans of color to move up front. One clipboard guy kept repeating, "Better seats up here," and pointing people forward like he was rearranging a photo op.

It didn't sit right.

"They're staging the optics."

A Black veteran walking beside me gave a small, wry laugh. "They want it to look like we belong up front. That's not the same as making room for us."

I didn't respond. But I understood. The contrast wasn't just visible. It was structural.

Then Obama took the stage.

The applause was loud. The room fell quiet. When he spoke, it wasn't performative. No skirting around the truth. He spoke of trust, of the bond between a nation and its veterans.

"Upholding our trust with veterans is not just a matter of policy. It is a moral obligation."

He talked about the need to fix the VA. To make it faster, better, and more transparent. And then he turned to transition assistance.

"We're going to make it easier for servicemembers being treated for mental-health conditions to continue their care as they transition to the VA. We're going to keep helping our troops transition to civilian life. Because if you can do these jobs in a war zone, you sure as hell can do them back home."

I was back in that office. Back in the meetings, the late nights, the policy memos, spreadsheets, and stakeholder calls. The work I'd helped lead, the work I'd believed in, the work I'd been let go for defending.

Hearing it from that stage was disorienting. I wanted to feel proud. I did, somewhere, but what I felt more immediately was grief. Quiet, sharp grief. Because I knew how hard it had been to get the military to take transition seriously. I knew how often they deprioritized and dismissed it, how little support commanders provided to prepare their troops for leaving the service. It wasn't worth it, not in their eyes. I also knew what it had cost me to fight for that work.

Now here it was. Championed, applauded, validated. Just like that, I was another face in the crowd.

I stood anyway, and I clapped. Not for the spectacle or the vindication.

I clapped because the mission had always been bigger than me, because the work had always mattered, because servicemembers deserve better. And someone had the courage to say it out loud.

And with that, I let it go.

The agency may have cast me aside, but they never took away what I stood for.

So I stood there, hands still, heart clear.

Chapter Ten

When I got back to DC, my mind felt clear in a way it hadn't in months. I wasn't waking up tense or replaying the same scenes out of habit. I had National Guard duties to keep up with, letters still making their way through the military's channels, and a job search unfolding at its own slow pace as my savings thinned. The constant mental noise had quieted. I could focus again.

Most nights that summer, I sat at my kitchen table drafting yet another letter to someone in the chain of political leadership who ought to wield authority or assume responsibility for taking action. These weren't casual notes. They were appeals to the people we surround with paneled offices, carved seals, and staff who carry their binders for them because we believe they're the ones who can cut through the inertia of the system. Assistant secretaries, deputy under secretaries, service-level policy directors, and associate administrators scattered throughout the Pentagon's upper floors.

I wrote to all of them carefully and respectfully. Giving each one the benefit of the doubt, assuming that if my request simply reached the right desk, someone would see the problem clearly enough to intervene. I believed those positions existed for that reason. The people at the top were supposed to prevent individuals getting ground up by the system.

But once the letters left my hands, they disappeared. Nothing came back. Just the long silence that makes you realize access and accountability aren't promises here.

So I turned my attention to the one place where the silence didn't feel suffocating: the law. More specifically, the first case I had ever accepted as an attorney. It was a case that had nothing to do with my own circumstances and everything to do with who I was.

***

Months earlier, before my life tilted on its axis, I'd made a quick trip back to Oklahoma to collect a freedom of information award I'd earned as a student reporter but never picked up. I planned it as a brief stop on the way to somewhere else, nothing more than a quick errand.

But the moment I stepped onto the University of Oklahoma's Norman campus, something in me slowed. It felt like walking back into a chapter I'd set aside but never fully closed.

Things had changed.

Under President Boren, the University of Oklahoma was always in motion. Construction cranes were practically part of the skyline, and every year brought a new building, a new renovation, a new name etched in stone. Coming back after a few years away felt like returning to a hometown that had rearranged itself while you weren't looking.

Gould Hall was among the first things that caught my eye. The old architecture building I remembered was dark, cramped, and perpetually under renovation. They had transformed it into a modern, light-filled space with clean lines, wide glass panels, and airy studios. It finally looked like a place that forged architects.

Farther down, the Zarrow School of Social Work had taken over what used to be a quiet corner of campus. The building was sleek, all contemporary brick and glass. An intentional shift toward openness and community. It was the structure that looked like it wanted people to feel welcome inside it — an unusual sentiment for a university that once shoved certain departments into whatever space remained.

And then there was Headington Hall.

Nothing prepared me for that. Headington was a massive residential complex rising where there had once been nothing but parking lots and older dorms. It looked part luxury hotel, part recruiting strategy. Red brick, tall windows, landscaped courtyards, athletic facilities tucked within reach. It was clear what purpose it served. The University of Oklahoma wasn't just modernizing, it was competing.

Even the Memorial Union had changed. The renovations had smoothed out its rough edges, expanded the food court, and redesigned the interior so sunlight poured through spaces that used to feel cave-like. The Union had always been the campus crossroads, but now it carried a polish that made it feel more like the center of a flagship university and less like a relic from the 1950s.

Boren's fingerprints were everywhere. Build, expand, beautify, repeat. The campus I knew was still underneath it all, but it had grown layers in my absence.

Walking past those new structures made the familiar parts feel even more vivid.

The Oval still stretched out in front of Evans Hall, a broad ring of green so precise it looked maintained with a ruler. The red-brick buildings that circled it rose with their comforting mix of pointed arches and pale stone trim. Those classic Cherokee Gothic facades. Even on a hot day, the bricks looked saturated, deep, almost iron-rich, glowing under the Oklahoma sun.

The flowers were everywhere.

The University of Oklahoma has always prized immaculate landscaping, but coming back after a few years away made it impossible to ignore how intentional it all was. Beds of seasonal flowers lined every walkway. Riotous patches of color that looked freshly planted because, most times, they were. The university rotates flowers constantly thanks to a dedicated beautification endowment. A fund earmarked only for landscaping. The result is almost theatrical. Tulips in spring, petunias in summer, pansies in winter, each one arranged as if the entire campus were being staged for an opening night.

Even knowing the reason, it still felt extravagant.

Oklahoma is a place that shaped the roughness of my childhood and laid the foundation for my adulthood in equal measure. Walking through campus again reminded me how much of myself I formed here. Norman taught me to think critically, to argue with purpose, and to question the rules instead of accepting them just because someone older or louder insisted they would never change.

It was the place that taught me institutions weren't monoliths. They were arrangements of people, policies, habits, and choices. People invite challenges. Rules change when someone refuses to let them calcify. Authority answers when someone calls it to account.

I had tested those boundaries often as a student.

I helped pioneer the Student Veterans Association, pushed for better representation in student government, and served on the State Regents' advisory board. A bylaw barred students without prior Senate office experience from running for Senate Chair. I didn't accept the logic.

I remember standing before that room full of students and saying, "If the Senate trusts someone's qualifications, why shouldn't they be allowed to choose them? Why should a small group get to decide who's even allowed to stand for election?"

Oklahoma was where I learned that challenging the rules wasn't rebellion but a responsibility.

In the evening, I picked up my award, and the journalism department hosted a small question-and-answer session. I slipped in quietly, blending into the back row while a handful of students asked the questions that used to keep me up at night — how to get agencies to answer them, how to find the story behind the "official version," how to push without burning sources.

When the event wrapped up, most students shuffled out in clusters. One stayed behind.

He wasn't lanky or sharp-edged the way people imagine student reporters to be. Joey Stipek was broad-shouldered, overweight, with an earnest, open face that made him look younger than he was. He held his folder close to his chest — not protectively, but like someone who had been carrying the same problem around for so long that it had become a part of him.

He approached me with careful confidence.

"Mr. Harrison?" he asked.

I turned. "Just Nick."

"I'm Joey Stipek with the *Oklahoma Daily*. Your old columns were a big part of why I got into this work," he said. "And your open-records pieces. People said you'd sometimes stop by when alumni visited the newsroom."

There was something vulnerable beneath his straightforward tone — not insecurity, but the awareness that he was asking something big from someone who didn't owe him anything.

"What's going on?" I asked.

He took a breath. "I've been requesting parking violation records for student athletes. People had caught other campuses fixing tickets, so my editor asked me to investigate OU." He opened the folder, his hands steady. "The university denied everything. They said FERPA."

I could feel my eyebrows lift. "Of course they did."

"And the *Oklahoman* and the *Tulsa World* tried a few years ago, and the universities refused their requests," he added quickly. He seemed to want to pre-empt judgment. "They didn't sue. Everyone said it wasn't worth the fight. That football is… well…" He trailed off, searching for the polite version.

I finished it for him. "Untouchable."

He nodded.

In Oklahoma, that wasn't hyperbole. Football wasn't just a sport but an identity. The athletic department's gravitational pull distorted everything around it. People learned quickly which questions were "acceptable" and which ones were career-ending.

Joey swallowed. "I think something's wrong. But if the university can just refuse and everyone shrugs, then…" His voice dipped. "Maybe I'm wasting my time."

I've always been unable to ignore the quiet resignation of someone who knows he's right but believes no one will ever listen.

"May I?" I asked, gesturing to the documents.

He handed them over.

The request was clean and tightly framed. The denial was sloppy — citing FERPA for records that no reasonable court had ever considered "educational." I recognized the move. Bureaucratic stonewalling dressed up as legality.

"You're not wasting your time. They're hoping you think you are."

He blinked, disoriented by the certainty in my voice. "So… you think I should keep pushing?"

"If you want the truth, yes. If you want transparency, yes. And if you expect this university to live up to the same standards every other public agency in Oklahoma follows, absolutely yes." I closed the folder. "Football doesn't exempt anyone from the law."

He hesitated. "I heard you're not admitted yet."

"That's true," I said. "I'm still waiting for my bar results."

"So you can't represent me."

"Not today," I said. "But I can help you think through this. And once I'm sworn in, if you still need help, you'll have it."

Something settled in him — relief, determination, maybe even a little defiance.

"Thank you," he whispered. "I didn't know who else to ask."

I nodded, because I understood that too. People often assume institutions correct themselves.

"Send me everything," I said. "We'll figure out the next step."

And just like that, the first case of my legal career began.

* * *

After I took my oath and joined the Oklahoma State Bar, everything moved quickly. I met with Joey again, this time with the authority to represent him formally. We signed a representation agreement that same afternoon. The document was simple, but it meant Joey finally had counsel and launched my legal career.

I filed the complaint naming David Boren in his official capacity. The University of Oklahoma responded with a predictable procedural maneuver, insisting Boren wasn't the proper party. The court agreed and dismissed without prejudice, so I refiled against the University of Oklahoma itself. Within a few weeks, the university removed the case to federal court, where they immediately moved to dismiss again. This time, they argued that FERPA barred disclosure altogether.

I drafted our response and cited the cases they preferred to ignore. Decisions from around the country had rejected that exact interpretation of FERPA. A few weeks later, the federal judge issued a concise order. The claims were plausible. The case would go forward.

Support didn't arrive in a single wave but gathered in fragments from people who had been watching these fights unfold for years. Attorneys from Maryland and North Carolina emailed us their briefs, court orders, and research. The very lawyers who had litigated the now-famous Diamondback case at the University of Maryland and the University of North Carolina football records fight. They had forced their universities to release the ticket records after courts rejected FERPA as a shield.

One of the Maryland attorneys wrote in his email:

"Your fact pattern is almost identical. Don't let them bluff you."

A lawyer from North Carolina added:

"The University of North Carolina tried the same argument. The court rejected it."

Those messages mattered legally and morally. They told Joey that he wasn't imagining the obstruction. They told me that the university wasn't relying on the law but on the culture of deference that surrounds football programs in places like Oklahoma.

The local press started reaching out. National outlets put in queries. Reporters who had once hit the same wall now wanted to know whether Joey might finally break through it.

During that same stretch, I kept writing letters of my own. One to the Army's G-1, another to a Deputy Assistant Secretary of Defense, another to a medical policy officer whose name I'd found buried in an old Department of Defense directive. I drafted them whenever I could carve out the time: after drill weekends, between job applications, in the quiet spaces left over after legal work. Joey was fighting for transparency in his world while I was fighting for the right to serve in mine. In different ways, we were both trying to force massive systems to acknowledge the obvious, and both systems were hoping we would just stop pushing.

Freedom of Information Oklahoma awarded us a small litigation grant. Enough to keep copying costs and filing fees from becoming a burden. Symbolically, it meant far more: someone outside the university believed this fight was worth it.

I also reached out to one of my fraternity brothers. A Sigma Nu who helped establish our chapter with me at the University of Central Oklahoma. Years later, we ended up as classmates in the part-time evening program at the Oklahoma City University School of Law, before I deployed to Afghanistan. When the case moved forward, I needed to affiliate with local counsel under Oklahoma's rules, and he agreed to serve as my appearance attorney.

Once the court resolved the preliminary motions, discovery began in earnest.

Interrogatories went out. Requests for production followed. Responses trickled in. Narrow, evasive, and worded with the precision that signaled the university intended to fight disclosure inch by inch.

And then the University of Oklahoma noticed depositions.

That was the moment the litigation shifted from paperwork to confrontation. The university's attorneys wanted to probe everything. His reporting, his motives, his conversations with the *Oklahoma Daily*, even whether a student had standing to demand public records at all.

No college student should have had to face that kind of institutional pressure alone.

* * *

Opposing counsel scheduled the depositions for a Friday. I flew back to Oklahoma the night before on the late flight where the cabin lights stay dim, and everyone keeps to themselves. It gave me too much time to think. Not about the case, but about Joey. He was young, smart, earnest, and completely unprepared for what a deposition actually feels like.

Most people outside the legal world imagine depositions as orderly, almost clinical. The reality is nothing like that. Under fluorescent lights, they become invasions that probe your credibility, your memory, your stability, even the person you are when no one is watching.

And for a student reporter challenging one of the most powerful institutions in the state? They probe even deeper.

The next morning, Joey showed up in a pressed shirt that didn't quite fit, carrying a notebook he kept checking even though it was mostly empty. He looked like someone trying to prepare for a test for which no one had given him the study guide.

Before we went in, he pulled me aside in the hallway outside the conference room.

"What if I mess this up?" he asked quietly.

"You won't," I said. "And if you stumble, we regroup and keep going. That's how this works."

He nodded, but his hands were tight around his pen.

Inside, the university's attorneys came at him from every angle.

"Have you ever used illegal drugs?"

"Have you ever plagiarized anything you wrote?"

"Are you in a romantic relationship?"

"Has the university ever disciplined you?"

"What is your GPA?"

"Has anyone ever treated you for a mental-health condition?"

"Have you ever lied to a professor?"

"List every job you've ever held."

They wanted to rattle him, to make him small, unsure of his own memory. Institutions attack the kid asking the question when they can't defend their actions.

And then the questioning took a turn I hadn't expected.

"Did you make the records request as a private citizen," their lead counsel asked, "or as a representative of the *Oklahoma Daily*?"

Joey hesitated. "I made it as well, I mean—I work at the *Oklahoma Daily*, so—"

"That's not my question," the lawyer cut in. "Which capacity? Student? Employee? Individual requester? Which hat were you wearing when you submitted the request?"

I leaned back, watching. They weren't asking because they genuinely needed the answer. They were revealing the only argument they thought they had. If Joey had made the request as a journalist, the *Oklahoma Daily* should have sued instead of him. It was a distinction without a difference, but it told me exactly where they were planning to take the fight next. And it told me who I needed to talk to after this deposition.

When the session finally wrapped, Joey looked hollowed out the same way most people look after a deposition. Even when you tell the truth, the process pushes you to believe you've done something wrong. He had spent hours being cross-examined about every corner of his life, as though requesting public records made him suspect.

When the door closed and the attorneys disappeared down the hall, he let out a long breath and slumped back in his chair.

"I feel like I did everything wrong," he murmured.

"You didn't," I said, moving my chair closer. "This is what they do. They make the process so invasive that you question your own motives. It's meant to wear you down."

He rubbed his palms against his knees. "It worked. I feel like a mess."

"That's because you care," I said. "And because you told the truth under pressure. That's harder than people realize. But they never touched the core issue. Not once."

He looked up. "You mean the records request?"

"Exactly. You asked for public records. They refused. Everything today was noise meant to distract you from that."

Joey exhaled slowly, some of the tension leaving his shoulders.

"Joey," I added, "there are two kinds of people who challenge big systems. The ones who assume they can't lose, and the ones who know they might, but push anyway. Only one of those types ever makes anything change."

He swallowed. "Which one am I?"

"You tell me."

* * *

After the deposition, I walked the familiar stretch of pavement along the South Oval. At that hour, the sidewalks that were usually packed between classes were mostly empty. A few stragglers cut across the lawn, but otherwise it was quiet.

The *Oklahoma Daily*'s newsroom was still in the old journalism building. Inside, it looked almost exactly as I remembered: long rows of open desks, computers lined up in neat grids, no walls or cubicles, just an open work floor where everything felt exposed.

In the center of the room, on a bulletin board that had somehow survived several generations of editors, was the 11x17 sheet I had put up during my last semester. Plain white paper, black marker, curling at the edges. My handwriting.

I stepped closer and tapped the corner with my finger.

Across the top, I had written: ASK EVERY WEEK

Below it were the three headings I'd scrawled years earlier:

WHAT WE SHOULD BE REQUESTING:

- Crime logs
- Parking citation data
- Regents' agendas
- Major contracts
- Title IX complaints

HOW TO FILE A REQUEST:

- Put everything in writing
- Use statutory language
- Track deadlines
- Follow up in writing

WHAT WE SHOULD REPORT EVERY WEEK:

- How many requests did you file
- How many remain unanswered
- Which ones are the most delayed
- Which offices aren't responding

I didn't design it to be pretty or inspirational. The poster was a reminder that open-records work is relentless and unglamorous. An institution's silence is itself a story. Accountability exists only when someone will demand it.

I was still looking at it when a student reporter glanced up.

"Hey — are you looking for someone?"

"The editor-in-chief," I said.

"She's out right now. Want me to leave a message?"

I scribbled my name and number and stepped back out onto the South Oval. The sidewalks were nearly empty. The air felt flat, and the campus felt strangely still.

About ten minutes later, my phone rang.

"Hi, Nick? This is the *Oklahoma Daily*'s editor. You stopped by?"

"I did. I just left Joey's deposition. We need to talk."

"Is he alright?"

"He made it through," I said. "But the university showed its hand, and it's not subtle. They're going to argue he didn't make the records request as a private citizen but as a reporter."

"That's ridiculous."

"It is. But it's the only path they have left. The motions are going nowhere. The precedent isn't on their side. So they'll reframe the entire case around who counts as a requester."

She was quiet for a moment, taking that in.

"And if they convince a judge he didn't have standing…"

"They'll move to dismiss," I said. "Hard. Quickly. And without the *Oklahoma Daily* joining, they might get traction."

Another pause. Not uncertainty, but calculation. The silence that comes from feeling the weight of an institution leaning back at you.

"You want us to join the lawsuit."

"I'm asking whether you'll consider it," I said. "Joey shouldn't be standing alone against the university. And you know exactly what this fight is about. Transparency, accountability, and whether the administration gets to decide which laws apply to them. That poster inside your newsroom wasn't just decoration."

She exhaled slowly and steadily. "I'll talk to our adviser tonight. And the board. We meet tomorrow."

"Take the time you need. Just know the university isn't waiting."

***

It didn't resolve quickly.

For the next several days, there were emails, questions, and clarifications. The editorial board wanted to understand the risks. The student media adviser wanted to know the legal exposure. Someone asked whether the university might retaliate against the newspaper's funding.

All the while, the University of Oklahoma kept laying groundwork. More silence from the General Counsel's Office, more procedural hints that a dismissal motion was coming. Everyone knew we didn't have much time left.

By the end of the week, she called back.

"We're in," she said. "The editorial board voted. We're signing on as a plaintiff. And we're writing a front-page editorial explaining why."

I let myself smile. The genuine kind, not the tired professional one.

"That's the *Oklahoma Daily* I remember."

"It's still us," she said. "We just needed the reminder."

***

By the next morning, the campus was buzzing. Word spread across the state by afternoon.

The *Oklahoma Daily*'s front-page editorial hit stands at dawn, a full-throated declaration that they were joining the lawsuit. They named the university's refusal to release the parking-ticket records for exactly what it was. Obstruction wrapped in the language of privacy. The editorial moved fast. Student papers across the country picked it up. Freedom of Information organizations reposted it. Reporters from North Carolina and Maryland emailed Joey congratulations. These were the very people who had fought versions of this battle before.

And within twenty-four hours, the impossible happened. President David Boren issued a public statement.

He announced he had reviewed the matter and was directing the university's Open Records Office to release the student-athlete parking ticket records. FERPA did not apply, he admitted. These were violation records, not educational ones. And the public had a right to know.

But twenty-four hours after that, Oklahoma State University's president issued an almost identical statement. The two public institutions in the state had stonewalled the *Oklahoman* and *Tulsa World* for years. Both reversed course because one student refused to be ignored.

Joey Stipek had accomplished what the two largest major state newspapers couldn't.

* * *

I was back in DC by then, sitting in the passenger seat of a car packed with coolers and beach towels as my kickball team made the familiar drive to Rehoboth Beach for a long holiday weekend. The windows were down, the air carried salt and sunscreen, and for the first time in months, I felt something like ease.

My phone rang. The university's general counsel. I answered. A polite voice. Formal. Controlled.

"Mr. Harrison, I'm calling to notify you that the university will release the requested records. We are also prepared to pay reasonable attorney's fees under the Oklahoma Open Records Act."

There it was. Decades of foot-dragging were undone by a twenty-year-old reporter and a lawsuit that everyone had predicted would drag on for years.

Oklahoma's open-records law carried actual force. One of the few in the country guaranteed attorneys' fees for plaintiffs who prevailed. That provision gave ordinary people a real chance to fight back. It meant that suing for public records wasn't symbolic but viable. And that mattered because transparency shouldn't depend on the size of your bank account.

When we got to Rehoboth, the team scattered toward the water, the bars, everyone ready for a rare weekend of sun and distraction. I was still processing the phone call when one of my teammates walked straight up to me, grinning. The only other person from Oklahoma in the league.

"Dude," he said, pointing at me with a bottle of beer, "did you seriously just take on the University of Oklahoma and win? My mom texted me this morning. It's all over the Oklahoma news."

I laughed, caught between disbelief and pride. "It wasn't me. Joey did the hard part."

"No," he said, shaking his head. "People back home are talking about it like it's some kind of earthquake. The University of Oklahoma never backs down. And Oklahoma State University flipped, too? That's huge."

We stood there a moment, the waves crashing somewhere beyond the dunes, the boardwalk humming behind us.

For a second, I let myself take it in. What it meant for Joey, for the *Oklahoma Daily*, for transparency in a state where football culture often swallowed accountability. A student had demanded answers. The press backed him. The institutions blinked.

Chapter Eleven

The extended drill weekend began in the motor pool auditorium. It was a cavernous maintenance bay with rows of metal folding chairs set up facing a portable projection screen. The cold made every breath visible, and the sharp smell of diesel drifted in from the line of vehicles idling outside. Soldiers shuffled in, jackets zipped, hands tucked into their sleeves, trying to stay warm.

Beside me on a table, several black binders sat in neat rows, one for each vehicle commander and driver. Inside each binder were full-color satellite images, laminated strip maps, turn-by-turn instructions, checkpoint descriptions, danger areas, alternate routes, and radio procedures. I had spent hours putting them together, building them exactly like the convoy packets we had used overseas.

Most of these soldiers had never deployed. They had never seen what a real convoy brief looked like. If they were going to learn anything this weekend, I wanted it to start here.

Once the company sat down, I opened the first binder and began.

"This is the route from the DC Armory to the training site," I said, holding up a satellite photo. "You've all driven it before, but today you're going to see it the way we planned convoys downrange."

I explained each segment of the route, pointing out blind intersections where convoys bunched up, the overpass that created a natural choke point, the wooded stretch that limited lateral observation, and the wide turn where spacing became critical. The room grew quieter as the soldiers realized this wasn't the usual "follow the lead truck" briefing.

In the back of the room, Lieutenant Colonel Michael Funderburk and Major Amber Ellison stood together, arms folded, listening. They said nothing, but I could see their expressions change from curiosity to something like approval. They hadn't expected this level of detail, but they knew exactly why it mattered.

When I finished the last page, I closed the binder and handed the stacks out.

"You don't need a packet like this for every convoy," I said, "but you should know what a real one looks like. You won't know when someone is taking shortcuts if you're unfamiliar with the right way to do things."

The room stayed quiet. Soldiers flipped through the binders.

I dismissed them to their trucks, and we rolled out.

* * *

Two days later, the battalion we were supporting rolled into its capstone exercise. By then, the cold had sunk into everyone's bones. They had been running lanes for days with short nights, long hours, icy wind cutting through every layer, and their discipline was slipping in small but noticeable ways. People were slower in getting out of trucks, and leaders were less sharp in their orders. Every movement showed fatigue.

But the mission for this final lane couldn't have been clearer. The S-3 had briefed it multiple times, written it down, and even reiterated it over the radio that morning:

Drive to the mock village. Stop. Establish a security cordon. Dismount. Distribute humanitarian aid. Maintain accountability of personnel and equipment.

It required no complexity, only deliberation.

When the unit approached the village and received simulated contact, I expected them to halt, fan out, return notional fire, and start moving into position. That was what the lane called for. That was what the orders required.

Instead, their NCOs said, "Push through! Keep going! Don't stop!"

And the whole formation obeyed.

Trucks sped up, soldiers kept jogging, and they blew straight past the village without even slowing down. They didn't set a cordon, dismount, or distribute a single bag of notional aid. The village itself slid past their windows as they rushed to be finished.

Right in the middle of that chaos, one of their crews stalled a truck; the vehicle fell behind, pulled to the side, and the crew abandoned it.

The gunner didn't stay with it. The dismounts didn't secure it, and no one keyed the radio to report it.

The abandoned truck just sat there in the cold, engine off, doors unlocked, equipment still inside.

One of my specialists stopped beside me and stared at it.

"Sergeant, that's one of theirs, right?"

"Yeah," I said. "It is."

He looked down the lane as their formation dipped out of sight. "They're really just leaving it?"

"Looks that way."

The lane was still active, and the opposing unit was long gone, without recovering the truck or even acknowledging they'd lost it.

I turned to my squad, the cold crunching under my boots.

"Gloves on," I said. "Move out."

And we stepped off toward the abandoned vehicle.

* * *

My soldiers jogged to the abandoned vehicle and immediately began stripping it of radios, dummy sensitive items, weapons mounts, ammo cans, cargo straps, and toolkits. They worked fast and efficiently. They didn't need an explanation; they knew exactly why we were doing it. This was what an enemy would do. Abandoning equipment invites exactly this response.

About five minutes in, I heard heavy boots pounding on frozen ground. Two senior NCOs were storming toward us, a sergeant first class and a first sergeant. Both were red-faced, breath smoking in the cold, already yelling before they even reached the truck.

The sergeant first class got to me first.

"Harrison! What the hell do you think you're doing?" He stepped right up into my space.

"We're OPFOR, Sergeant First Class. You abandoned your vehicle. We're treating it as enemy materiel."

"You don't touch our equipment. Put it back. All of it."

Before I could respond, the first sergeant shoved forward.

"You're done here. Stop what you're doing. Put every piece of that gear back in the truck. Right now."

I came to parade rest. Heels together, hands behind my back, chin lifted, eyes straight ahead. Calm and steady.

"First Sergeant, with respect, no. We're playing OPFOR. Their crew left the vehicle unsecured. We are executing our orders."

Her voice shot up in pitch and volume. "Don't you 'with respect' me. I am telling you to stop."

I didn't move.

"First Sergeant, my orders come from my chain of command. If you have an issue, you'll need to take it up with my commander."

The sergeant first class shouldered in beside him now, practically vibrating with anger.

"You don't tell a senior NCO no!" Soldiers turned to look.

I kept my posture. I kept my tone.

"Sergeant First Class, I am executing my orders."

They both lost their bearing completely, shouting over each other, jabbing fingers toward the truck, demanding we reverse what we'd done. The more they yelled, the quieter I became. There was no argument, no escalation, no movement. I stood at parade rest and let them tire out.

Behind them, their junior soldiers had stopped moving, staring at the scene with wide eyes. They had never seen a sergeant stand his ground calmly while two senior NCOs let their tempers run wild.

Finally, the first sergeant jabbed a finger at me.

"This isn't over, Harrison."

"Understood, First Sergeant."

They stormed off, still yelling as they went, kicking frozen clumps of mud out of their way.

I turned to my squad.

"Keep working. Finish it."

One of my specialists stepped up, shaking his head in disbelief.

"Sergeant, I've seen nothing like that."

I shrugged. "Just do your job. Let them handle theirs."

He nodded, still processing what he'd seen. "Yeah, but they were losing it. And you didn't even blink."

And we went back to work.

* * *

That evening's after-action review took place in a drafty canvas tent, the kind the Army drags out for winter field problems. Two industrial heaters roared in opposite corners, filling the air with the smell of diesel and damp gear. One row of benches held the opposing unit, another our military police company. At the front, an observer/controller stood with a clipboard, waiting for the room to settle.

Squad leaders from the other battalion went first. They spoke like people selling success.

"Overall successful movement. Maintained momentum through contact. We didn't allow ourselves to get bogged down. Completed the scenario efficiently."

Listening to them, you would've thought they had executed every step perfectly.

When they finished, the OC looked straight at me. He already knew I had something to say.

"Sergeant Harrison. Go ahead."

I stood.

"With respect, you failed the mission."

That got attention. A few soldiers shifted on the benches. One of the squad leaders turned slightly.

"The stated task was to enter the village, establish a full security cordon, dismount, and distribute humanitarian aid. None of that happened. The element bypassed the village entirely. And during simulated contact, you left a vehicle behind without reporting it or attempting to recover it."

One of their NCOs: "We were coming back for it."

I shook my head. "No. You exited the lane. You never returned."

Just the facts. The same way we documented deficiencies downrange. I went on.

"In combat, you don't have time to think things through. You don't stop to think and then decide to do the right thing. You run on adrenaline and muscle memory. By the time you realize you shouldn't be doing something, it's already too late because you're already doing it."

For years, the Army documented versions of this in its lessons learned. Paratroopers hit the ground and rolled up their parachutes because the Army trained them to do it on every drop zone. Leaders knew actual contact required leaving the chute and moving. Wounded soldiers removed their helmets because the Army taught us to signal someone out of the fight that way. Enemy fire exploits that exposure and kills them.

"What soldiers practice becomes reflex. What they've rehearsed."

I looked back at the lane diagram.

"When leaders bypass a task because they're cold and tired, those leaders set the standard. When soldiers see a crew abandon a vehicle in contact and everyone ignores it, the unit normalizes that failure. And when training gives way to an actual fight, people fall back on the standards their leaders trained them to accept."

The tent went quiet.

The OC nodded once. "All valid points."

Across the benches, some of the junior enlisted from the other battalion were nodding too. Subtle, almost hidden, but unmistakable. They knew exactly what they'd seen out there.

The battalion commander said nothing. He just gave a small nod.

The after-action review moved on after that, but the tone had shifted.

* * *

By the time we rolled back into the city after that field exercise, exhaustion settled deep in my joints and lingered long after the cold faded. The confrontation on the lane, the after-action review, and the unspoken tension between right and wrong standards of leadership lingered with me on the drive home.

It wasn't a simple transition. In the field, you understand your purpose, know your duties, and every hour contributes to the mission. Back in DC, everything felt uncertain. The Army was still fighting me. My future in uniform was unresolved. And the civilian world, the world I'd moved here to build a career in, no longer felt solid beneath my feet.

Out in the cold, the mission answered for you. You met it, or you didn't. You recovered what belonged to you or watched it disappear. Leaders answered in real time, and consequences followed immediately, ready or not. Even in the chaos around that abandoned vehicle, nothing felt ambiguous. You acted, you adapted, you upheld the standard.

Back in Washington, nothing worked that way.

There were no lanes, no OCs, no clean evaluations of performance. People didn't solve problems but let them drift, multiply, or push them down the line until paperwork diluted them into nothing. In the field, even bad news carried clarity. In DC, uncertainty settled in like weather, heavy and persistent and impossible to fight through. The systems I depended on responded with indifference, crept, and ignored urgency. The shift from a world where everything mattered to one where almost nothing seemed to was disorienting.

And that was the hardest part. I had returned to a city I barely understood, one built on process rather than purpose, where prestige mattered more than performance. The law felt just out of reach.

For most people who come to Washington, DC, the law is something they studied once, not something they expect to practice. People arrive chasing federal careers, roles tied to national influence, not local courtrooms. People know DC as the place where lawmakers make laws, not the place where residents live under them.

I was no different. When I moved here, I never imagined I would end up practicing law in the District of Columbia. I assumed my legal credentials would sit quietly in the background while I built a federal career, served my country, and worked toward senior leadership. I had other plans. And none of them involved standing before a DC judge, hand raised, swearing an oath. But life has a way of narrowing our choices until only the essential ones remain.

After the fight with the Army, the fallout from challenging the government's discriminatory HIV policies, and the unresolved battle to stay in uniform, I found myself in a precarious place. My bank account was shrinking, my future was uncertain. Every door that had once felt open now seemed firmly closed. Going home to Oklahoma was no longer an option. I had endured too much, survived Afghanistan, and spent a lifetime trying to rise above the circumstances I was born into. Practicing law in DC wasn't my dream. It was my lifeline.

The process of waiving into the DC Bar is deceptively simple. You fill out an application, mail in a stack of documents, and wait.

People treat DC politics as fast-moving, but the legal world moves at a glacial pace. Your application sits untouched for nearly a year. It doesn't matter how urgent your situation is or how desperately you need work. It doesn't matter whether you're trying to pay rent while fighting your own government for the right to serve. The process is what it is, passive, unmoving, immune to desperation.

To complete the application, I needed my MBE and MPRE scores sent directly from the Oklahoma Bar Examiners. I dug out the old contact information and emailed, expecting a perfunctory reply. Instead, I received something entirely different. A moment of human kindness in a year defined by institutional indifference.

A message popped up from a woman in the office of the Oklahoma Board of Bar Examiners.

"Mr. Harrison, of course, I remember you."

I blinked at the screen, surprised that anyone remembered my name. Much less my circumstances. When I called her office to follow up, she answered with a warmth I hadn't expected.

"You're the young man who emailed me from Kuwait, aren't you?"

"Yes, ma'am. I deployed during the bar exam window."

"I remember. We rarely get requests from overseas war zones. I'm glad you made it home safely. Give me a day. I'll prepare the letter and get it sent to DC."

It was such a small thing, and yet it brought a lump to my throat.

Most veterans don't ask for much, but when someone helps you quickly and without suspicion, the gesture lodges deep inside you.

The rest of the process wasn't nearly as kind. Months passed with no action on my application. During that time, my financial situation worsened. Without a waiver into the DC Bar, I couldn't practice. Without practicing, I couldn't build a stable income. And with the ongoing fight against Army policy consuming my energy and my attention, it felt like every option I had was being squeezed into nothing.

Occasionally, I would check the DC Bar's portal even though I knew it wouldn't change. Months passed with no updates, no requests, no acknowledgement that I existed.

Meanwhile, the bills came, and the job offers didn't. The sense of humiliation grew heavier by the day.

It is a strange and painful thing to stand on the edge of your own profession and be told you cannot enter, not because of merit, but because of process. Money. Arbitrary barriers erected generations ago and preserved under the guise of "professionalism."

People like to pretend the legal profession is a meritocracy. It is not. Survival through law school requires money. Months off to study for the bar, application and background check fees, bar exam fees, and the ability to sit and wait while paperwork gathers dust.

And if you don't come from money or if you don't have a military salary or GI Bill benefits or a deployment savings account to fall back on, the profession becomes a series of closed doors.

I was one of the lucky ones. It didn't feel like it, but the Army had given me things that cushioned the fall. Discipline, determination, a sense of purpose, and enough savings from deployment to keep me fed.

But for most people, the barriers are insurmountable.

After nearly a year, I finally received a letter from the DC Bar Examiners. I tore it open and instead found a problem I never expected. They had found "another" Nicholas Harrison in Oklahoma. He had multiple evictions, and they needed me to prove that I wasn't him.

I remember staring at the page in disbelief and muttering,

"You've got to be kidding me."

But pride found no room. Anger found no room. Training drove my response. Quick, clear, and complete.

I pulled old leases, bank statements, deployment orders, anything to anchor me in time and place. Anything to prove that my life was not someone else's.

Weeks passed before anything reached me. A background check controlled my future, my ability to practice law, and my financial survival.

But eventually, the letter arrived. I cleared the check, and the court scheduled my swearing-in.

I stood in my apartment with the notice in my hands and whispered,

"Finally."

It had taken a year.

* * *

The morning of the ceremony was sharp with cold, the air that stings your lungs and heightens your awareness. I walked through Judiciary Square, my breath rising in pale clouds, until the building emerged before me. It was solemn, monumental, older than nearly everything around it.

The District of Columbia Court of Appeals, housed in what was once Washington's first City Hall, stood like a stone guardian of the city's legal past. Its sandstone façade, weathered by nearly two centuries of history, carried the quiet confidence of a structure that had watched Americans argue, deny, expand, and redefine justice.

I climbed the broad marble steps, running my gloved hand along the column beside me. I had read about this place. Construction started in 1820, expanded through the 19th century, and it had adjudicated everything from routine municipal disputes to cases under the Fugitive Slave Act. Here, enslaved people once stood before judges who decided the course of their lives. Abolitionist lawyers pressed arguments that would echo through history. Judges denied justice in this building, and lawyers and the enslaved fought to reclaim it.

Inside, the warmth enveloped me immediately. The lobby was quiet at this early hour, save for the sound of footsteps and hushed voices echoing through its vaulted corridors. Signs posted along the walls told the building's story of city politics, of Civil War-era cases, of its transformation from a practical municipal hall to the symbolic heart of the District of Columbia's judiciary.

Since I had arrived early and alone, I wandered the corridors slowly, letting my fingers trail across the cool surfaces of the gray marble banisters. Most of the others being sworn in had family with them. Clusters of parents, siblings, and spouses all dressed in their finest, snapping photos under the grand archways. Their laughter filled the hall like music. I kept my hands in my pockets, watching with warmth and distance.

A security officer noticed me reading one of the historical plaques.

"First time here?" he asked.

"First time," I said. "Feels strange to be joining the bar in a place with this much history."

He chuckled. "Son, this building has seen everything. Triumphs, tragedies, and a lot of in-between. You'll fit right in."

There was something grounded in his tone.

As court staff finally called us in, I stepped through the heavy wooden doors into a space shaped by nearly two centuries of Washington's legal history. The room rose high above us, lit from a broad skylight that cast a pale winter glow across the paneled benches and the pale stone walls. Tall arched windows echoed the Greek Revival façade outside, and pairs of Corinthian pilasters climbed toward a crisp plaster cornice that circled the room like a quiet architectural drumbeat.

Everything felt deliberate. The symmetry, the restraint, the sense of order that came from an older age. Oil portraits of long-gone judges lined the upper walls, their steady gazes fixed on the crowd as though measuring each of us. The space carried a gravity that settled into my bones. It was dignified rather than ornate. It felt like a room that remembered every argument ever made within it.

I took my seat alone.

My suit, ordered years earlier from an Afghan tailor who visited our base in Darul Aman, felt like a quiet tribute to the strange, winding path that had brought me here. I smoothed the fabric, straightened my tie, and waited.

When the judges entered, the room rose in unison. A clerk read the formal introductions, her voice echoing off the plaster vaults. Then came the moment that would change everything.

We lifted our right hands.

The oath was familiar to me. Echoes of other oaths I had taken in desert outposts, military offices, and parade fields. But this one carried a different weight, one that tied me not only to the Constitution I had sworn to defend, but to the community I was pledging to serve.

"I, Nicholas Alexander Harrison, do solemnly swear or affirm that as a member of the Bar of this Court, I will demean myself uprightly and according to law; and that I will support the Constitution of the United States of America."

The words resonated through my chest. They landed as something lived, not promised.

In that moment, standing beneath the ornate plaster ceiling, surrounded by the carved oak and the murmured pride of families, I felt a shift inside myself. I had not come to practice law. But DC had become the place where I fought, endured, rebuilt, and insisted on belonging.

When the ceremony ended, people embraced their families, posed for photos, and wiped tears. I retrieved my coat and walked back into the frigid January air alone, but carrying something I hadn't felt in a very long time.

As I descended the marble steps, the city presented itself differently. Washington never softens, but it felt sharper, more legible, as the oath cut through years of blur and brought its lines into focus. The same cold that once bit through my uniform in the field now pressed against my suit, but it no longer acted as an adversary. It felt like the air of a place I had chosen at last, even when it had resisted choosing me in return.

For years, I had kept a certain emotional distance from this city, living here but never letting myself inhabit it. Washington was where I worked, where I struggled, where I fought the Army, where I waited for decisions that never came. But belonging? I had never allowed myself that word. Maybe I didn't think I deserved it. Maybe deep inside, I was still the kid from Oklahoma who expected every institution to say no. Maybe because DC itself had made me earn every inch of ground.

But as I walked away from the courthouse, something steadied inside me. Thoughts turned to the cold field exercise, the abandoned vehicle, and standing my ground while senior NCOs shouted in my face. The months of bureaucratic silence, the misidentification, the financial fear, the humiliation of waiting on a system that treated urgency as inconvenience. How easy it would have been to leave, to go home, to start over, to shrink my life into something smaller and safer.

And yet I hadn't.

I had stayed, persisted, and fought for a place in this city with the same stubbornness the Army had taught me in far harsher conditions. The battlefield was different, quieter, lonelier, hidden behind forms and hearings and waiting rooms. But the endurance required was the same.

Over the next few days, the transformation formalized. My Oklahoma driver's license gave way to a DC one. Voter registration followed. My name was added to the roll of attorneys allowed to practice in the jurisdiction where the next battles would unfold. On paper, these were ordinary acts; in truth, they were declarations of identity.

Something fundamental had shifted. I no longer saw myself as someone passing through, someone whose life in this city was temporary or conditional. The waiting for permission had ended. So had the waiting for the Army to decide my worth, or for bureaucrats to acknowledge my existence. In every sense that mattered, I was now a Washingtonian.

Chapter Twelve

The exhilaration of being sworn into the DC Bar carried me for a few days, but it wasn't long before reality reasserted itself. The glow of the oath faded quickly when stacked against the numbers in my bank account. My fellowship was over. My unemployment benefits had expired. And the job market had shown me no mercy. The truth left no room for interpretation. I needed work. With a DC Bar number finally in hand, I could start looking in earnest.

Document review was the most realistic starting point. It wasn't glamorous, but it was honest legal work. And it paid. Most staffing agencies in DC wouldn't even talk to you until you took the oath. "Pending admission" might as well have been a scarlet letter. But now I could walk through those doors.

One of the first places I reached out to was a document-review professional staffing service on F Street, just down from the National Press Club. The neighborhood carried a sense of importance. Reporters crossed 14th Street with coffee in hand. Government workers streamed toward the Metro escalators. The Press Club's stone façade rose above the sidewalk, its brass doors and blue awning impossible to miss. Across the street, Art Deco fronts and older brick buildings pressed together. The air held the smell of roasted chestnuts from a street cart mixed with early-morning exhaust.

I stepped into the firm's suite carrying a résumé that still felt too thin and an urgency I failed to hide.

A woman in her fifties greeted me with a practiced, professional smile. She wore her long, dark-blonde curls loose, paired a tailored navy blouse with a simple pearl necklace, and carried the calm confidence of someone who had spent decades placing other people where they needed to land.

She introduced herself by first name only and shook my hand. "You must be Nicholas," she said, sizing up what I needed before I said a word.

"Yes, ma'am," I said. The military reflex slipped out before I could stop it. "Thank you for meeting with me."

She laughed lightly. "No need to 'ma'am' me. Have a seat. Let's look at what you've got."

I handed her my resume. She scanned it with quick, practiced eyes, nodding as she reached the lines about my military service, my Afghanistan deployment, my bar admission.

"Well," she said, setting it down. "You're exactly what we need, and we're always looking for attorneys who show up, work hard, and don't bring drama."

She spoke without preface or posture, and made it easy to listen.

"Can you start on Monday?" she asked.

The question caught me so off guard that I almost didn't process it. "Monday?" I echoed. "Absolutely. I can start anytime."

"Good," she said. "I'll submit you for the next project. Doc review is never glamorous, but it'll give you steady hours. And steady hours mean steady pay."

She stood, shook my hand again, and added, almost as an afterthought, "I know things are hard out there for new attorneys right now. We try to make this a soft landing."

* * *

On the first day of the project, they asked us to arrive in suits. It felt ceremonial, almost like another oath. A quiet acknowledgment that, even if the work didn't require courtroom polish, we were still lawyers. After that day, business casual was fine; no one cared much what you wore as long as you showed up and worked.

The project site sat a few floors up in a bland downtown building. The kind a committee clearly designed. Inside, rows of computers stretched across a large, open room. A makeshift legal factory humming with fluorescent lights and the soft clicks of dozens of mice. It was not the dream job any attorney imagined when they passed the bar. But for many of us, it was a lifeline.

What struck me most was the understanding built into the culture. Everyone knew document review wasn't a calling. It was a bridge job for people between law firm positions, or for attorneys who needed something steady while they chased their next opportunity. No one judged you for looking elsewhere. No one punished you for interviewing. They wanted you to say something before you quit.

"If you're leaving, give us a little notice so we're not shorthanded."

It was the most reasonable thing any employer had asked of me.

And they paid overtime happily, even gratefully. The work was repetitive, but it was honest. When you needed the hours, they were there. When you needed a break to attend an interview, they understood.

For the first time in months, I felt a sense of stability. Not success, but stability.

* * *

I was in my room after another long evening of document review when my phone buzzed with a number I didn't recognize. The kind where the screen blurs if you look at it too long. Normally, I would have let it go to voicemail. This time I answered.

"Good morning, this is Lieutenant Colonel Conreau Williams."

Her voice carried the calm authority of someone accustomed to making decisions that mattered. I straightened instinctively.

"Yes, ma'am. Sergeant Harrison."

She didn't waste time. "I've read your memorandum. Your request for an exception to policy regarding your HIV status." There was a brief pause, followed by a quick, genuine laugh. "And I have to say, your line about the Army acting like it's still the 1980s, that one was right on target."

It was strange hearing a senior officer speak so plainly. But she shifted immediately back to business.

"Here's the issue," she said. "You wrote a strong memo, but you didn't submit a packet. And without full supporting documentation, no one can act on anything."

I felt the weight of that sink in. Months of work on that memorandum, and I was now learning it hadn't even placed me at the start line.

"That said," she continued, "it is a perfectly reasonable request. There's nothing improper in what you're asking. It just has to be documented correctly."

Her tone was factual. Then she said, "They assigned me to help you assemble the packet. It's going to require comprehensive documentation. Medical records, treatment history, lab results, service documents, evaluations, everything. It needs to be complete and in the proper format."

"Yes, ma'am," I said. "Tell me what you need."

"I'll send you the list," she replied. "You should begin gathering everything. Some of it you'll have to request, and that can take time."

There was no promise in her voice, no suggestion of where this might lead. When she ended the call, the room felt suddenly quieter, the glow of my laptop screen unchanged.

The work in front of me had gone nowhere, but I had a new job now.

* * *

The list Lieutenant Colonel Williams sent me was long enough that I had to read it twice before it fully registered. It wasn't a checklist so much as a full inventory of my life: medical, military, academic, legal. None of it existed in one place. Each piece required its own request, its own follow-up, its own wait. And every piece had to be exact.

I started with the memorandum. The version I had sent to the Army G-1 months earlier suddenly felt thin. Under her guidance, I rewrote it, clarifying dates, tightening the justification, and laying out the regulatory framework the way she told me a reviewing officer would expect to see it. I didn't do creative work. I did compliance work, making sure no missing detail gave anyone an excuse to dismiss it.

The medical portion was the worst. I needed a letter from my infectious disease specialist confirming my diagnosis, explaining my treatment regimen, documenting my lab history, and stating clearly that I was medically stable. But that wasn't enough. I also had to request years' worth of records. Initial diagnosis, viral load results, CD4 counts, treatment notes, and medication changes. It took multiple calls, releases, follow-ups, and more patience than I had.

I didn't expect one part of the requirement: the Army needed a medical opinion from its own contracted physician. Someone I had never met reviewed my file independently. When that opinion came back, it was blunt and to the point: there were no medical contraindications to my service as a Judge Advocate. It was a statement that the Army usually hides behind layers of vague phrasing. This one was clear. Even the contractor had written my status did not impair my ability to serve.

Alongside the medical records, I had to gather everything else that proved I was qualified. I collected diplomas, transcripts, my bar admission letter, my ERB, and every NCOER I could find. Letters from supervisors and attorneys I had worked with. Anything that might show I wasn't asking for a favor. I wanted to do a job I had already proven I could do.

The packet eventually took shape. Nothing about it felt triumphant. It felt like assembling an IRS audit file. The weight, the detail, the endless anticipation of what someone three levels up might want checked. But it eventually reached the point where even Williams said it was complete.

She sent it forward to the Army Surgeon General's office for their review. Weeks passed. Months. When the answer finally came back, it was almost absurd in its simplicity. The Surgeon General's office agreed with the contractor. They found no medical basis to prevent my service. No restrictions, no disqualifying conditions. Nothing justified the barriers I'd been fighting.

There wasn't much time to process the news. Almost immediately, I learned that Lieutenant Colonel Williams' assignment in the G-1 had ended. She was gone. The staff who had handled my packet were gone with her. And with her departure came a new directive: if I wanted the process to continue, I would have to route the entire request back through my chain of command. Starting from the bottom and walking it up, level by level, all over again.

* * *

I brought the packet to my company commander early one morning, half expecting the conversation to be awkward. It wasn't. He waved me in, skimmed the first page, and said, "State surgeon already briefed me. They told me you can do anything. No restrictions. From my standpoint, you're good."

"That's what the contractor's medical opinion said, too."

"Then I don't see the problem." He signed his endorsement on the spot. "Battalion will take it from here."

For a moment, it looked like the process might actually be straightforward. But it wasn't.

At the battalion, everything slowed. The staff didn't oppose my request. They just didn't want to touch it. They responded with polite hesitation, cosmetic suggestions, and endless contradictory questions about routing. A major wanted me to rewrite sections "to match battalion format." Someone else thought it should go through medical. Another suggested NGB directly. None of it was in regulation or required. It was bureaucracy looking to rearrange something instead of moving it.

After a week, the battalion sergeant major pulled me aside.

"Your packet's making people nervous," he said. "Nobody wants to be the one who moves it the wrong way."

"I don't need it rewritten," I told him. "I just need it endorsed and pushed up."

He nodded. "Yeah. I know."

And then nothing moved. Drills passed. Everyone weighed in, but no one had ownership. I couldn't push. It was too early for someone of my rank to escalate without it looking insubordinate. So I waited, watched the stall become undeniable, and finally did the only thing left:

I requested an open-door meeting.

* * *

Lieutenant Colonel Funderburk greeted me warmly. He already had my packet on his desk. I had seen this warmth in the field.

"Sir," I said, "the battalion has had this for several months. Every drill brings a new suggestion to rewrite this or reroute that, but G-1 helped me build it exactly the way the reviewing authority requires. The Surgeon General's contractor cleared the medical portion. I just need the endorsements so it can move up."

He flipped the pages. "State surgeon told me you can do anything," he said. "So the battalion has not acted on this for three months?"

"Yes, sir."

"Too long."

"Route this straight to Troop Command," he said. "Make no rewrites and allow no delays."

He used his authority decisively.

As I walked out, I knew my timing had to be perfect.

* * *

When the packet reached Troop Command, I let myself believe the worst was over.

It wasn't.

Within a month, I was seeing the same pattern repeat. Emails volleyed back and forth between sections, trying to send the packet to anyone except themselves. Personnel said it belonged with medical. Medical said the Staff Judge Advocate. The Staff Judge Advocate said they didn't review medical exceptions. No one cited the regulation. Everyone deferred responsibility.

And again, I couldn't push because I was a sergeant. Not yet. I had to let the record show that the delay was theirs, not mine.

By the third drill cycle, the stall was obvious.

One morning, Major Ellison spotted me in the hallway.

"I saw your packet downstairs," she whispered. "Why is it still at Troop Command?"

"They're still debating where it should go, ma'am."

She raised an eyebrow. "The G-1 told you exactly where it goes."

"Yes, ma'am."

She exhaled, annoyed. Not at me, but at the system. "I'll talk to some people. Do nothing yet."

It was the first time in months that someone with rank said out loud what I'd been living with. This wasn't confusion. It was avoidance.

Two days later, I got a call.

"Sergeant Harrison? This is Captain Donald Cravins. The Trial Defense Service assigned me to help you."

He spoke without rushing or qualifying his words, and the room settled around him.

"I'll track your packet," he said. "Too many offices are handling it, and that causes breakdowns. Send updates directly to me. Call if anything shifts."

Support that mattered.

Later, Major Ellison pulled me aside again. "The Chief of Staff agrees. This goes to the Specialty Branch Recruiter next. Don't wait for the staff to figure that out. I'll push it."

Within a week, the recruiter emailed. He needed every email I'd exchanged with G-1. Every instruction, every attachment, every clarification. I stayed up half the night pulling everything together and sent it as a single, organized packet.

I forwarded the update to Captain Cravins.

"Good," he said. "Now we track it."

* * *

By the time the packet had made its way through the 372nd MP Battalion, the 72nd Troop Command, and the Land Component Command, it had been in circulation for months. I had examined, questioned, adjusted, and resubmitted every memo, every endorsement, and every supporting document more times than I could count. And it was finally ready for the Commanding General.

Or so I thought.

Instead of landing on the general's desk, the packet came back down the chain and landed in my inbox with a message from the Specialty Branch Recruiter. He wrote in a clipped, precise tone:

"Sergeant Harrison, a senior officer said you will need to get original ink signatures for all memoranda and supporting documents if we want this request to receive serious attention. Electronic signatures will not suffice. Scanned signatures will not suffice. You must also change all dates on the memoranda and the DA 4187 to reflect August."

I read it twice, then a third time, because it made little sense. Months had already gone into routing the packet, staffing it, and collecting endorsements from commanders at three different levels. Everything matched G-1's instructions, down to the exact format they required. Now, at the very end, someone demanded that I redo every signature by hand and change the dates to make it appear that I had written the memos last week instead of half a year earlier.

It was bureaucratic theater for show.

The recruiter continued: "Please print the DA 4187, sign it in ink with a fresh date, and return the original to me. Once I have your ink-signed document, I will FedEx the packet to Lieutenant Colonel Funderburk for his original signature. The other commanders are standing by, so getting their ink signatures will not be an issue."

It was all treated as though the problem had never been the months of inaction but merely the color of the ink. The recruiter wrote the commanders were "standing by," as if they hadn't already signed the same documents months earlier, as if the entire issue turned on whether the signatures were wet or digital.

There was no arguing, no appeal, no alternate route. If I wanted the exception request to reach the general, I had to comply. So I did what the system demands of enlisted soldiers: I swallowed the irritation, printed every document, and started again.

Re-signing everything I had signed before, I rewrote the dates to match whatever month they wanted the paperwork to claim and coordinated with the recruiter to get ink signatures from officers who were local. We then overnighted the packet to North Carolina, waited for Lieutenant Colonel Funderburk's signature, and had it shipped back.

Each step was unnecessary. Each step was a repeat of something already done. Each step costs more time.

Once I gathered all the signatures in real ink and updated the dates, the Specialty Branch Recruiter compiled the packet again and moved it to the Staff Judge Advocate for legal review. The Staff Judge Advocate took one look at the request and announced that it "needed to be cleared by the Army Surgeon General."

I pointed out that the Army Surgeon General's contractor had cleared it months earlier. That the medical review already existed and that a favorable recommendation sat in the G-1's office. They hadn't known, hadn't looked, or hadn't bothered to ask.

The ink signatures alone consumed weeks, and the freshly rewritten dates conveniently erased any visible record of how long the packet had been sitting untouched. And somehow, despite all of it, despite the medical review already completed and every requirement already met, we had arrived back at the same circular problem.

*　*　*

By the time the packet finally made its way back to the Specialty Branch Recruiter, it had been a year since I first sent my request to the G-1. A full year of routing, rerouting, staffing, restaffing, halted packets, and delayed decisions. Open-door meetings, misplaced documents, signature drama, ink demands, date changes, reprinting, and explanations no one read but still insisted on giving. It had taken so long that I could track entire seasons by who was drilling in what uniform.

When the notification came through, it was a simple email. Just another message in an inbox filled with bureaucratic correspondence. I opened it without bracing for anything.

The first line hit like a steel rod to the chest.

"The Commanding General has disapproved your request."

I read it again, slower, as if the words might rearrange themselves into something survivable. They didn't. The email explained that forwarding the request to the G-1 remained an option, but the G-1 rarely grants policy exceptions over a command's objection.

That was it. After a year of effort, that was the last word.

I sat there for a long moment, staring at the screen, letting the implications collapse inward. The legal career I was trying to build, the uniform I had earned, the calling I had shaped my life around, and the chance to serve as a JAG officer. Erased by a line in an email from a recruiter who was quoting someone else. A year of my life was undone by something no one even bothered to explain.

I forwarded the email to Captain Cravins and texted him: "Sir, please call when you can."

He called within five minutes.

"What happened?" he asked.

I read him the message.

He offered no sigh or reassurance, only a crisp and controlled: "I'll look into it."

Within an hour, he had already spoken to someone in the Commanding General's office. By that evening, he had called me back.

He said, "the Commanding General did not deny your request."

I didn't understand. "Sir, the email said."

"No," he said firmly. "Major General Errol Schwartz denied nothing. He said it wasn't within his authority. Someone misinterpreted his note." A brief pause. "And then they told you it was a denial."

It wasn't anger I felt. It was a kind of hollow shock. After a year of obstacle after obstacle, this one wasn't even real. It was a clerical misreading. An assumption. Someone saw a line they didn't understand, filled in the gap with whatever made the process easier for them, and passed the wrong interpretation down the chain.

The next morning, I was CC'd on an email from the Staff Judge Advocate's Office, correcting the record with blunt clarity:

"The Commanding General did not disapprove the request. It is not within his authority to grant or deny an exception to policy. Only the Army's G-1 can do so. This is not a matter of the command's preference."

The message from the Staff Judge Advocate's Office clarified that no denial had ever existed. The Commanding General lacked the authority to approve or deny an exception to personnel policy, and someone should never have sent the statement suggesting otherwise.

Once the office corrected the record, everything suddenly unlocked. Major General Schwartz's staff tracked down the packet and returned it to his desk so he could sign his endorsement and push it to the National Guard Bureau, where it belonged. It had passed through so many offices that tracking it down was no small task.

Later, Captain Cravins called again.

"I briefed the Commanding General on the timeline," he said. "Everything. How long it's taken, what you've done, what's happened at every level."

He paused, letting the weight of what came next land properly.

"He said the organization failed you."

I felt that in my bones. No satisfaction, no vindication. Just truth finally spoken aloud by someone whose rank made it matter.

Captain Cravins continued, "The general said the delays were unacceptable. It should never have taken this long."

"And he told me to tell you personally: Until the approving authority grants the exception, the JAG office will hold the slot for you. You earned it. He's not letting it go to anyone else."

I said nothing for a moment. For the first time in a year, someone at the very top of the chain saw what had happened, named it plainly, and took responsibility for fixing it.

Chapter Thirteen

I was doing everything I could to hold the rest of my life together while my packet was slogging its way through the Army's channels. The process had gone quiet, and I had no sense of whether anyone was even looking at it. To pay the bills while I waited, I was still grinding through document-review work in cramped rooms, scanning emails, coding documents, and wondering how long I'd be stuck in that holding pattern.

It was during this stretch that Captain Harvey reached out.

He said his boss at the Pentagon wanted a briefing on the small-business programs I had worked with at the Small Business Administration, and he asked if I could do him a favor. It sounded simple, a favor for a solid commander I respected. I didn't hesitate.

Even after a full day of doc review, I stayed up late pulling together a proper slide deck, handouts, and notes. It felt good to work on something that involved actual policy and real people rather than litigation data dumps. I wasn't expecting anything from it. This was just helping my old commander.

When I arrived at the Mark Center, I set up my laptop, arranged the handouts, and got ready. The Associate Director of the Office of Small Business Programs came in with a few members of his team. I delivered the presentation the way I would have briefed a field grade officer.

The briefing covered my work at the Small Business Administration, explained how the programs operated, why they mattered, and how they supported small businesses breaking into federal contracting. I presented the material plainly, exactly as I understood it, and let it speak for itself.

A few minutes in, the Associate Director stopped me.

"That's enough," he said. "You carry yourself well. You're smart. Have you ever thought about working here? You don't have contracting experience, but you can pick that up. The way you think can't."

It caught me completely off guard. I had come in thinking I was doing someone a favor, but I hadn't realized I was being evaluated.

When the meeting ended and the Associate Director's team left, Harvey finally cracked a smile. "You didn't think I asked you here just to give a PowerPoint, did you? I wanted him to see you. If I'd told you it was an interview, you would've prepared too much and made it harder than it needed to be."

He wasn't wrong.

I'd spent months fighting to get the Army to even look at my packet, trying to prove I was worth a chance. Meanwhile, my former commander had quietly opened a door for me because he believed in what I could do.

* * *

The Associate Director spent most of his day in his office with the door partially open, hunched over thick binders or draft policy documents, reading in silence. Despite how busy he always was, he never made me feel like I was interrupting him. If I walked in with a draft or a question, he'd look up with that huge grin of his and wave me inside. That grin lit up his entire face.

I was still learning the defense acquisition world and needed guidance on everything. How to structure an acquisition strategy, what program managers cared about, and which traps to avoid in policy language. Whenever I showed up in his doorway with a question, he leaned back in his chair, laced his fingers behind his head, and nodded toward the stack of thick, dog-eared books he kept within arm's reach.

"Well." He reached for the Federal Acquisition Regulation like it was scripture. "Let's see what the FAR says."

He flipped straight to the right section, tapped the page with the back of his pen, and walked me through how the rule actually worked in practice.

"Read that and tell me what the actual issue is."

He stayed calm and unhurried, guiding me through each problem as if he had all the time in the world, even when he didn't.

After a few weeks, our conversations drifted. We joked about the absurdity of some regulations, about how a flagship contractor had turned every requirement into a proprietary part. He enjoyed hearing how I broke a problem down. "You always see something I missed."

Sometimes he pushed back and squinted at the paragraph I'd written. "That can't be right. That doesn't sound right to me."

"Okay," I said. "Call another attorney and ask them."

He did, and without fail, he'd come back later that afternoon, leaning into my doorway with that wide grin of his.

He always checked, and he always came back with the same result. Sometimes he'd just stop by my desk, holding his phone or a notepad, and say, almost offhandedly, "You were right. They read it the same way." There was no performance, no theatrics. Just confirmation, delivered with a quiet, amused grin.

He liked the predictability of the legal mind, the structure and logic. When he asked how lawyers all seemed to think the same way, I explained it the way one of my professors once had.

"It's like walking down a path and picking up pebbles. Each pebble is an issue. You recognize it because you've seen the pattern before. You set it aside and keep moving until you've gathered everything that matters.

"Then you work through them one by one: name the issue, pull the rule, apply it to the facts, draw the conclusion, and move to the next pebble. That's all lawyers are doing. It's a method, not a mystery."

He nodded, thinking it through. "So that's why you sound like the other lawyers. You aren't guessing because you're following a pattern."

"Yeah, we all learn it the same way. It doesn't matter whether you went to Harvard or City College. If it's ABA-accredited, you study the same cases in the same order. Any lawyer can usually tell where you are in the semester just by how you frame the problem. We all walked through the same fact patterns at the same pace. We're trained the same way, so we land in the same place."

From then on, he leaned on that pattern. When something needed precision, he brought it to me. When he met with someone senior, a congressional staffer, or a program manager known for being combative, he stopped by my desk.

"Help me think this through and tell me what they're really asking."

He trusted that I'd see angles he didn't.

He also trusted me with every packet that left our office. I took the time to make the materials look right. Clean formatting, logical structure, polished language. The Associate Director understood how much that mattered. "Presentation is the first judgment people make," he'd say.

And when he'd go into meetings, he stayed self-deprecating. That disarmed everyone. He'd settle into a chair, fold his hands over a briefing packet, and say with that Alabama drawl:

"Now listen, I'm just a slow country boy from Alabama. Can you help me understand this?"

They always laughed, and then they always respected him. He wasn't actually asking for help. He was steering the conversation and giving them room to reveal what he needed them to acknowledge.

By the time the Mentor–Protégé Program's twenty-fifth-anniversary conference arrived in Atlanta, the Associate Director and I were running on weeks of preparation. We had built the agenda, coordinated the sessions, talked through every panel, and handled every crisis that inevitably hit in the days before a major event.

Over four hundred people showed up. Small business innovators, big-name primes, government program managers, staff from the Services, university research teams, and even a few congressional staffers floating quietly in the back. It felt like the center of the acquisition universe for four days straight.

The Associate Director moved through the conference as if he'd been doing it all his life. Laughing, greeting people, effortlessly switching between technical talk, policy debates, and casual conversation. Every time he walked into a room, people straightened up. Some of the program managers had been in the field for decades, but they treated him like someone whose judgment mattered.

My job was to keep him armed with everything he needed: the talking points for a breakout session, a packet summarizing the Government Accountability Office's latest findings, the schedule for the protégé presentations, and the data sheets for the panel discussions. I spent half my time handing him materials before he went onstage and the other half of my time answering questions from small businesses trying to break into the system.

The conference ran better than anyone expected. People stayed late for the networking sessions. Panels ended with standing discussions instead of polite applause. Several of the protégés met with primes who wanted to continue the partnership beyond the program's requirements. The Mentor–Protégé Program did what it set out to do: grow the base, build relationships, and bring new players into the defense ecosystem.

At the end of the fourth day, after the last breakout room had emptied and the conference staff started rolling away tables, the Associate Director approached me with that wide, amiable smile.

"Good work," he said. "I couldn't have pulled it off without you."

The conference ended, and people shook hands, exchanged cards, and headed for their flights. I went back to DC.

But when I got home, the reality I'd been avoiding was still there.

* * *

By early 2016, my request for an exception to policy had finally reached the Army's G-1. I had handled the process exactly the way the Army teaches you to. The frustration was simmering underneath, but I stayed measured, deferential, disciplined.

I hadn't come in trying to blow up the entire policy. AR 600-110 was already under review, so I stayed in my lane. Working groups were dissecting it line by line. The ask wasn't to rewrite the regulation or overhaul accession standards overnight. It was one narrow exception, the accommodation the Army had granted thousands of times for other medical conditions.

They would not involuntarily separate me. And if the Army wasn't comfortable sending me back to an infantry company anymore, then the least they could do was let me serve where my education and skills were actually useful. In a courtroom. That was the only thing I asked for, permission to continue the career I had already earned. They could finish their broader review of the policy.

And because I knew the larger revision effort mattered too, I put my shoulder behind that work instead of fighting against it. I reached out to other HIV+ servicemembers through OutServe-SLDN and collected their experiences, their frustrations, and their recommendations. We weren't trying to write a manifesto. We were giving the Army input from the people affected.

I encouraged everybody to write their ideas and send them to me. Some people typed long paragraphs; others sent bullet points; a few called me on the phone and talked through everything while I took notes. I organized it all into one coherent packet and sent it up to G-1, thinking I was helping the process along.

A few days later, someone from the office called me.

"Sergeant Harrison, we can't accept these recommendations as-is."

"Why not?"

"They need an O-6 or GS-15 endorsement. That's the requirement for consideration by the working group."

I sat there and took it in. I was dealing with bureaucracy, not hostility, and I knew how to navigate it.

So I turned to the one person I trusted to give the packet a careful, honest review. My primary care provider, Dr. Czarnogorski.

"Ma'am, are you a GS-15?"

She laughed. "Yes, Nick. Why? What are you up to?"

"I drafted recommendations for the AR 600-110 rewrite. They want an O-6 or GS-15 endorsement. I need you to look at them. Strike anything you disagree with. If the substance holds, I need someone senior willing to sign."

"Send it over, and I'll read it tonight."

She did, and she called the next afternoon.

"These are solid, practical, medically accurate, and reasonable. I'll endorse them."

And she did without hesitation. Her signature was what the Army required. The right rank, the right position. We resubmitted the packet properly, through the channels the Army said it respected, into the very working-group process designed to fix the regulation.

It was the soldier's way of doing things. Follow the rule, meet the standard, and work within the machinery so the institution could do what it insisted it wanted to do.

* * *

The conference hall that spring was loud in the way only military conferences get. Bursts of laughter, uniforms brushing past one another, the clatter of chairs being reset between panels. OutServe-SLDN's annual leadership conference was always a chance to reconnect, but that year felt heavier. The policy review had stalled; my packet was somewhere in the machinery, and everyone I talked to seemed stuck in the same holding pattern.

I took a seat near the middle of the room as Amanda Simpson stepped up to the podium. She didn't need a long introduction. Everyone there knew who she was. The highest-ranking openly transgender woman in the Administration. Someone who had taken hits I could only imagine and kept going.

Her speech wasn't flowery. She spoke plainly about service and integrity, about the simple expectation that people who met the standard belonged there. I nodded along because she wasn't selling inspiration. She was stating the obvious.

I hung back while the line to greet Amanda Simpson formed and then slowly inched forward. People wanted selfies, hugs, and little speeches about how inspiring she was. I wasn't there for any of that. I waited until the room thinned out and she finally had a few free feet of space around her.

When the last person stepped away, I approached quietly.

"Ma'am?" I kept my voice low. "Do you have a moment?"

When I stepped up, she gave me a quick once-over and said, "What's on your mind? You look like you didn't wait in line for a handshake."

I introduced myself and told her straight about my exception-to-policy request, that it had reached the Deputy Chief of Staff, G-1, and that I'd kept my ask narrow on purpose. She listened with that expression she had when she was sizing someone up while pretending she wasn't. Her head was slightly tilted.

When I finished, she said. "G-1. Well, that explains the glacial pace."

I must've made a face. She chuckled. "This is nothing. Try being the highest-ranking openly transgender woman in the Administration. I get late-night jokes for dessert."

She shifted her folders, leaned in slightly, and dropped her voice.

"You're knocking on the wrong door. A Deputy Chief of Staff isn't the ceiling."

"Ma'am, that's the approving authority."

"On paper. You want to move something that's stuck? You go to the person who outranks the person holding it."

She let that sit, then added, deliberate and precise.

"Debra Wada. She is the Army's Assistant Secretary for Manpower and Reserve Affairs."

I nodded. She kept going.

"She muscled through the transgender service changes. Smart, effective, not afraid to tell the Army when it's wrong." A small grin. "An Assistant Secretary beats a Deputy Chief of Staff. Every time."

There was nothing sentimental about it. It wasn't encouragement. It was instruction.

I thanked her. She waved it off with a flick of her hand. "Go, ask, and see what happens."

* * *

Over the next few weeks, I drafted a letter to Assistant Secretary Wada. No theatrics, just the facts, the bottleneck, and the narrow exception I was requesting. I mailed it, then followed up through the main line to her office.

A few days later, her staff called me back.

"Sergeant Harrison? We received your correspondence."

"Yes, ma'am."

"Your packet hasn't made it up here yet. But we're tracking it."

"Understood. Thank you."

"We'll monitor its movement. Once it lands in this office, we'll let you know."

That was all she offered. No promise, no fix, no leverage pulled in my favor. Just confirmation that the Assistant Secretary's office now knew the packet existed.

* * *

A few weeks later, a letter finally arrived in my mailbox. A single sheet of paper, signed by a general I'd never met. It contained two sentences:

"Your request for an exception to Army Regulation 600-110 was not favorably considered. After review, taking such action is not in the best interest of the Army."

That was the entire explanation.

A point of contact sat at the bottom of the page. I called.

169

"Office of the G-1. Colonel Douglas Stitt."

"Sir, this is Sergeant Harrison. I'm calling about the denial letter I just received."

"Yes, I'm familiar with your packet."

"Can you explain the basis of the decision?"

He didn't hesitate.

"There is a Department of Defense policy that governs in this area. This isn't an issue where the Army has broad discretion."

He paused. Long enough to signal reluctance.

"And the National Guard Bureau did not concur."

"The National Guard?" I said. "They offered me the JAG position."

"That was their official recommendation." Flat. No elaboration.

"Alright. Since you're citing Department of Defense policy as the controlling authority, please forward my packet to the Under Secretary for Personnel and Readiness."

"No. Your packet has gone as far as it can go. It's being sent back to your unit now."

The call ended there. I called the Assistant Secretary's office next. The same staffer answered.

"I've been told the packet won't be elevated and is being sent back down. Is there anything the Assistant Secretary can do?"

She chose her words with care.

"If she intervened, she would take the matter out of the G-1's hands. People would read that as a loss of confidence in his judgment."

"So she won't get involved."

"She's not prepared to take that step."

Political appointees existed to cut through bureaucracy. No one would do it.

Fine. If the Army wouldn't forward it to the Department of Defense, I would.

I mailed the entire packet directly to the Office of the Under Secretary for Personnel and Readiness. A week later, another one-page letter arrived.

"The policies were reviewed and reaffirmed in 2013. We cannot grant favorable consideration to your request. Thank you for your service in the DC National Guard."

I expected it. But it was still jarring to see months of effort reduced to two sentences that didn't address a single fact in my request.

Chapter Fourteen

Captain Donald Cravins caught me after drill, lowering his voice just enough to signal that this wasn't a hallway conversation.

"Got a minute?" he asked.

We slipped into an empty office. He closed the door softly.

He stood there in uniform, carrying the easy gravity of someone who had lived long enough inside both command and politics.

"Did you hear anything?"

"Denied."

"No justification?"

"None."

He nodded once. Not surprised. Just registering the fact.

"You did everything right," he said. "Clean packet. Proper routing. You waited and respected the process."

"I kept it narrow," I said. "Handled it at the lowest level. I wasn't trying to challenge the policy."

"And that," he said, "was exactly right."

No judgment or suggestion I had misread the room. Just confirmation.

"You gave them every chance," he went on.

"And they still said no."

"That's what matters," he said. "When someone does everything correctly and the system still fails, no one blames them for what comes next."

I looked at him. "What is next?"

"You need institutional backing," he said. "An advocacy group. Someone who understands policy, optics, and Washington."

I didn't respond.

"This isn't about making noise or fighting the Army. It's about having support while you figure out what options are even on the table."

I nodded.

"You're continuing the process you already started. People who know how this level works."

I let that settle.

"Who?"

"The Human Rights Campaign. They have policy experts, legal people, and experience with this."

"I wouldn't even know what to say."

"You don't need certainty. What matters is laying out what happened, because the hard part is already behind you. You built the case correctly, respected the chain, and waited. That's what gives this weight, and that's why people will listen."

* * *

I dialed into the conference line five minutes early. The line sat quiet except for the faint hum of a computer microphone somewhere. At precisely 2:00 p.m., the beeps began.

A few voices introduced themselves in quick succession. Policy, government affairs, advocacy. Names slid past.

Then a fourth voice, measured and clear.

"This is Sarah Warbelow. Legal Director. Nick, are you with us?"

"Yes, ma'am." I caught myself. "Yes, I'm here."

"Great. Donald gave us a general heads-up, but we'd like to hear the details from you. Whatever you're comfortable sharing."

They listened without interruption. No one filled the pauses. It was quieter and slower than a military briefing. The pressure felt familiar.

I laid out the sequence, describing the packet, the medical documentation, the endorsements, the long wait, and the denial that came without explanation.

When I finished, a question came from the line. Had they offered anything at all? Any criteria unmet? Any guidance on the next steps?

"No. Just a denial."

A murmur on the other end. A chair shifting. Fingers on a keyboard.

"Okay. First, I'm really sorry you're dealing with this. And thank you for walking us through it so clearly."

Her cadence stayed steady and unhurried. She weighed each detail and slotted it neatly into place.

"I have a few questions, if you're comfortable."

"Sure."

"Did they explain whether this was Army policy or Department of Defense policy?"

"They said there was a Department of Defense policy that governs in this area."

"And you've been serving without limitations up to this point?"

"Yes."

"And the medical opinion supported your readiness?"

"Yes."

Typing again.

"Okay. That helps a lot. Now, one thing we should put on the table early, just so we understand your comfort level."

I straightened in my chair.

"On issues like this, there are two tracks. One is internal, working behind the scenes with policy staff, helping the military reconsider the decision. The other is public advocacy. We don't need an answer now, but we need to know whether you would ever consider that second path."

My stomach tightened.

There was no judgment in the question. No push. A lawyer defining the edges of the problem.

"I haven't thought that far."

"That's completely fine. We're not asking for a commitment. We just need to know how to frame the next steps."

I nodded, even though she couldn't see me.

"Right now, I'm just trying to understand what happened. And what options exist."

"That makes sense. Internal review is always the starting point. Public action is only ever a last resort."

Another voice chimed in. Realistically, nothing was likely to move until after the election. Major decisions are frozen. No one wants to touch anything controversial.

Someone else agreed. Getting OSD to return a call was nearly impossible. Everyone was waiting to see how the election turned out.

"We'd like to keep talking. Maybe in a few months. Let things settle. In the meantime, if you get any new paperwork or communication from the Army, send it along. It helps us understand the landscape."

"Of course."

A few final logistical questions followed. Points of contact, copies of memos, and whether the denial was standard or tailored. I answered what I could.

Then, almost abruptly, the call wrapped up.

"Thank you again for speaking with us, Nick. We'll be in touch."

"Thank you."

The line went dead.

* * *

The day before the election, the polls still showed Clinton ahead. Everyone said it would be tight, but predictable. In DC, that kind of confidence becomes background noise. On impulse, I shared a joking post on Facebook: a photoshopped image of Donald Trump sitting behind the Resolute Desk. I captioned it, "What if he wins?"

I did not intend it as a prophecy. It was dark humor Washington indulges in whenever we think we have the world figured out.

I had supported Hillary Clinton from the beginning. I had admired her since she was First Lady, a brilliant, forceful woman. People vilified her for the simple offense of refusing to be small.

But I also didn't hate Donald Trump. Truthfully, I'd grown up with him in the cultural background. I read *The Art of the Deal* as a teenager. My family played the Trump board game around the dining room table. He was a brash New York Republican. Not an ideologue, more of an entertainer in politics' clothing. Nobody thought he was going to govern. Even the establishment of his own party kept him at arm's length.

He said outrageous things. He doubled down on mistakes. But that was part of the spectacle. Many people assumed he was running for visibility, not victory. What none of us inside the Beltway grasped was how deeply people outside it resented Washington. The elitism, the stagnation, the feeling that nothing ever changed. Trump tapped into that anger, and he did it better than anyone expected.

But on election night, none of that mattered. Everyone felt shock.

The tone on television shifted around 9:30 p.m. The anchors' confidence thinned out, replaced by something cautious, measured. My phone buzzed on the coffee table.

A friend from college texted, "Are you seeing this? Please tell me this is just early-night noise."

Moments later, my LGBTQ+ friends started messaging. "Is everyone okay?" "This is bad." "I'm shaking."

Their fear was visceral. Elections come and go, but for our community, the stakes were always more intimate. When you see rights debated, granted, clawed back, and defended through every administration, you understand they aren't abstractions. When you've lived long enough to see progress treated as optional.

I called one of my closest friends because the messages he was sending felt panicked. He answered immediately. Raw fear, no hello.

"Nick, people are terrified. I've already gotten texts asking if they should scrub their social media. What happens now?"

"I don't know yet," I said. "But no one saw this coming."

He exhaled shakily. "It feels like the country voted on whether we matter. And we lost."

And in that moment, with texts piling up, anchors speaking in careful tones, and friends' fear bleeding through the phone, the only thing I could think about was the handwritten note George H. W. Bush left for Bill Clinton in the Oval Office on his first day.

I remembered reading it years earlier, struck by its grace. Bush didn't agree with Clinton. He didn't vote for him. He had just lost to him. And yet he wrote:

"You will be our President when you read this note. I wish you well. I wish your family well. Your success is now our country's success. I am rooting hard for you."

It was an acknowledgment that the office was bigger than ego, party, or resentment. That the country needed its President to rise to the moment, no matter who he was or how he got there.

"He's going to be President. And we hope he rises to the occasion. If he succeeds, the country succeeds. That includes us."

"I hear you. But tonight it feels like the country told us exactly what we're worth."

"That's why we have each other. Tonight we're scared. Tomorrow we stand together."

And I meant it. Because even in that moment of fear, I understood that what I was fighting for wasn't partisan. It couldn't be. The military's HIV policies weren't wrong because Democrats or Republicans said they were wrong. They were wrong because they violated basic fairness and logic. Those failures had persisted under both parties. The people who could fix them didn't always say the right words into a microphone.

* * *

The first time I met Baraq wasn't at some candlelit dinner or carefully arranged moment. It was at the Mid-Atlantic Leather convention, the big kink event held every Martin Luther King holiday weekend in downtown DC.

If you've never been, it's impossible to describe without sounding like you're exaggerating. Thousands of people from up and down the East Coast pack into a hotel that becomes a cross between a trade show, a nightclub, and a giant, barely controlled social experiment for one weekend. The upper floors can get wild. Everyone in the community wanders through at some point, even if only out of curiosity.

I was wandering, fully in rebound mode after a painful breakup. I was open to distraction, open to connection, open to just feeling something again. Someone invited me upstairs to a jockstrap party. I went. Many people packed the crowded, humid space with blasting music.

After about ten minutes, I decided I'd had enough. I pulled my shorts back on and was about to slip out the door when it happened.

Our eyes met. Just a brief look, but enough.

He stepped toward me, and instinct carried me the rest of the way. Words never really found a foothold, and the space between us collapsed into a kiss that was quick, messy, and impulsive. The kind you give a stranger there because the moment invites it and nothing more. He registered as part of the convention crowd, an out-of-towner passing through for the weekend before disappearing again. That assumption kept everything light and unexamined. Meaning stayed at a distance. There wasn't room for it, and I wasn't looking to make room.

The moment filed itself away as nothing important, just a rebound impulse that didn't ask to be carried forward. The night continued downstairs, with a plan to stop by the convenience store and then call it done.

Then he found me again.

I was standing in the aisle debating between chips and a terrible hotel sandwich when I saw him walking toward me. Same guy, same expression, like he'd gone looking for me on purpose. He stopped a few feet away, a little breathless.

"Hey."

"Hey."

We spoke just enough to acknowledge that whatever had happened upstairs wasn't finished.

"Is it okay if I give you my number?"

The question caught me off guard, in a good way. That wasn't how these nights usually ended.

We texted almost immediately.

"Where are you staying?"

"Home. I live in DC."

That got my attention.

"Out with friends. It's my birthday weekend."

Then the line that made me stop.

"I work for the Human Rights Campaign."

He wasn't an out-of-towner, a one-night curiosity, or someone destined to disappear without a trace.

We didn't talk long, just enough to establish that there was something worth following up on. We agreed to set up an actual date once the chaos of the weekend settled. I remember walking back to my room feeling a strange combination of lightness and caution. Intrigued, pleasantly surprised, not ready to assign meaning, but not ready to dismiss it either.

* * *

We didn't hook up the night we met. We didn't hook up after our first date either. That alone made this different.

Most gay men won't admit it openly, but we all know the truth: it rarely takes long to decide whether we want to sleep with someone. A few minutes of conversation, a glance, a vibe. That's often enough to know whether it's a one-off, a maybe-later, or a "don't waste my time."

But with Baraq, there was space. We actually dated. Dinner at Dupont Italian Kitchen. Kickball league night. A movie, Nocturnal Animals, the artsy, unsettling film you watch with someone you're still figuring out.

And in between those things, we talked. Not long confessions, just the normal back-and-forth of two people circling around each other, testing warmth, testing humor, testing interest. He told me he'd seen me around DC before, but I'd never noticed him. I told him about the new job prospects I was juggling. He mentioned his work at the Human Rights Campaign almost casually.

We were moving toward something slowly and intentionally.

And that meant something else too. Something I could feel creeping closer each time we said goodbye at the end of a night.

I was going to tell him.

People outside the community don't understand how much calculation goes into dating as an HIV+ man. You're always weighing things.

The questions stacked up fast. Was this just fun, or a one-night thing that would dissolve by morning? Did this feel like someone worth seeing again, someone close enough to trust with actual information about me, or close enough to complicate my life in ways I didn't want? And underneath all of it sat the bigger calculation: if this turned sexual, where did it stop, what rules applied, what stayed protected, what stayed exploratory, and how far would I let it go?

When someone with HIV is undetectable, HIV transmission is impossible through any type of sexual contact. This is a medical fact, not a probability. But logic rarely controls how people react. Disclosure opens a door to uncertainty, and once it's open, anything can happen. Reactions scatter across a spectrum: some men take it in stride, others vanish without explanation, some spiral over risks that never existed, and a few respond as if disclosure should have come with a permanent warning label etched into your skin.

And once sex happens, you can't roll anything back. You can't disclose later and hope they don't freak out retroactively. You can't go back to "just casual."

Disclosure turns the key in a lock. Whatever's on the other side, you live with it.

When the night finally came, it arrived quietly after weeks of getting to know each other, and I felt it settle over me.

This is the time. Tell him now, or don't go any further.

I sat on the edge of the bed, my heart doing that heavy, deliberate thud that comes right before a leap you can't undo. He looked at me, confused by the sudden silence.

"I should tell you something before we... before anything happens."

His expression shifted. Not alarm. Attention.

"I'm HIV+. Undetectable. Have been for years."

A beat passed. Long enough for my body to brace for the catalog of reactions, judgment, recoil, the tiny flinch you learn to watch for.

None came.

He nodded once. "Okay. Thanks for telling me."

Then, just as simply: "I'm on PrEP. I know what undetectable means."

Relief washed through me so fast it almost made me dizzy. Not because I thought he'd run, but because I'd let him into a place very few people ever reached. That kind of trust has its own nakedness.

We talked a little more. Nothing like the sweeping, cinematic conversation the old version of this scene once pretended existed. We exchanged questions and answers about treatment, how it worked, and what it meant, and he listened without moralizing, tiptoeing, or reducing me to a risk calculation.

"This changes nothing for me."

He said it the way someone said the sky is blue. Plain and unperformed.

Only then did things move forward, not just physically, but emotionally. It wasn't about getting each other naked. It was about whether what we'd been building could hold the weight of something real.

When he didn't bolt, didn't panic, didn't treat my disclosure like a trap I'd sprung, when he simply stayed, I let myself consider that this might be more than filling space after a breakup.

It wasn't perfect or cinematic. It was honest. That mattered more.

After more talking, we closed the distance between us. Nothing rushed or performative. Just two people choosing to trust each other a little more than they had the night before.

Later, when the room went quiet, and we lay there catching our breath, the conversation shifted again. Not heavily, but authentically. The way it only does when there is nothing left to perform.

He asked about my life beyond interviews and the National Guard, and for the first time with anyone I was dating, I told him what I was fighting for. I talked about the commission I had earned, the waiver they kept sitting on, the slow bleed of bureaucracy, and the policies that treated people like me as disposable or dangerous. I had planned to say none of it. Exhaustion and a stubborn belief in change surfaced together and carried me through the telling.

He listened in the same way he had earlier.

"Can I ask you something?"

"Yeah."

"Promise me you won't stop."

I didn't quite understand.

"No matter what happens with us," he said, choosing each word, "or where this goes, or if it goes anywhere at all, promise me you'll keep pushing. Keep fighting. It matters."

"I will."

That was it. Not a revelation. Just an answer to a question he took seriously enough to ask.

We settled into a peaceful quiet afterward. The kind that comes after the conversations are done. We talked a little longer about ordinary things, work, schedules, and a movie we'd seen weeks earlier.

Chapter Fifteen

About six months after we returned from Atlanta, the Associate Director left for another position, and the agency restructured the contract. That's the reality of government contract work. The official you support takes a new job, fresh leadership arrives with different priorities, or budget cuts eliminate your funding entirely. One day you're building relationships and settling into meaningful work, the next you're back on the market. I found myself doing document review projects again, scanning job boards for the next government contract that might offer something more substantial than temporary legal work.

While I was numbly scrolling through job boards I couldn't bring myself to apply to, a Facebook notification blinked at the corner of my screen. It was a message from someone I hadn't spoken to since Oklahoma, the attorney who'd run the HIV Project at Legal Aid back when I was studying for the bar.

When I'd come home from my last deployment, I'd wanted to do something useful while I prepped for the exam. Before I'd ever become HIV+ myself, I'd volunteered with Other Options, the food pantry for people living with HIV. Later, when law school ended, he took me on at the Legal Aid HIV Project. It was unglamorous work. I dealt with discrimination complaints, housing issues, employment problems, and insurance denials. These were the kinds of cases nobody in big law brags about but that keep real people afloat.

I hadn't seen his name for years.

He opened with a simple "How have you been?"

We caught up through quick, efficient messages. I asked about Oklahoma, and he immediately corrected me. He hadn't lived there in years. He was in the South Pacific now, working for the Attorney

General of Micronesia. The way he described it, it barely sounded real. Warm ocean water, slow days, hills so green they didn't look natural, a tiny island you could walk across, no traffic, no political insanity. He sent photos. Palm trees against a flat blue sky, empty beaches, European tourists wandering around shirtless and sunburned. The scenes you only see in travel ads.

Everyone spoke English, he said. The islands had once been a U.S. trust territory, and they still had deep ties to the United States. They were always short of American-trained lawyers.

"You'd be valuable here on day one," he wrote. "You could do criminal, civil, contracts, maritime law, anything. We teach each other as we go. Nobody shows up knowing maritime law."

I asked how things were out there.

He wrote back that it was paradise.

Then he asked how things were for me.

His message arrived at exactly the wrong moment. Or perhaps the right one. DC felt like a city I was orbiting without ever making contact, a place that used to feel electric but had gone dim on me. I'd spoken with Cravins about needing help and a special interest group, but nothing had changed yet. I was still in the same apartment, on the same couch, staring at the same job boards. So when he asked how I was doing, the question hit deeper than he probably intended.

I told him the truth. At least the version that didn't require telling someone everything half a world away. Getting fired from the Small Business Administration had left me between contracting gigs, doing document review to keep the lights on, far from what I had moved to Washington to do.

He asked about the Army.

That part was harder. I wrote that they denied the commission packet, that every avenue I tried felt like a dead end, and that nothing seemed to budge, no matter how many polite follow-ups I sent. And then, I typed something I hadn't said out loud to anyone.

"I'm wondering why I'm still in DC. If I'm not doing the work I came here to do, what's the point of being here?"

He didn't hesitate. He asked if I'd ever consider moving to Micronesia.

I stared at the message for a long time.

I asked what I would actually do there.

"Anything you want," he said. "They'll treat you like gold. And if you ever come back to the States, maritime lawyers make a fortune."

He sent one last photo, a sunset taken from his balcony. The sky was all gold and orange, reflected on still water broken only by a few small fishing boats. The entire island looked quiet in a way the city never was.

It hit me harder than I wanted to admit. Part of me actually considered leaving, starting over, living on a tropical island where no one cared about Army waiver requests or bureaucratic holding patterns. A place where bureaucratic indifference no longer sets the ceiling.

The question I'd been avoiding took its full shape. If I wasn't doing the thing I'd moved to this city to do, then what was keeping me here?

I didn't have an answer yet.

That quiet, sun-drenched island glowing on my phone forced me to admit the question was real.

Asking whether DC was still worth it made me ask whether the Army still was. My life here extended beyond jobs or apartments and rested on the National Guard, the uniform, and an identity I had spent years building. When I faced myself honestly, the uniform stood at the sharpest point of friction in my life.

***

Most people who've never served assume the military is a strict meritocracy: competence rises, incompetence sinks, and everything else takes care of itself. Anyone who's worn a uniform knows better. Rank is shorthand for reputation, and reputation determines how people treat you. And in a National Guard headquarters company, nobody bothers to look deeper.

When I first came into the DC National Guard, they let me run the military police platoon. It made sense. I had deployments, leadership experience, and enough credibility to keep a tactical operations center running. Everyone assumed the commission was imminent. But as the months dragged on and nothing happened, people tilted their heads at me in that quiet, military way that says: Why is this guy still a sergeant?

My old company commander tried to help. He asked if I'd take a contracting NCO slot at Joint Force Headquarters. They felt I could learn something useful while waiting for my JAG commission to process. I had priority for the position because of that pending commission. At a minimum, it would keep me useful.

But JFHQ is its own ecosystem. Headquarters companies eat their young. I walked in as the lowest-ranking NCO in the building, which meant one thing. Every shit detail rolled downhill into my hands.

The orders kept coming. Pick up the water, inventory the janitorial closet, and clean the storage cage.

The logic was purely military. A man my age, with my education, still wearing a sergeant's rank? That alone marked me as someone who had failed. In the military, presumed screw-ups invite correction, and humiliation becomes quality control.

There were days I stood there with a clipboard while NCOs who'd never left the country laughed as they gave me extra tasks. I had two graduate degrees, fifteen years in uniform, a Combat Infantryman Badge, and somehow I'd become the catch-all for chores no one else wanted. Limbo turns even competence into suspicion.

The only consolation was the idea that maybe I could get certified as a contracting specialist. Something to justify the wait. Something to make the months feel less wasted.

For a while, the slot felt like neutral ground. Not progress, but not another slide backward. It let me pretend the Army still saw a future for me. So when they told me I was being moved again, it didn't feel like a routine reassignment. It felt like the floor was tilting beneath me.

They wanted to send me to school to become a truck driver.

I pushed back, respectfully pointing out that I had priority for the contracting billet because I was waiting on my JAG commission. That was why they'd placed me there.

The contracting officer exploded.

"How dare you say that?!" he said, loud enough for the entire office. Then he jerked his keyboard toward him and started typing out an email with the fury of someone trying to win an argument through sheer force of keystrokes. When he hit send, I glanced at the CC line.

He'd copied the U.S. Property and Fiscal Officer. The man was a full-bird colonel, along with half a dozen names I didn't recognize.

I said, "Sir, who are these people? We don't need the entire fiscal chain of command for this."

He glared. "You don't even know who the USPFO is?"

I didn't take the bait. By then, I'd learned how Washington worked: skip the theatrics and go straight to the decision-maker.

I emailed the colonel directly.

Sir, I'm not sending this explanation to the contracting officer because he isn't showing the maturity or discretion to handle it appropriately. For your awareness: They placed me in this billet because I am HIV+ and awaiting an exception to policy on my commission packet. Until they act on that, this position is where I belong, and I have priority for it.

He replied almost immediately.

Thank you for the clarification. I understand, and I support what you're doing.

Within the hour, the contracting officer backed down, not kindly and not with an apology.

I said the quiet part out loud to someone in the chain of command, and the truth moved something. Only later did I recognize it as the seed of a strategy: stop hoping the system behaves and start forcing it to look at itself.

The relief didn't last. I still couldn't attend contracting school because they considered me non-deployable, and without the school, I couldn't do the job. I was stuck in a position without the training, in a unit that didn't know what to do with me, while my commission packet sat somewhere gathering dust.

That's when I walked into the chaplain's office.

No one goes there first. You go there when JAG shrugs, when Admin shrugs, when the First Sergeant shrugs. When every answer is "not my lane" or "we'll look into it." The chaplain is the only door not barricaded by ego.

He gestured for me to sit. "What's going on?"

I explained everything: the school I couldn't attend, the move that made no sense, the months of limbo. As I talked, his eyes drifted to the Combat Infantryman Badge on my uniform.

"You're infantry?"

"Yes, sir. Two deployments."

"And on the civilian side?"

"I'm an attorney. JD-MBA, PMP."

He paused. "PMP?"

"Project Management Professional."

Something shifted. The sudden realization was that the command had been wasting someone with actual skill.

"Would you be open to working for me?" he asked. "If I go talk to them right now?"

"Yes, sir."

He didn't ask for paperwork. He just stood, walked out, and went straight to the commander. Ten minutes later, he returned.

"I'll take you," he said. "If you want it, you can move here. Today."

Someone in uniform treated me as if I had value instead of pushing me aside or hiding the problem.

The chaplain didn't fix the policy or clear the bureaucratic fog. He didn't give me clarity, a commission, or a path forward. But he removed me from a situation that was curdling into hostility and disrespect.

He gave me space. Not salvation, just runway. Just enough room to take the next hit without breaking.

* * *

I carried that tension with me everywhere. Even on the nights that felt warm and ordinary, like Tuesdays with Baraq, part of me was still standing in a fluorescent hallway at JFHQ waiting for someone to decide where I belonged. He didn't always ask, but he always saw it.

On that Tuesday, he came over as he always did. I had a pot roast going in the crockpot. Garlic, onions, and slow-cooked meat make the apartment feel warmer than it ever actually was.

We sat on the couch with plates balanced on our knees, *Game of Thrones* murmuring in the background. The show everyone was watching then, the one we'd started watching together. Tuesdays had become that kind of ritual for us, steady and familiar, something that felt like a small piece of stability in a city where nothing else seemed fixed.

Somewhere between bites, I said:

"I got a Facebook message this week. From someone I haven't talked to in years."

He glanced over. "Yeah? Who?"

"A guy I worked with back in Oklahoma. After my last deployment, while I was studying for the bar. He ran the HIV Project at Legal Aid, and I volunteered with him for a bit. Completely random message."

"What did he want?"

"He doesn't even live in Oklahoma anymore." I set my plate down. "He moved to the South Pacific. Works for the Attorney General of Micronesia now."

That drew his attention fully. "Micronesia? The islands?"

"Yep, actual tropical islands. Beaches. Warm water. Slow pace. He says it's basically paradise. And apparently they always need American-trained lawyers."

He blinked, working it through.

"And he asked if I'd ever consider moving out there."

"Would you?"

The shrug I gave wasn't casual. "I don't know. Everything stalled. After the Small Business Administration fired me, I picked up that contracting job with Rob for a while, then he left for another position, and the contract ended. Suddenly, I was right back where I started. Document review. Waiting for something to break my way."

He listened attentively.

"They denied my commission. Nothing's moving. I keep pushing every angle, and the system grinds you down until you stop bothering."

I let out a long breath.

"Some days I really wonder why I'm still in DC. I came here to work in government, to be part of something bigger. Now I'm not doing any of it. I'm living in the most political city in the country and spending my days coding documents for lawsuits I don't care about."

I looked at him.

"It feels like nothing I wanted is happening, and nothing I'm doing is leading anywhere."

He nodded, thoughtful, without trying to fix it.

The question I'd been circling since that message finally came out.

"If I went, would you consider coming with me?"

He froze, not in fear or disbelief, but in real consideration. The kind that pulls someone inward toward a life they've never imagined.

"Me? In Micronesia?"

"Yeah." I kept my voice low. "If I left, would you want to go too?"

He studied his plate, then looked back up.

"It sounds incredible. Beautiful. Simple. Like stepping out of the noise for once."

The pause came from him, not me.

"But I don't know what I'd do there. You're a lawyer. You'd have a job waiting, and you'd be valuable. I plan political fundraisers. That doesn't exactly translate to a small island in the Pacific."

He turned it over carefully, trying to imagine a life reshaped around mine, and came up empty.

"I'm not saying no," he said. "I'm open to the idea. I just can't see where I'd fit."

We sat there in the soft light of the TV. Plates cooling, garlic still hanging in the air. Whatever was happening on screen barely registered. What mattered was that, for the first time, the idea of leaving wasn't something locked inside my head. I said it aloud. And he hadn't dismissed it. He'd actually thought about it.

But once the conversation settled, the reality settled too. He couldn't go with me. Not without giving up work, community, and everything he'd been building. And I couldn't pretend that wasn't part of the equation.

We decided nothing that night. The possibility just forced me to look harder at why I wanted one.

And that thought cracked open something I hadn't let myself think about in years. Something an NCO once told me in a moment I never understood. A man I hated, a conversation I never expected to remember, and a lesson that surfaced now, uninvited, because it made sense.

* * *

In the days after that conversation, I kept circling the same questions.

Why stay and keep fighting a system that had made it clear it didn't want me?

I had options. I had degrees and deployments. I could have left the military, doubled my salary, vanished into the private sector, and let someone else wrestle with the mess.

But the more I imagined leaving, the more it forced a second, heavier question. If I walked away, who was I leaving behind?

And that was when an old, unwelcome memory broke through. A memory of someone I could barely stand.

An NCO from my first deployment. The guy who prowled around looking for crooked name tapes just to make junior soldiers do flutter kicks until he got bored.

He rarely bothered me, since pulling me away for push-ups would have made the entire tactical operations center fall apart. Not a mentor or a role model, but he remained a background presence who still taught me something I wouldn't understand until years later.

Toward the end of that deployment, we were all worn thin in the way only deployed soldiers understand. An order came down that anyone on tower or gate duty had to wear Kevlar for the entire shift. Twelve hours in a concrete box in 120-degree heat with straps carving into your forehead, sweat burning your eyes. Officially for safety, but really just one more miserable rule added to a stack of miserable rules.

That night, they paired me with a newly promoted sergeant still learning how to balance authority with common sense. After a couple of hours roasting in that stagnant oven, I leaned over and said, "Look, take it off for a bit. We're still alert. Nobody's going to die if we breathe."

He hesitated, but competence has gravity, and for months I'd been carrying most of the tactical operations center. If I said it was fine, it felt like permission.

So we took them off and set the helmets on the bench.

That was when he appeared.

A bored staff sergeant charged up the tower stairs like he was conducting a raid and stepped inside wearing a triumphant look, as if he'd caught two fugitives instead of two exhausted soldiers trying not to pass out. He walked away satisfied with the catch.

After the shift, the lieutenant went straight for the new sergeant. Responsibility, example, judgment. I watched the panic in his eyes as a brand-new NCO about to get punished for something I'd told him to do.

And I saw it clearly. How blame rolls downhill to the person with the thinnest armor.

So I cut in, deadpan.

"Well, sir, in his defense, the platoon leader does usually do whatever Specialist Harrison suggests."

Silence. Then the suppressed smiles from the lieutenant, squad leaders, and even the poor sergeant. It was funny because it was true.

The temperature shifted. The lieutenant dismissed the sergeant with a warning, then turned to me with a look that said, You made this mess. He told me to grab my helmet and pull another twelve-hour shift.

It was miserable, but I took it without complaint because I could. That sergeant couldn't. I knew how power actually circulates in a platoon. Not by rank, but by who can absorb the hit without breaking.

I didn't understand it then. It felt like another small injustice in a place with many. But something in it stuck anyway, lodged under irritation. Taking the hit isn't always about blame. Sometimes it's about who can take it.

Months later, back home, he demonstrated the same lesson again in a moment so ordinary I almost missed it.

We were in formation waiting for the first call. The Army was phasing out BDUs and moving to ACUs, but supply had no budget and no guidance. Most soldiers had already bought their own uniforms, the quiet financial pressure that lands hardest on nineteen-year-olds.

Except him.

He stood there in an old BDU top like the changeover didn't apply to him at all. In a formation full of digital camouflage, he looked like he'd dropped in from a different war.

I asked him why.

"I've got ACUs at home," he said. "But if I wear them, every private will to feel like they have to buy theirs too. Supply's supposed to issue uniforms. So I'm not wearing a damn thing until everyone gets one."

It wasn't a speech. He didn't announce a principle. He just stood there in the wrong uniform, day after day, becoming more conspicuous as everyone else shifted into grey. By the end, he was almost alone, a stubborn reminder of the system's failure.

He looked ridiculous. He also looked right.

That was the moment I understood the NCO corps in a way no leadership course ever taught. Not as disciplinarians barking orders, but as the people who absorb pressure so the youngest soldiers don't have to. Quiet resistance without medals or recognition. Just a little borrowed dignity for the people beneath you.

I never liked the man, but I never forgot that.

I thought he was being stubborn. Years later, I realized he was shielding people who couldn't shield themselves.

Standing in my apartment years later, thinking about Micronesia and escape and the fantasy of starting over in a place untouched by Washington, that memory resurfaced with sharp clarity. Not because he was admirable, but because the lesson finally made sense.

If someone in my position didn't push back, the people who actually needed protection never would.

Most HIV+ servicemembers couldn't risk raising concerns with the chain of command. Fear defined the margins of their lives. Exposure, career collapse, and being labeled problems. Far from cities with U=U posters and lacking graduate degrees or civilian careers to fall back on, their livelihoods depended on staying invisible.

They couldn't afford the hit. I could.

Once I recognized that difference, I couldn't unsee it.

The Army had already denied my commission. My career would not collapse any further if I stood up for myself. If I didn't fight the policy with all the insulation I had, I couldn't pretend anyone with less protection would be able to.

Staying wasn't suddenly noble. It didn't come with a plan or a promise that it would work. It just stopped being passive. Leaving would have been an escape. Staying meant taking the hit on purpose.

That realization fixed nothing. It didn't make the Army's decision less humiliating or my future less foggy.

I just wasn't ready to disappear.

Chapter Sixteen

When I was in college, the University of Oklahoma was trying to reinvent itself. President David Boren had arrived with a plan: higher admissions standards, more National Merit Scholars, a campus that looked and felt like a flagship research institution. All of that required money, and he wasn't shy about saying so.

The university talked about the fact that our tuition was the lowest in the region as if it were an indictment, not a reflection of the state's economy. They didn't say, "We should keep college accessible." They said, "We're leaving money on the table."

And they wanted all of it — money from increased state appropriations and higher tuition rates. Everything they could get.

Most of the student government leadership lined up behind the president, drawn by invitations to meetings at Evans Hall, the photo opportunities, and the easy proximity to power. Actual representation of the students never drove it; appearing "reasonable" and "mature" did.

I did not oppose improving the university. I just knew what a two-thousand-dollar jump meant in a state where most families lived close to the edge. None of the people pushing the increase ever talked to the ones who'd have to cover it.

So, I went to the State Capitol.

I walked into each office, handed over a packet I had written explaining what the increase would mean in real numbers, and asked if the legislator had a few minutes.

Most did. Others gave me more time than I expected.

One legislator asked me straight out, "Why are you here by yourself? Usually, the students come in with somebody from the administration."

"I'm not representing the administration," I said. "I'm representing the students who can't afford this."

He motioned for me to sit.

We talked about rural families, about first-generation students, about how fast costs had already been rising. I wasn't giving a speech. I was telling him what the increase would mean for people I actually knew. When I left, he said, "You've got my vote."

I heard that enough times to think the bill could fail.

It startled people that one student, not a coalition or a lobbyist, was cutting into the margins of a coordinated push by administrators from every public college and university in the state.

On the day of the vote, I walked into the gallery thinking it might actually fail. Enough legislators had told me directly that they were with me that it didn't feel impossible.

When the board lit up, I saw the shifts in real time. Three legislators who had committed to voting against the increase switched their votes. I didn't know why until afterward. The university presidents in their districts had leaned on them. These were political heavyweights. Several of them were former governors or former U.S. senators, people with far more influence than a single student walking from office to office.

But the increase passed by only three votes. That was the closest anyone had ever come to stopping it.

I gathered my packets and walked out without saying a word.

* * *

Between government contracts, I suddenly had a lot of free time. I was living in Washington, and the Armed Services Committee offices were a short train ride away. But this differed from anything I'd done before.

If I handed them a packet with my name on it identifying me as an HIV+ servicemember, it became public record. There was no taking it back.

Still, nothing else was moving. So I sat down and built the packet.

I printed everything cleanly: the policy, the reports Congress had already required, the military's own data, the denial of my exception to policy, and a brief narrative explaining exactly how the system trapped servicemembers like me. I stapled each one neatly and stacked them on my kitchen table. Then I pulled the membership lists for the House and Senate Armed Services Committees, mapped out every building, and wrote myself a route like I was planning a ruck march.

On the morning I started, my hands were shaking just a little. It was the first time I had ever told my story directly to anyone in government outside the Army's bureaucracy. I kept thinking about the horror stories I'd heard about careers ruined because someone's HIV status got out. But the packet would not walk itself up the Hill. So I took a breath, picked up the stack, and stepped into the first office.

My routine became the same each time: smile, walk to the front desk, hand over the packet, ask for a staffer's business card before anyone asked me anything too direct. Most interactions lasted under thirty seconds. I didn't linger. I didn't want to.

In one office, though, it went differently.

I handed the packet to the staff assistant, thanked her, and asked if the legislative assistant's card was available. Before she could answer, another staffer walked up behind her, picked up the packet, and started reading it right there. She was mid-twenties, professional, sharp.

Not skimming. Reading.

She didn't look up. She focused on the page as if the words hooked her. Every second made my stomach tighten. I got the business card as quickly as I could and slipped out of the office, wanting to put distance between myself and whatever reaction was coming.

I was halfway down the marble hallway when I heard heels hitting the floor behind me at a steady, deliberate pace.

"Excuse me, sir? Are you Nick Harrison?"

I braced myself. I had no way of knowing what was coming.

"Yes, I'm Nick."

She reached out her hand before I could say anything else.

"Thank you. Thank you for doing this."

Confusion must have crossed my face, because she continued before I could respond.

"I have friends who are HIV+. One of the hardest parts of advocating for them is that no one wants to put their face or name out there. I don't blame them. But these policies don't change without actual stories, without someone willing to step forward."

I nodded. She had run after me.

"You're doing something important. Please keep going."

I walked away feeling steadier. It was the first time anyone had said out loud that telling my story mattered.

Over the next few weeks, I worked systematically through the committee lists, marking off the offices that reached back out. Staffers emailed. Others called. A few scheduled longer conversations where they asked detailed questions about deployment restrictions, medical classifications, and how the policies worked in practice.

People in Washington like to make Capitol Hill sound inaccessible, a place where nothing moves unless you have connections, influence, or a former title. But the truth is simpler. You walk into an office, hand someone a packet, and if the issue is real, people talk to you. I never spoke to a single Member of Congress, and it didn't matter. Staffers are the ones who write the legislation each year. They draft the report language, shape what goes into the NDAA, and decide what gets attention and what doesn't.

By the time I finished, I had spoken with staff in fifty-four offices.

Reactions weren't uniform, but the pattern was consistent. Republican staff approached it as a readiness issue; Democratic staff approached it as a civil rights issue. The perspectives were different, but the questions were the same: why the policy still existed, what purpose it served, and why the military hadn't updated it.

* * *

I didn't know it, but while I was walking packets around the Hill, another kind of momentum was starting in another part of Washington. On the fourth floor of the Human Rights Campaign headquarters, Baraq decidedly did not belong.

He'd spent the morning doing what he always did: juggling donor calls, reviewing gala budgets, texting state directors about venue contracts. But the whole time, one thought kept circling back. Nick is doing all of this alone.

Finally, he stood up, walked to the hall, and headed for the elevator.

He rode the elevator up two floors and stepped into a quieter hallway. He stopped outside the legal offices he almost never visited. Without a plan in mind, he noticed the open door he'd been searching for and knocked lightly on the frame.

Sarah Warbelow looked up from a stack of documents. Her glasses were low on her nose, expression instantly warm.

"Oh, hey!" she said. "You're far from the fundraising floor. Come in. What's going on?"

He stepped inside, aware of how far outside his lane this was.

"This is a little outside my job description. But I wanted to talk to you about someone I'm dating."

She set her pen down. "Okay. Say more."

"His name is Nick Harrison. He's in the DC National Guard. He's HIV+. He's been trying to commission as a JAG officer, and the Army keeps blocking him."

Recognition flickered across her face.

"Yes, I remember him." She nodded. "We spoke before the election. I meant to follow up, but then…"

She gestured upward, as if the entire Trump Administration existed somewhere above the ceiling tiles.

"Everything turned into fire drills. Constant defensive posture. We lost track of a lot of threads."

"I know," Baraq said. "I just didn't want you to lose track of him."

"Actually, he's come up a few times recently, and it has not been from inside the Human Rights Campaign."

That surprised him.

"What do you mean?"

She leaned back, shifting into the analytical mode people trusted.

"We've been getting calls from staffers on the Hill. Mostly from the Armed Services Committees. They aren't asking general policy questions. They're asking specific ones about why the military still treats HIV this way, whether anyone is working to change it, and whether we're connected to a servicemember named Nick Harrison."

A smile crossed her face.

"And every time they call, I keep thinking someone is making noise up there. Someone got their attention."

203

"That's him," Baraq said. "He's been walking into those offices. Alone. Dropping off packets with his name on them."

She exhaled softly. Not with pity, but with respect.

"Well. That explains a lot."

Her hands folded on the desk.

"If Hill staff are calling, the issue landed. They're looking for guidance, and they expect us to have answers. And if they're hearing about Nick, they're hearing about the policy gap."

She tapped thoughtfully against her notebook.

"This isn't something we should handle solo. If we pick this up, we need the other HIV groups like NMAC, Sero, and Lambda Legal. Alignment matters before the issue gets bigger."

Baraq nodded. This was exactly what he'd hoped to hear.

"And we should talk to him again. Really talk. Not the pre-election half conversation we managed last time. It sounds like he's been doing the work of ten organizations by himself, and we need to catch up."

She looked at him with appreciation and reassurance.

"I'm glad you came up here. Most people don't walk into someone else's department to flag something like this. But you were right to."

He shrugged, a little shy.

"He doesn't ask for help easily."

"That's fine. It doesn't mean he shouldn't get it."

She was already rearranging priorities.

"We'll set something up."

* * *

Within a few days, the ripples from that conversation reached me from two directions at once.

After drill, Captain Cravins caught me in the hallway and asked if I had a minute. We stepped into his office, and he closed the door.

"So," he said, leaning against his desk with that sly half-grin he used when he knew he had news worth sharing, "you'll never guess who I ran into at a fundraiser last night."

I shook my head.

"Chad Griffin," he said. "We started talking, I mentioned you, and he said he'd give his folks a gentle nudge to get a meeting set up. Nothing heavy-handed. Just enough to make sure it doesn't get forgotten."

I didn't need a civics lesson on what a 'gentle nudge' from the President of the Human Rights Campaign meant.

The next morning, an email landed in both our inboxes from someone at the Human Rights Campaign's legal team. The tone was brisk but warm. Sarah had started a follow-up with Chad's nudge behind it.

"Hi Nick and Captain Cravins, we'd love to reconnect and hear more about the recent developments. Do either of you have availability over the next few days? Here are a few windows that seem possible…"

They listed three options within the next week. Each would normally require reshuffling a soldier's and a lawyer's schedules.

I typed a carefully worded response when Cravins' reply popped up:

"I can make any of these times work. Just tell me where to be."

He was a full-time officer with a demanding calendar; he didn't say things like that lightly. He was putting this above everything else.

I deleted my half-hedged draft and wrote:

"Same for me. I will make any of the proposed times work."

A few hours later, another email arrived:

"It looks like one time works for all parties. Meeting invite attached. We'll see you both at the Human Rights Campaign headquarters."

That evening, I called Cravins to talk through logistics.

"You ready for this?"

"As ready as I can be. Do you think I should wear my dress uniform?"

He didn't even pause.

"Yes. Absolutely. I'm wearing mine."

"You sure? I don't want to look like I'm trying too hard."

"This isn't trying too hard. It's showing them exactly who you are and what the Army stands to lose by keeping this policy in place. You stop being an abstraction or a case file and become what you actually are."

His voice stayed steady and certain.

"Your record includes deployments overseas and combat experience, all of it earned. Let them see that the moment you walk in."

I swallowed. Hearing him say it aloud made the meeting feel bigger than just an introduction or a follow-up.

"Okay. Dress blues."

"Good. We'll go in there, tell them the story straight, and let them ask whatever they need to."

* * *

The following week, Captain Cravins and I arrived at the Human Rights Campaign headquarters in dress blues. People glanced at us in the lobby with the reflexive curiosity uniforms always draw in civilian spaces.

A staffer led us upstairs. The conference room had a view over half the city, with the White House in one direction, the Capitol in the other. It felt like a place where decisions actually mattered.

We took seats at one end of the table. Before I could introduce myself, Cravins leaned forward slightly. He was composed, deliberate, owning the room without forcing it.

"Before we begin, I want to introduce Sergeant Harrison properly."

My spine straightened. His voice carried a quiet authority that he used when he wanted the room to listen.

"Nick isn't just a National Guardsman navigating a flawed policy. He's a combat veteran, an NCO before law school. He has an operational deployment to Afghanistan in 2006 and later deployments to Kuwait and Iraq. He has earned everything this uniform represents."

He paused long enough for that to land.

"Between those deployments, he put himself through law school. JD-MBA. No shortcuts. No special advantages. And after all of that, the Army still won't allow him to serve as a JAG officer because of a policy that hasn't kept pace with medical reality."

No theatrics. Just clarity.

"At one point, they suggested he transfer into a trucking MOS. A truck driver for someone with two graduate degrees, years of leadership experience, and a documented record of exceptional service."

Knowing looks passed around the table.

"He's not here asking for special treatment. He's here because this policy costs the Army exactly the talent it should be retaining. And because the impact goes far beyond him."

A nod in my direction. "Nick, go ahead."

I swallowed. "Thank you." I slid copies of my packet across the table. "I want to walk you through how I got here, because this wasn't my first step. It was the last."

"I worked with the G-1 collaboratively, and they agreed the request made sense. They told me to take it up the chain, so I did for an entire year, while everyone kept insisting the policy update was coming. During that time, I waited. I avoided escalation, stayed out of the press, and refused to attack the system. I followed the process exactly."

"And then they shelved the rewrite. After a year of doing everything right, I received a denial. Two sentences. No explanation."

Stillness settled over the room.

"That's when I started digging into the NDAA language Congress had already passed. Representative Barbara Lee required the Department of Defense to study whether these policies were still medically justified."

I shrugged.

"They dismissed her."

A few nods. They remembered.

"The summary said the standards 'remain medically appropriate' and 'consistent with existing research.' No analysis. No engagement with the science."

"It was a punt," someone said.

"That's how it read to us, too," said another voice.

"So when it became clear internal processes weren't going anywhere, I walked the Hill. I contacted every Armed Services Committee office on the House and Senate side."

"How many packets did you actually drop off?"

"All of them. Every Member's military legislative aide."

"And follow-up?" Andrea Levario asked.

"Every office. I've spoken with fifty-four so far."

That landed.

"And the responses?"

"Republicans frame it as readiness. If someone can do the job, let them. Don't pay them to sit on the bench. Democrats see it as civil rights. Different language, same conclusion. The policy makes little sense."

Heads nodded. Not surprised, but confirmed.

Andrea turned to Sarah. "If we take over the legislative strategy, we'll need a full debrief. Which offices are engaged, who's ready to lead, who asked the right questions."

"I can walk you through all of it. I kept notes."

The speakerphone lit up.

"Hi everyone, this is Scott Schoettes from Lambda Legal."

After the greetings, his voice cut in again.

"Nick, thank you for your presentation. Your story is compelling. It's exactly the narrative courts understand."

"Thank you."

"I'd like to speak with you privately after this. One-on-one. Not on a group call. I want to talk about the possibility of litigation and hear more details directly. It will also help preserve the attorney–client privilege."

"Of course. I'm open to that."

"Good. We'll connect after the meeting."

The room shifted back into strategy. Sharper NDAA language, targeted questions, no more room for the Department of Defense to hide behind vague references to "current research."

When it wrapped, hands were shaken, and follow-ups were promised.

As the elevator doors closed, Cravins looked over.

"Good job. You handled that exactly right."

* * *

After the meeting, once I'd stepped outside and the cold air hit my face, my phone buzzed. A Chicago number. I stepped away from the building and answered.

"Nick? This is Scott Schoettes — we spoke briefly on the call."

His voice was steadier and warmer than it had sounded through the speakerphone. A lawyer's voice, but human underneath it.

"I wanted to follow up," he said. "I've been wanting to bring a case against the military for a long time, ever since we helped get things changed at the State Department. We've considered several people, but your situation… your case is strong. Especially because you've already gone through the trouble of exhausting every administrative avenue."

"I did everything I could think of," I said. "I even filed with the Army Board for Correction of Military Records. Have heard nothing. They're backlogged for months."

"That's exactly the record we're looking for," he said. "Courts like seeing that you gave the institution every chance to fix itself."

There was a pause. Not hesitation, but preparation.

"So let me ask you something," he said. "If we move forward, will you step forward as a named plaintiff, or stay unnamed? Each option carries tradeoffs. An unnamed role preserves your privacy. A named role turns the case into a public story." He let the thought hang for a moment. "That visibility creates pressure, but it also invites scrutiny and harassment."

I stood there watching cars pass, the city moving around me as if none of this mattered. I thought about the exception to policy request and how many hands it had passed through. How it felt knowing my medical condition wasn't a guarded secret anymore but a running commentary up an entire chain of command.

"I appreciate the warning," I said. "But honestly? I crossed that line a long time ago. That packet moved through a battalion-sized element before it ever reached the person who denied it. Half of the building knew my status. And when I started talking to Congress, I knew everything I sent became a public record. Privacy was gone the minute I asked the Army to follow its own rules."

"So you're comfortable being named?"

"I am," I said, and it surprised me how certain the answer felt. Then I said the part that mattered: "Someone has to be."

He was quiet, listening in that deliberate lawyer's way.

"Most soldiers in my position will not step forward," I said. "They're too afraid of what happens if their status spreads. And the military counts on that fear. They've built the entire system around it. The paperwork gauntlet, the exceptions, the denials. No sergeant should have to send their medical history through a chain of command to the Under Secretary and the Deputy Chief of Staff level just to get a waiver considered. Most won't. And that's how the policy survives."

Scott didn't interrupt.

"I've already taken the hits," I said. "My career stalled. The worst consequences have already happened. But the nineteen-year-old kid at Fort Riley? Or the specialist in Alabama who doesn't have a law degree or a civilian safety net? They can't risk this. They can't afford to become the face of anything."

I took a breath.

"I can."

"Alright," he said. "Then I'll draft a memo laying out the case and present it to our committee. They make the final call on what cases we take, but I'm optimistic. Your case is strong. Your background is strong. And the timing feels right."

"What do you need from me?" I asked.

"For now? Nothing. Just be ready for the possibility that we'll move quickly once we get the green light."

We talked a little longer about logistics, timelines, and the architecture of what would come next. When we finally hung up, I stayed there on the sidewalk a moment longer, phone still in my hand.

Chapter Seventeen

I discovered the first reports almost by accident. Early talk that the Pentagon was considering a new "Deploy or Get Out" approach to readiness. It wasn't official yet, just the quiet policy chatter that shows up before anyone puts their name on it. But the outline was clear enough to recognize: a rule that would allow the services to separate anyone who had been non-deployable for twelve consecutive months.

Even in that rough form, the implications were hard to miss. The policy left no room for nuance. It ignored effective treatment and refused to consider conditions that were stable and fully controlled. It relied instead on a blunt instrument aimed at a predictable target.

I read the piece again, slower this time, making sure I wasn't overreacting. I wasn't. If this idea solidified into policy, HIV+ servicemembers would be among the first pushed off the books.

There were a handful of offices on the Hill I trusted, and one of them needed to hear about this immediately. Months earlier, when I first met with that staffer, he had talked about the massive number of servicemembers sitting on permanent profiles who couldn't deploy.

"The military must address this."

I remembered my reply. "Then they need to make sure their HIV policies actually match the science."

A nod followed. "They certainly can't ignore it forever."

So when I saw the article, that was the first office I reached for.

Before scheduling anything, I sent the link to Scott with a quick note: "We need to get in front of this. I can go back to a few offices."

His response came almost immediately.

"You can't go alone anymore. As a plaintiff, you need to go with one of our attorneys. I'll send Sasha Burnett. She's in our DC office."

The words landed, and the weight of them took a moment to settle. Years of walking those hallways alone had trained me to set meetings, build relationships, and carry the argument myself. Now, rules and guardrails framed every step in unfamiliar ways.

Somewhere in the back of my mind, I had known that becoming a plaintiff would mean surrendering some control, but I hadn't felt the weight of it until then.

I wrote back: "Understood. But we need to hurry."

Sasha met me downtown the next morning. As we walked toward the Cannon Building, she set the tone. "Let's keep this tight. Stick to what we can document."

The staffer skipped small talk once we sat down.

"I saw the article. It looks exactly like the direction we discussed."

"It is. If they implement it as written, every HIV+ servicemember ends up labeled non-deployable, even after a decade of stability."

Sasha laid out the legal implications. I covered the operational reality. Promotions, assignments, career derailment, and the permanent profile issue that was now being weaponized instead of reformed. He took notes and asked targeted questions about scope, timing, and how the services might respond.

That afternoon, the same conversation unfolded twice more in two other offices, carrying the same urgency and concern. A shared recognition that a single poorly drafted policy memorandum could inflict damage that no one could undo later.

By the time Sasha and I stepped out of the Cannon Building, the reality had settled in that this was no longer my terrain, at least not in the way it had been. The freedom to walk the Hill at will, drop into an office when someone finally returned an email, or push an issue forward through sheer persistence had disappeared. From that point on, coordination shaped every step, deliberation framed every conversation, and each word carried consequences for a lawsuit not yet brought.

I was beginning a different fight.

* * *

A few days later, I sat down with Andrea Levario at the Human Rights Campaign to make that shift real. She'd booked a small glass-walled conference room. The kind felt exposed during the day but stayed mercifully quiet after hours. A few minutes in, the Executive Director of OutServe-SLDN, Matt Thorn, stepped through the door, gave a quick nod, and took a seat across from me.

Andrea opened her notebook. "Okay," she said. "Walk us through what you've been doing on the Hill. Everything. Who you met, what they said, what they asked for."

I pulled out my notes. The pages I'd been carrying around for months. "All right," I said. "I'll start with the Armed Services Committees. I've spoken with staffers at almost every office. Some of them already understand the science. Others don't know much. A few are genuinely curious. But some are just indifferent, though polite about it."

Andrea kept pace, typing rapidly. Matt listened with his arms crossed, expression neutral.

The explanation continued, moving through the service fellows who understood the medical system, the chiefs of staff who pressed with sharp follow-up questions, and the offices that failed to grasp the waiver process at all. It mapped who held real influence over personnel matters and who had the attention of the uniformed liaisons.

When I mentioned Representative Sullivan's office, Matt cut in.

"I'd avoid them."

I looked up. "Why?"

"They're not allies. He's been awful on transgender issues. We're not partnering with people who attack our community."

A slow nod. "I'm not defending his record on trans issues. But he sits on the committee that actually deals with personnel matters. People listen to him, especially on the Republican side."

Andrea shot Matt a look to let me finish, and I kept going.

"I'm not saying we put him on a poster. But if he's willing to discuss HIV policy, I don't think we can afford to ignore that."

A shake of the head. "I don't trust him, and I'm not asking our organization to legitimize him. There are lines we don't cross."

I chose my words carefully. "Democrats have controlled the Department of Defense for years. They haven't fixed this. If we want change, we need to talk to the people who actually have the power to move something, regardless of party."

Matt exhaled sharply. "Nick, that's not your call to make anymore."

Andrea said nothing, but the shift in posture was enough. The conversation tightened around me.

She closed her notebook. "Your role is changing. You're about to be a plaintiff in a major federal case. That comes with limits. We appreciate everything you've done, but from here forward, the policy work has to run through the organizations."

"Including deciding who we meet with."

I leaned back. "So I'm supposed to step back now."

A small, sympathetic nod. "Yes. We take the reins from here."

The blunter version followed. "You've brought us incredible groundwork. Now let us handle the Hill."

My eyes dropped to my notes. Pages of relationships, conversations, strategy, all built piece by piece. Nothing said it belonged to me at the top, but until that moment, they had felt like they did.

I closed the notebook. "All right. But if someone's willing to talk, regardless of party affiliation, you should use that door. These policies harm people across party lines."

No response from Matt. Andrea met my gaze with respect, but also finality. Just like that, the handoff had begun.

* * *

If losing control felt frustrating, what came next made it feel necessary.

A few days later, I met with Matthew Rose at the National Minority AIDS Council. We met in a quiet corner of the NMAC office, a small conference room with a window overlooking a stretch of downtown DC. He shook my hand with the serene confidence of someone shaped by years in federal buildings while remaining rooted in community work.

"I wanted to meet you in person," Matt said, motioning for me to sit. "I've heard about the work you did on the Hill this summer. Staffers were talking about you."

"That's… surprising," I said. I didn't think of myself as someone people talked about.

"No," he said, "what's surprising is that you did it alone. Most organizations don't get that much traction in an entire year."

He leaned back in his chair, studying me for a moment. Not like someone assessing strategy, but like someone curious about how the pieces of a person fit together.

"I also wanted to talk because we're drafting an amendment to the NDAA," he continued. "Language that forces the Department of Defense to address HIV specifically. Not vague readiness language, but actual requirements. They ignored it in last year's report. We will not let them do that again."

That startled me. Until now, everything felt piecemeal. Legal theories in one corner, individual advocacy in another, policy staffers writing questions no one answered. This was the first time someone said plainly: We're going to write language that forces their hand.

"Do you think it'll make it in?" I asked.

"It might," he said. "But even introducing it changes the conversation. It tells the services we're done letting them hide behind euphemisms."

He paused, then shifted to something more personal.

"You know why NMAC cares about this issue, right?"

"I assumed because it's HIV," I said.

"That's part of it," he nodded. "But the bigger reason is the military itself. For a lot of minority communities, the military is one of the few ladders left. A place where you can get an education, stability, a middle-class life, and health care. A way out."

He softened his voice.

"You know that better than most."

I didn't answer immediately. But he was right.

The military had served as my exit ramp out of Oklahoma and away from a future that felt small and predetermined. Through it, I gained an education, a move to Washington, and access to law firms, government offices, and contracts that would otherwise have remained closed. The experience forced me to grow up and gave me financial stability for the first time in my life.

And now, the same institution that had lifted me was holding the door shut because of a virus they understood better than almost anyone.

Matt continued:

"The irony," he said, "is that the Department of Defense has the best HIV science in the country. They have the biggest longitudinal cohort anywhere. Hundreds of thousands of medical records going back decades. Their researchers were publishing data years before the rest of the country understood how undetectability worked, how transmission risk dropped to zero. They knew. Yet, they kept the old policies."

I nodded, but it didn't feel like agreement. It felt like something clicking into place.

The thing I couldn't quite articulate yet was that they weren't reasoning through it at all. They were acting as if it were simply their prerogative. This was the decision the military was used to having deferred to. They had always set the standards, and no one had ever made them justify or explain them.

"That's what gets me," I said. "They had the evidence. They had better data than the CDC and the NIH. But they didn't apply it to their people."

"That's why we're here," Matt said. "Your case matters. The military closes a door millions of marginalized people rely on for opportunity."

I sat with that for a moment. It felt like he had given me language for something I'd sensed but never articulated. My fight wasn't just about fairness or my commission. It was also about protecting the ladder that had allowed me to climb.

He smiled, not unkindly.

"Nick, the work you did on the Hill moved things. You gave people the foundation to build on. But now you have a different role. Being a plaintiff changes everything. The visibility, the stakes, the legal precision required. It's another world."

"I know," I said. "I'm getting used to the idea of letting other people take it from here."

"That's the right move," he said. "Let someone else handle the advocacy. Hold your position. Let us do the messy coordinating. You stay steady. The entire case will orbit around your story."

He stood and shook my hand, and there was something in the gesture that suggested he expected me to draw strength from it.

"You've done good work," he said. "Now let us build on it."

He meant it as reassurance, but it didn't land that way.

* * *

Several months had passed since my call with Scott. Lambda Legal had still filed nothing. Still circling. Still "working through internal steps." I had stepped back as everyone asked. No more Hill laps, no more back-channel pushing. But the waiting was feeling like its own static.

So when OutServe-SLDN held their annual leadership conference, I showed up feeling restless and relieved to be around people who actually understood the landscape.

It didn't take long for Matt Thorn to spot me.

"Nick." A hand waved me over. "There's someone you need to meet."

He steered me toward a small cluster near the buffet tables. The familiar swirl of uniforms, suits, and name badges signaled both clout and exhaustion. Among them stood a man with shoulder-length reddish-brown hair and a neatly trimmed beard. His navy blazer was paired with an open-collared shirt, giving him the look of someone who was comfortable straddling the line between formal and relaxed.

"Nick, this is Peter Perkowski, our Legal Director."

A firm handshake. "I've read the summaries. You're the National Guard servicemember challenging the commissioning policy, right?"

"That's me. Lambda Legal is still reviewing the case on its end."

A nod. "Scott and I have been in touch. He mentioned your situation."

The question came next, direct but not brusque. "So where are they in the approval process?"

I exhaled. Plenty of people had asked that lately, but he was the first who sounded like he might actually do something with the answer.

"They're still moving it through whatever internal structure they use. It's slow. They're interested, but it's a process."

Before any response could land, Matt Thorn stepped in.

"Peter." His voice dropped just enough to carry weight. "You know them. Tell Lambda Legal we're going to file this if they don't move."

A blink. "You're serious?"

No hesitation. "Yes. This needs to happen, and it needs to happen soon. You tell Scott that we're prepared to go forward with this case. OutServe-SLDN will file if Lambda Legal doesn't."

My stomach tightened. Silence felt safer than speaking, and I didn't trust my voice not to give away what that moment meant.

Matt kept going.

"Lambda Legal has been circling this for months. Nick's case is strong. The record is clean. The facts are in place. If they're dragging their feet, we're done waiting."

Peter looked from me back to Matt, measuring the statement.

"I'll talk to Scott. He needs to know we're ready to step in."

A nod, satisfied. "Good."

Peter peeled off to join another group. Once he was out of earshot, Matt turned back to me.

"You've waited long enough."

There was no edge, just certainty. The kind that came from someone used to forcing momentum.

* * *

Eric Fanning's reception was the usual conference choreography. Short remarks, polite applause, then a crush of people lining up to shake his hand. I hung back against the far wall, watching the line snake past the bar and thin out. No reason to ask him anything in front of an audience.

When the crowd finally drifted away, I stepped forward.

"Mr. Fanning." I offered my hand. "Nick Harrison. I wrote to you a few times when I was trying to commission into the JAG Corps. I received no response."

A practiced, apologetic smile. "A lot of letters come through that office. I'm sure someone reviewed it."

"Maybe. I wanted to talk to you about the HIV policies while you were Secretary of the Army."

His posture shifted, still polite but suddenly guarded. "We looked at it, but any change has to come from the legal and medical communities."

I cut in before he could finish. "Legal and medical communities have aligned for years. Law and science settled this long ago. Political appointees were the ones who needed to push it forward."

One blink. Caught, but unwilling to engage. "Well, I'm not the Secretary of the Army anymore. It was nice meeting you."

He ended the conversation and walked away.

I stepped back into the reception area and rejoined a few friends from the conference. One of them smirked.

"So, you waited around as if you wanted a moment alone with him."

"I confronted him over the HIV policy while he was Secretary."

Another voice cut in, eyebrows raised. "You should be careful. He'll probably be the next Deputy Secretary of Defense."

I didn't hesitate. "Then, he needs to pull his head out of his ass."

They laughed, the moment passing as quickly as it came. But when the conversation shifted back into small talk, I felt myself drift.

They did not know what I was stepping into.

* * *

Toward the end of the conference, I slipped into a panel on HIV in the military. Advocates, a handful of uniformed attendees, and servicemembers who carried the quiet, tired look of people shaped by the policy rather than the literature filled the seats.

At the center of the table sat Lieutenant Colonel Ken Pinkela.

I understood the outline of his case, from the accusation and investigation through the court-martial and conviction. The record showed no transmission, no risk, and no science to support it, yet someone claimed they "felt" endangered, and the military treated that feeling as fact. It cost him his career, his rank, his pension, and everything that followed.

Seeing him made it harder to keep that story at arm's length.

When his turn came, Pinkela stayed still and spoke without ornament. He had repeated the same nightmare too many times to soften it. His account moved from the charge to the speed with which the institution he had served for decades turned on him, and then to the isolation that followed. A stigma that refused to fade even when the facts remained on his side.

He said, "They didn't care that there was no risk. They cared that someone said the word HIV."

It landed in the room like a dropped weight.

Other panelists picked up the thread. Criminalization statutes, outdated service regulations, and commanders interpreting policy however they wanted. They talked about how the military charged servicemembers with crimes that made no medical or legal sense and punished them simply for being HIV+ in the wrong unit under the wrong commander.

No one called on me, and I volunteered nothing. I just sat there listening, my jaw tight, because I understood exactly what all of this meant for me once my name became public.

Pinkela wasn't a hypothetical. He was a warning.

When the panel wrapped, people drifted toward the hallway. Someone near me said, "God, imagine going through all that when there was zero risk." Someone else responded, "The military doesn't need risk. They just need a reason."

I stayed in my seat a little longer than everyone else. I wasn't afraid in the cinematic sense. I wasn't imagining handcuffs or headlines. It was subtler than that. That moment brought the realization that suing and putting my story out would lead people I'd never met to form opinions. Someone with a grudge or a misunderstanding could say something, and suddenly I'd be living inside the machinery I just watched destroy a man's life.

The policy fight was one thing. The consequences were another.

Walking out of the room, the thought stayed close: If this goes sideways, the science won't matter. Someone could decide I'm a danger, and the institution would move before anyone bothered to check the facts.

Chapter Eighteen

It didn't begin with a plan. It began with a simple ask: Could I watch Yuki while Baraq was out of town for a week?

My apartment suited her immediately.

It always had that effect on people and, apparently, on cats too. It was a 1930s Art Deco building. The building had survived every wave of redevelopment by sheer force of character. The nonprofit foundation that owned it kept the units surprisingly affordable, but the real treasure was the space itself. High ceilings, wide rooms, and closets big enough to qualify as small apartments in other parts of the city. Light pooled in the corners. The air felt open. You could exhale there.

Yuki acted as if she'd just upgraded from coach to first class.

Within hours, she had claimed the walk-in closet as her personal annex, curling up on a pile of sweaters like she'd been looking for this spot her entire life. She wandered the apartment with the relaxed entitlement of someone who had come home after a long time away. She even found a vantage point near the windows where she could survey the city's skyline outside.

By the time Baraq returned from his trip, she wasn't just settled. She was thriving.

He scooped her up the moment he walked in, and she nuzzled into him without hesitation. Even while he held her, his eyes wandered through the apartment, taking in the space, the light, and the way she had made herself at home.

He set her down, and she trotted straight back to the closet, vanishing into the sweaters. After watching the doorway where she disappeared, he said, almost to himself, "She really likes it here."

He wasn't wrong. His place in Anacostia felt cramped and dim by comparison. Fine for a single guy who rarely spent time at home, but not ideal for a creature that needed territory. Here, she had room to explore. Room to roam. Room to breathe. And he could see it written in her posture, her confidence, the easy way she moved.

He watched her disappear back into the closet and let out a quiet, conflicted laugh. "She's just really comfortable here," he said. "I feel bad uprooting her now." He wasn't angling for anything. He meant it. She'd settled into the apartment so naturally that moving her back felt wrong.

"Well," I said, "you don't have to uproot her now. We're both on holiday break. You're both welcome to stay here and hang out. That way, she can stay put."

That was how it shifted, not through a big conversation, but through the simple practicality of what already felt right. Yuki settled into the space, and he stayed because he didn't want to uproot her.

It was December, and Civilization VI had just come out. He'd been excited about it for weeks but wasn't sure it would run on his computer. He didn't celebrate Christmas, but that gave me an excuse to buy it "as a gift" and install it on my computer so he could camp out and play while I read or caught up on work.

That became our rhythm. Quiet parallel lives unfolding in the same room. We didn't fill the silence. We didn't need to. He'd sit at my desk strategizing his empire while I sprawled on the couch reviewing memos or simply letting my mind drift. Hours passed, and nothing felt forced. It was the first time in a long time that being with someone didn't mean performing for them.

Before this, he'd been splitting his evenings. Rushing home to take care of Yuki, then coming back across the river to spend time with me.

It always left him stretched thin. So I told him he didn't have to keep choosing. He could stay here with both of us.

Yuki approved immediately.

And at night, when he and I finally crawled into bed, she'd wait until we'd settled before joining us. She'd climb up quietly and tap his back with a single, insistent paw. A gentle summons. He'd turn to face her, and only then would she curl into the crook of his arm, purring like she'd orchestrated all of this from the beginning.

I'd reach over and rest my hand on her, completing the arrangement. Three creatures, sharing a bed, perfectly still and content.

That was the real beginning.

* * *

Lambda Legal sent over the retainer agreement in early April. It arrived with a brief, friendly note confirming everything we had already discussed. I printed it, signed it at my dining table, and scanned it back. There wasn't any ceremony to it, but the moment still felt like stepping across an invisible line. Something that had lived mostly in conversations and documents was now turning into an actual case with my name.

A few days later, I heard from Ian Wilhite. His email took its time, inviting me to talk and offering "a few thoughts before things move on the communications front." The tone felt steady and unhurried rather than urgent or transactional. When we finally connected, his tone was steady and reassuring, the kind that makes complicated things feel manageable.

"I know this is a lot. My job is to make it feel less like a lot."

He wasn't giving orders. He was mapping the terrain, pointing out where the footing was solid and where it wasn't, so I wouldn't stumble over something avoidable.

"Once the filing happens, reporters will reach out. Ideally, they'll come through us first. Most of them know to do that. We screen the requests, make sure they're legitimate, and set things up so you're not walking into a conversation cold. It also lets us loop in the right people on our end so everyone stays coordinated. This isn't about protecting you from something you can't handle. It's about making sure no one ambushes or blindsides you."

I told him that made sense, because it did. It felt less like being managed and more like having someone watching your back.

"Everyone has a role in this. I know you're a lawyer, so your instinct will be to comment on the legal arguments when they come up. Anyone in your position would. But that's not your job here."

He let that land before continuing.

"Your job is to give this a human dimension. You're the only one who can tell the personal story. When the conversation turns to legal questions, that's when you hand it off to Scott. Let him take the mic. It gives him the opening he needs, and it keeps you where your voice carries the most weight."

He paused, his tone easing another notch.

"And look at your social media. Not because there's anything wrong with it. There isn't. But from here on out, you don't want to weigh in on things that pull you off message. You're about to become the face of this issue, regardless of whether you planned for that. People will read everything you say through that lens."

"Keep it to the case, or to things no one can twist. Travel. Dinner. The cat. You don't want someone who might otherwise support you deciding they can't stand behind you because of an opinion that has nothing to do with what we're fighting for."

The advice carried the weight of experience, closing nothing off. It felt like someone checking the forecast and handing me a jacket before I stepped into the storm.

Before we ended the call, he added, "We'll take this one step at a time. You're not in this alone, Nick."

A few days later, he emailed again about photos. Lambda Legal needed a set of images to offer to media outlets once they filed the case. Clean and dignified photos of me in uniform without making it a performance. We decided to use Arlington National Cemetery as the backdrop. The place already carried its own gravity.

The morning of the shoot opened under a muted gray sky. Arlington National Cemetery lay quiet in its familiar way, with trimmed grass, long rows of headstones, and the soft echo of footsteps somewhere in the distance. The air seemed to hold its breath.

Ian met me near the entrance with the same amiable smile he'd had on the phone. "She's set up in one of the quieter sections," he said, leading me along one of the winding paths. The photographer looked up as we approached and waved. She had an understated, grounding presence that made the whole thing feel less like a photo shoot and more like a moment someone was documenting.

I ducked into the public restroom and changed into my dress uniform in a stall, then stepped back out. She studied the light, adjusted her lens, and began offering gentle direction. Tilt a little this way, step forward, look past the rows. Nothing forced. Nothing theatrical.

Between shots, Ian watched quietly from a few yards away, hands in his pockets. Every so often, he glanced at the photographer's camera and gave a small nod, as if to say the frame held together and the moment had landed.

Walking between the headstones, I felt the familiar weight of the place settle around me. Arlington National Cemetery reminded you of all the people whose service had shaped the story of the country, and of why it mattered that the military treat every servicemember with dignity.

When the photographer finished, the three of us wandered for a bit. We stopped near the Tomb of the Unknown Soldier just in time to catch the changing of the guard.

* * *

It started, as most things in my life seemed to at that point, with a sense of responsibility creeping in at the edges of everything else I was juggling. After a few seasons playing Stonewall Kickball, I decided I owed something back. When the league announced it needed a treasurer, I put my name in, and the players elected me.

Stonewall Kickball wasn't just a sports league. It was the engine that kept queer DC from feeling lonely and transactional. People showed up not knowing anyone, and suddenly they had teammates. Fresh off the bus from somewhere, they had learned to keep their guard up. Now, they had people to grab drinks with after games, people to flirt with, people to date, people to crash on a couch with when everything fell apart. It was where friendships formed, exes learned to coexist, and chosen families quietly assembled themselves one Sunday at a time.

I knew how much that mattered. I'd watched enough people arrive in DC with nothing but a suitcase and a Human Rights Campaign bumper sticker, trying to figure out where "their people" were. Stonewall Kickball gave them something to hold on to. Volunteering as treasurer felt like the least I could do for a structure that had given so many a place to land.

Stonewall Kickball's fiscal sponsor was the DC Center, and the DC Center itself was a kind of accidental institution. A patchwork of everything left behind after Whitman-Walker's financial overhaul years earlier. Across the country, LGBTQ+ centers had grown out of the wreckage of the AIDS crisis. People rejected by their families, dying alone, leaving whatever they had to the clinics and organizations that had cared for them when no one else would. Those bequests became buildings, staff, and programs. The physical proof that if no one else claimed us, we would at least claim each other.

In DC, Whitman-Walker had been the anchor. When the clinic stabilized its finances, it shed most of its LGBTQ+ programming. Support groups, arts and cultural events, and youth programs. Anything that wasn't directly tied to its healthcare mission. The popular, self-sustaining programs spun off on their own. Pride, the youth league, the sports leagues. Everything else landed on the DC Center's shoulders.

It wasn't glamorous. It was stabilizing work. The quiet infrastructure that keeps communities from unraveling when no one else is watching. The support groups, the drop-in hours, the tiny offices where people came out, broke down, or figured out how to start over. None of that made headlines, but it kept people alive.

After a couple of kickball seasons handling Stonewall Kickball's books, the DC Center's leadership asked the league to spin itself off as an independent nonprofit. It was a headache. New bylaws, new bank accounts, new everything. But they invited me to join the DC Center's board as its treasurer. It felt like stepping into the machinery that kept queer life in the city going. So, I said yes.

By then, the case moved quietly in the background, and I had no sense of how any of it would collide. I couldn't predict how the people I played with, flirted with, or had casual hookups with would react when my name appeared in national stories about HIV and the military. What I knew was this: if I wanted to belong to this community, I needed to contribute to the work that held it together, not just enjoy the parts that felt easy.

That need pushed me to seek guidance from someone who understood what visibility meant in a community that could both embrace you and pass judgment. The board was actively recruiting new members, and I remembered chatting with Amanda Simpson during the Outserve-SLDN conference. I'd followed her career. Her appointment as the first openly transgender woman to a senior government position, her work in aviation, defense, and diplomacy. She carried an experience you couldn't manufacture. Visibility earned the hard way, and resilience carved out of necessity.

I reached out to see if she might be interested in serving on the DC Center board. We traded a few emails. She said she was willing to consider it but wanted to hear more about what the role involved, so we scheduled a meeting. Even if she wasn't ready to commit, I knew I wanted to hear whatever she would share.

We met at a quiet coffee shop near Dupont, near the embassies. She arrived with the calm confidence of someone who has spent most of her adult life walking into rooms that were not always ready for her. We exchanged small talk. Her considering her next career move, me explaining the board's needs. The conversation drifted almost naturally toward the topic pressing most on my mind.

I talked about the case. Not the legal mechanics, but what it might mean once it became public. The interviews, the headlines, the questions I couldn't control. The way a name can feel like something other people get to handle. And underneath that, a quieter fear: how my community would respond. The people I organized with, the people I'd kissed in dark bars, the ones who only knew me as a teammate or a crush.

I asked her what it had been like for her. Being in the spotlight, navigating the scrutiny, carrying the weight of representation, whether she wanted it or not.

She listened in the way people do when they recognize a question they once asked themselves.

Finally, she said, "You're going to see stories written about you. And you're going to want to read the comments."

She paused long enough for me to understand that this was the part that mattered.

"Don't," she said. "You won't gain anything from them. They're not written for you, and they're not about the truth. They'll get in your head, they'll drain your energy, and they'll try to make you question yourself at exactly the moment you need to be steady."

I nodded, but she continued.

"You've already got enough on your mind. Don't give strangers the power to shape how you feel about what you're doing. You can't fight a battle and carry everyone's opinions at the same time."

The advice wasn't harsh. It came from a place of protection, the kind offered by someone who had already paid the price to learn it.

We talked for a little while longer about the DC Center, about the community, about showing up for people even when you're tired. But the heart of the meeting stayed fixed in that moment. She didn't tell me the spotlight would be easy, or that criticism wouldn't hurt, or that visibility came with any kind of shield. She simply gave me the clearest boundary I would have heading into the storm.

When we stood to leave, she said she was interested in the board but needed to see where her next role would land first. I told her that it made perfect sense. But what I walked away with wasn't a potential board member.

* * *

Scott pushed the filing date back a week, and the delay landed in my chest like an exhale I didn't know I'd been holding. It was just one more week before everything went public. One more week before reporters, before arguments, before the government said my name in court filings.

So, we took a road trip.

I left DC early, the spring light just spreading across the Potomac. Northern Virginia slid by in long stretches of green and old stone walls. Traffic thinned as the road curved toward Charlottesville, and by late morning Monticello appeared on the ridge. Familiar, but somehow sharper under the circumstances.

Jefferson's mountaintop retreat didn't feel like a plantation so much as the physical shape of a mind that never stopped spinning. French doors, Palladian symmetry, octagonal rooms, skylights he'd stolen from European architecture after years spent as minister in France. He built his obsessions into the walls. Displaying science instruments, designing his bookshelves, and tucking inventions into corners.

"Jefferson really was a Renaissance man." We stepped into the entrance hall.

"Yeah." Baraq let his hand skim the carved molding. "Brilliant in a lot of ways. Architect, writer, philosopher. He could do almost anything."

He paused, studying a portrait on the wall.

"But despite all that genius, he was a terrible businessperson. He ran himself into debt over and over, yet he kept the entire system going."

I nodded. "He saw the contradictions. He just wasn't willing to give up the wealth and comfort slavery gave him."

"Exactly. He understood the moral problem better than most of his peers. He wrote about it constantly. But he wasn't willing to dismantle the institution that supported his world."

"So he lived with the contradiction," I said. "And pretended it was unsolvable."

"Like many people." Baraq's voice stayed even. "It's easier to call something a 'complicated issue' when solving it costs you everything."

That was Monticello. Beauty and contradiction in equal measure. Brilliant ideas sitting on land worked by people who had no freedom.

We walked the terraces, with a view of miles of soft blue ridges, and let the breeze settle. By the time we drove into Charlottesville for the night, the sun was sinking behind the hills, and the town glowed with soft bar lights and the low hum of university life easing into summer.

The next morning, we headed toward Richmond.

Hollywood Cemetery wasn't subtle. It rose above the James River in sweeping layers, a garden cemetery designed to impress, to overwhelm, to make the living walk slower. Massive oaks arched over winding paths. Obelisks leaned slightly toward the sky. You could hear the river rushing below long before you could see it.

Just inside, we passed the structure everyone in Richmond calls the vampire crypt. The W.W. Pool mausoleum. Gray granite blocks, a barred iron door, stained glass long shattered. The legend says a vampire fled into it after a tunnel collapse in 1925, bleeding and with skin hanging loose. Standing in front of it, you could understand how the story survived. Even in daylight, it felt like something the cemetery tolerated but did not entirely claim.

Further in, the monuments grew grander as we climbed toward President's Circle. The view widened. The river on one side, the city skyline on the other, the cemetery's rolling hills in between. This was the plot Lewis Ginter bought for himself. Prime ground among presidents. And yet the first grave here was not his.

It was John Pope's.

He had started as a messenger boy at Ginter's company. A teenager delivering notes across Richmond. But somehow, over the years, they became inseparable. Living together, traveling together, working side by side, until Pope wasn't just an employee but the central companion of Ginter's life. Two lifelong bachelors sharing a home in a century that offered no words for what they were.

When Pope died in 1896, Ginter buried him here, in the plot meant for himself. The grave beside Pope's stood empty, reserved and waiting.

We stood at the edge of the circle, looking down at Pope's stone softened by decades of weather. The empty plot beside it was just grass, but it spoke louder than anything carved in marble.

"Do you think people understood what they were to each other?" Baraq asked quietly.

"People always understand. They just pretend not to."

A year after Pope died, Ginter followed him. But instead of being placed beside Pope, his family built the enormous mausoleum down the slope. Granite columns, stained glass, carved wreaths. A monument of wealth and legacy. Beautiful in its own right. But nowhere near the man he wanted to bury at his side.

The distance between their resting places hit harder than I expected. The hilltop soaked up the early afternoon sun, cicadas humming somewhere unseen, light settling into the quiet space between the two graves.

We lingered there, letting the stillness settle. It felt like a private corner of the world. A life shared, divided only by the hands that controlled what happened after death.

We eventually made our way back to the car and drove north toward Mount Vernon. The estate rose above the Potomac like a painting. White clapboard, red roof, the long veranda facing the river. It didn't have Jefferson's flourish. It felt steadier, more utilitarian.

"Very Washington." Baraq glanced at the mansion as we walked toward it. "Practical. Straight lines. No theatrics."

"Exactly. Jefferson wanted to reinvent the world. Washington just wanted to run it efficiently."

We moved through the house, past the formal rooms and narrow staircases, and out onto the grounds.

"You know, people talk about Washington wrestling with the moral problem of slavery, but he really spent little energy on it. Jefferson tortured himself in print. Washington just kept the books."

Baraq lifted an eyebrow. "He was a businessperson."

"A very good one. Mount Vernon was only one of several plantations he owned. He shifted enslaved people around like inventory. Counted them, traded them, logged every detail in his ledgers. No illusions. No philosophizing. Just the economics of the system."

We stopped where the path bent toward the family tomb. A breeze carried the smell of river water and damp earth.

"And he put the capital here, right next to his land. People call it vision. Today, people would call it self-dealing."

Baraq gave a low whistle. "Founding father corruption. They really cleaned that part up for the tours."

"And the dentures. Did you hear that explanation at the museum?"

A soft laugh. "About him paying enslaved people for their teeth?"

"Right. As if a ledger entry makes it ethical. As if consent means anything when you own the body you're bargaining with."

We kept walking, past the gardens and the spinning house, across manicured lawns that blurred what had happened on them.

"It's strange," Baraq said at last. "All this beauty built on top of something so brutal."

"That's the story of the country. And the military, in its own way."

He looked over at me, understanding more than I'd said.

By the time we drove back toward DC, the sun was low, and the air was cooling. The world looked ordinary again. Only I wasn't.

Chapter Nineteen

The case went in on May 30, 2018, while we drove back toward DC under a bright, expansive late-spring sky that made Virginia feel endless. My phone vibrated before the tone registered, and I glanced down to see Scott's name before opening the email.

It was short, almost abrupt in its simplicity:

"We're on file. Eastern District of Virginia. Complaint is live. Ian will connect you with the Times."

That was it. My name and diagnosis were now part of the federal record. The institution that had excluded me would have to answer for it in court. And I was nowhere near DC when it happened.

I did it on purpose. I planned the trip to give myself geographic distance before the story broke open across the city where I lived.

We drove a few more miles before the next call came.

Ian.

There was no preamble, no reminders, no instructions. We'd covered all of that already. His tone carried the same steady assurance he'd had from the start.

"Okay," he said, "Phillips is ready."

Because the groundwork was already done. Lambda Legal had been coordinating with the *New York Times* for weeks. Phillips had spoken with military physicians, infectious disease experts, and people who remembered the early years of HIV inside the services. This didn't begin a story. It marked the moment everything clicked into place.

The landscape blurred by while I lifted the phone to my ear.

Phillips sounded exactly like the reporter you hope for when your life becomes evidence in a case much bigger than yourself. Calm, informed, and already two steps into the material. He didn't waste time on introductions. He knew who I was and why this mattered.

He asked about my service, about commissioning, about the future I'd been building before the diagnosis.

Then he moved into the questions that mattered. The policy, the science the Army chose not to incorporate, the absurdity of calling someone non-deployable when their viral load was undetectable. The institutional distortions that let people with unmanaged, far more serious conditions move forward while I remained frozen in place.

He asked nothing inappropriate. He didn't seek lurid angles. His focus stayed on service, dignity, and the system itself.

Then, he asked, "What do you most want people to understand?"

"That I'm not asking for special treatment," I said. "I just want the Army to treat me like everyone else they manage medically. This isn't about risk. It's about stigma that never caught up with the science."

When we hung up, I felt that strange, sharp clarity that comes after finally speaking something aloud. The road stretched ahead in long ribbons of heat. Trucks passed, fence lines flickered in and out, a wheat field bent under a soft wind, all of it unchanged, though everything inside me had shifted.

I said to Baraq, "It felt like I just handed my life to the front page of the *New York Times*. But I am in excellent hands."

A few minutes later, a text from Ian arrived:

"Great. Phillips has what he needs. We'll keep things moving."

The machine was already turning, gears sliding into motion while we crossed another quiet stretch of highway.

* * *

It didn't take long. Maybe thirty minutes after the call with Phillips, while the highway bent toward Fredericksburg and the light softened into that late-spring haze, Baraq's phone buzzed with an alert. He glanced down, then turned the screen slightly my way.

"*New York Times* is up," he said. "Phillips moved fast."

Of course, he did. He had been ready. He structured the reporting weeks earlier. Conversations with former program leads, military physicians, and infectious disease experts already sat in the can. He had only been waiting for the filing and my voice, and once he had both, the story unlocked itself and stepped onto the page.

While I focused on the road, he opened the article and read it with the same quiet, concentrated posture he always took when something mattered. Without skimming, he stayed silent, eyes fixed ahead, turning the words over and testing where they would land. Every so often, a small nod gave him away, marking the moments when a paragraph hit harder than he expected.

After a few minutes, he said, "It's good. Fantastic. He treated you fairly. He treated the issue fairly."

Warmth and protectiveness carried in his voice as he kept the phone in his own hands, choosing to absorb more than he let out rather than passing it to me.

Then he said, almost gently, "Don't read the comments."

I hadn't asked about them. I hadn't even thought about them yet. But he knew where my mind would eventually wander.

"I'm not," I said.

"Good." He nodded once. "You don't need to. I'll read everything."

He didn't say it as a declaration. It was a simple truth. He would take in every piece of the world's reaction before I ever saw it. He would decide what reached me and what didn't.

I didn't know it then, but his phone wasn't just filling with headlines. His friends were reaching out too. Some of them with genuine affection, some with fear they didn't have language for, all of it shaped by the old shadows of HIV stigma that lingered in their generation.

They were worried about him, worried about what it meant for him to be dating someone with HIV who was suddenly the subject of national news. They told him to be careful, to take care of his health, to pay attention in ways that made sense to them but revealed how far behind their understanding still was.

He didn't share any of it with me. Not that day, not that week, not for months. He just absorbed it quietly while keeping everything between us steady and warm, never letting even a trace of their anxiety bleed into the space he was creating around me.

He scrolled further down the article while I watched the highway fold under the afternoon sun, taking it all in before letting any of it reach me. "There's an entire section about the old policy," he said, his voice quiet with the same long, careful attention he always gave a layered piece of writing.

"This reporter talked to the doctors and medical experts who actually oversaw the military's HIV program decades ago. One of them walked through why the military wrote the policy the way it was back then. How it reflected the science and expectations of that era. And then he said something that just undercuts the whole rationale for leaving it the same now."

He paused, scanning the screen again.

"He clarified that the scientific understanding has shifted dramatically. Treatments work, people live long, healthy lives with undetectable viral loads, the risk of transmission is essentially zero with modern therapy, and yet the policy acts like none of that ever happened. He said he was baffled the military's rules haven't changed along with the medicine."

His gaze stayed on the road as he worked through what he'd just read.

"It's damning in how it matters. The argument doesn't lean on emotion or a clever line. It lays out the science and the timeline, then exposes the difference between what they knew then and what they know now, showing how the policy kept one foot in the past long after the evidence had moved on."

Before I could respond, my phone buzzed. Not a journalist yet. Ian.

"*New York Times* piece is live. Others are about to follow. I've already got two outlets asking for interviews, both vetted, both solid. Do you want to take them today, or do you want some space between them?"

No pressure. Just structure. Control. A sense that he already held the map and was asking which door I wanted to open first.

"I'll take them."

"Both today?"

"Yes."

"All right. I'll send times and numbers. You just pick up when they call. I'll make sure you're not blindsided."

He hung up, and almost immediately another alert flashed on Baraq's phone. A military reporter jumped on the story within minutes. One outlet pushed a short piece live, another followed close behind, and a regional write-up out of Norfolk quickly gave way to national LGBTQ+ coverage and a veteran-focused publication.

Each time, he read before saying anything.

"This one sticks to the policy. Straightforward."

"This one tries to summarize too much, but nothing harmful."

"This one is not great, but it's not wrong. Just clumsy."

He wasn't filtering for accuracy. He was filtering for impact, making sure nothing landed in my lap that required emotional triage while the day was still unfolding.

My phone buzzed again. Ian.

"Okay. Public radio wants you for a short segment. Ten minutes. They already talked to Scott. They're good."

"I'll do it."

"And a national print outlet feature writer wants a longer conversation tomorrow or the next day. Again, already vetted. Let me know if you need space."

"I don't. Put it on the calendar."

A brief pause, just long enough to let something human show through the professionalism.

"You're handling this extremely well. Just remember, you don't have to say yes to everything."

"I know. But I want to."

"Then we keep going."

The line went dead.

The requests kept coming, spilling in from a DC television affiliate, a national morning show already scouting segments for later in the week, and a podcast that specialized in military equity issues. One reporter had clearly written his background paragraphs months earlier and now waited only for the filing to drop.

And each time before I opened my mouth to answer, a quieter truth settled in. Lambda Legal had put its weight behind me. Time, staff, strategy, credibility. They could have chosen anyone. There were countless others living the same injustice who would never have their stories amplified, never have a national reporter waiting for their voice. If the community had invested its resources, its platform, its hope in me, then the least I could do was honor that by showing up. Saying yes wasn't about exposure. It was about responsibility. It was about making the most of a chance that didn't belong to me alone.

Every time I felt the old instinct rise, the part of me that wanted to respond to each request, Baraq said, "You don't need to jump every time your phone buzzes. Ian's doing that part. You just stay in your lane."

But I kept saying yes, because the lane was wide now, widened by people who believed the story mattered. And if Lambda Legal had built a platform to carry one voice forward, I would not waste the lift.

Late in the afternoon, he showed me another headline. Not the story, just the headline. It was one of the larger outlets, one whose reach I understood instinctively.

"You're everywhere now."

The line hung between us for a moment. Not frightening, not overwhelming, just true.

He leaned back in his seat, still reading, still absorbing, quietly building the wall between me and everything I didn't need to carry yet.

"You're okay. This is happening the way it should. And you're okay."

"I think so."

He looked at me as if the answer had already settled. "You are. And if anything shifts, I'll tell you, but not before I have to."

Outside the window, the sun slanted lower across the highway, lighting the tops of the trees and stretching long shadows across the pavement.

The world was turning. And he had already put himself between me and the spin.

* * *

When I got back to DC, the air felt heavier. Not in a foreboding way, but in the way the city always feels when you return to it after something irreversible has happened. The *New York Times* story had already made the rounds. My phone still vibrated with messages I hadn't opened. And before I had even unpacked, Ian called to tell me the next piece of the rollout was already in motion.

"*Metro Weekly* wants to do a full feature," he said. "Cover story. We think it's the right move."

Metro Weekly wasn't just another outlet. It was the city's weekly LGBTQ+ magazine. The magazine you grab at coffee shops, bars, bookstores, and gyms. The thing people flipped through on their commute. If the *New York Times* told the country what was happening, *Metro Weekly* told my community.

Lambda Legal arranged everything. A date, a photographer, a writer, a quiet office in their building where we could do the shoot without interruption.

I remember walking into the room and seeing the lighting rig already set up. Soft boxes, a dark backdrop, and that stillness photographers create before they move bodies and equipment around. The photographer looked up and smiled in a knowing, almost nostalgic way.

"I've done a lot of these," he said as he adjusted a reflector. "Especially during Don't Ask, Don't Tell. I spent years photographing servicemembers who couldn't even show their faces back then. Maybe this will be the last one I ever have to do like this."

There was no bitterness in his voice, just history. The weight of it. The sense that each generation gets its own kind of fight to stand in front of a camera for.

We took a series of shots. Some casual, some head-on, some in uniform. For the cover, with Blood and Honor stamped across it in bold white type, the photographer chose the simplest setup. I sat at a table in my dress uniform with my hands clasped in front of me against a dark background, the light catching the gold on my insignia until it looked forged rather than polished.

The photographer kept adjusting the lighting until the shadows carved my face just enough to look deliberate but not theatrical. He stepped back at one point, studying the frame.

"There it is," he said. "That's the one."

He wasn't talking about posture or symmetry. He meant the exact intersection where sincerity meets resolve. The thing he knew how to capture because he'd spent years photographing people who were trying to tell the truth with their bodies, even when the military wouldn't let them use their names.

After the photos, we moved on to the interview. The writer asked questions with the curiosity that comes from living in a community that understood institutional exclusion. We talked about the case, about service, about the strange limbo of being told you're fit enough to fight for your country but not fit enough to advance in it. He asked about Baraq, too. How we met, how he handled the diagnosis, and what the past few weeks had been like with the case breaking open.

I answered honestly, without feeling exposed, and I felt understood.

A week later, the issue came out.

My face, uniform sharp, lighting dramatic, the headline Blood and Honor stretched across the bottom of the cover, everywhere. Coffee shops. Grocery stores. The front table at JR.'s. Stacks in the gym's corner. Even the mailbox alcove in my building.

It was impossible to avoid.

Metro Weekly wasn't just coverage. The magazine was a broadcast to the community that this story wasn't happening somewhere else or to someone abstract. It was happening here in DC, to someone who walked the same streets and lived the same life they did. Someone they might have brushed past at a bar or seen on the Red Line.

* * *

The call came a day or two after the *Metro Weekly* cover started showing up everywhere.

I was still getting used to seeing my face where I hadn't put it. The magazine rack by the register, the stack by the door at JR's, the corner of the gym where people flipped through it while waiting for a machine. I had done nothing differently, but the city felt closer somehow, like the walls had shifted inward.

My phone buzzed with a number I recognized.

"Nick," Donald Cravins said. "Do you have a minute?"

"Of course."

His tone stayed steady, the one he used for strategy and timeline. But a layer of formality sat underneath it, enough to signal this wasn't a casual check-in.

"I want to be upfront with you. The command asked me to call."

Leaning back against the counter, I waited.

"DC National Guard leadership pulled me in earlier today. They flagged some of the recent coverage, specifically the interviews where you're in uniform."

The familiar tightening settled in my chest. Not panic, but awareness. The moment when something moves from the theoretical to the real.

"They asked me to remind you of the regulations on wearing the uniform during media appearances. That's it. A reminder, not discipline or accusation."

A brief pause.

"I asked directly whether this affected your JAG slot."

"And?"

"It hasn't changed. The Commanding General was clear. You're still the plan."

I let out a breath I hadn't realized I'd been holding.

"There was something else. They mentioned the article where you talked about the Human Rights Campaign. And how I introduced you."

I smiled despite myself. "I hope that was okay."

"It was more than okay. I told them I felt honored, and I meant that."

Something shifted then, subtle but unmistakable, from message delivery to something personal.

"Nick, I want you to understand something. I'm a civil rights attorney in my civilian practice. If I were representing you right now, I'd probably be telling you to wear the uniform everywhere."

"That tracks."

"It's a compelling truth. And it matters. But they asked me to pass along the regulation, so I did. Professionally. Cleanly."

"I appreciate that." And I did.

Another pause, just long enough to register.

"I also wanted you to know I've been talking to my son about what you're doing."

That surprised me.

"He's at the academy. We've been having a lot of conversations about service. About what it actually means."

I stayed quiet.

"What you're doing is the truest form of patriotism I know. Serving a country even when it doesn't fully accept you, and insisting it live up to its own values."

He paused again.

"It's the same fight Black servicemembers have had to wage, over and over. Proving they belong while wearing the uniform. Loving an institution that hasn't always loved them back."

The kitchen stayed quiet except for the hum of the refrigerator.

"I just wanted you to hear that. Especially right now."

"Thank you." My voice came out steadier than I felt. "That means more than you know."

"You're doing the right thing. Just keep being smart. And keep going."

After we hung up, I sat with the weight of what remained.

* * *

The first wave of support came from a place so familiar it almost startled me. Not from lawyers or advocates or policymakers, but from the Stonewall Kickball team GroupMe. It was only a few hours after the *New York Times* story went live. I had barely settled back into my apartment when my phone buzzed with a notification.

It was one of my teammates. One of the more enthusiastic ones, someone who always overused exclamation points and sent GIFs at inappropriate times. He had dropped the article into the chat with a quick message:

"Y'all, look. Nick is out here taking on the Pentagon."

A beat passed. Then the chat exploded.

"Hell yes, Nick." "We've got your back." "This is badass." "Proud of you, dude." "Holy shit, this is incredible."

A rainbow-heart emoji appeared first, followed by a flexing arm beside a tiny gavel. Then someone joked, "Kickball lawsuit fundraiser when???" and the absurdity of it made everything feel even more real.

I stared at the screen, unsure how to respond. Part of me had been bracing for awkwardness, silence, or uncomfortable questions people reach for when they don't know what to say. Instead, something warm and uncomplicated came through. Pride, support, solidarity.

I typed, Thanks, everyone. I really appreciate it. Anything more felt like it might break the spell.

The messages kept coming, even hours later. People I hadn't talked to in weeks reached out privately. A few mentioned sharing the article with friends or partners. One teammate wrote, "If you ever need anything, you know where to find us."

None of it felt forced or rehearsed.

The *Metro Weekly* cover landed a week later, and the next ripple moved through the league.

The Commissioner called that morning.

"Nick, oh my God. Have you seen this?" Pages rustled on the other end of the line. "This cover is iconic. This is going to be in bars all over the city. It's like you're about to walk onto the floor of the United Nations."

I laughed, partly at the enthusiasm, partly because he wasn't wrong.

"Can I share it on the league page? Like… immediately? Please?"

"Of course."

He didn't wait. The post went up before we hung up.

"And by the way," he said, dropping his voice with the delight of someone who'd just found a new puzzle, "I pulled your case filings. I'm reading the complaint right now. Halfway through the declarations. My God, they structured this beautifully."

Only an attorney would admire the architecture of a lawsuit like that.

The excitement wasn't performative. It ran deeper than the usual congratulations for a new job or engagement. This felt like recognition of someone from the community taking on a fight that mattered to all of them.

When the cover hit the league page, the comments poured in.

"OUR TREASURER." "Hell yes, Nick." "Blood and Honor. Let's GO." "This is history." "Proud doesn't even cover it."

Scrolling through it, I realized how much fear I had carried into this moment without noticing. The worry that people would pull back, that HIV stigma, even softened by time and medicine, would still make them hesitate around me, and that stepping into the spotlight might mean stepping away from the community that grounded me.

But none of that happened. Not even a hint of it.

If anything, the opposite occurred. The community moved in closer.

They shared the articles in the spaces where we actually lived our lives. Group chats, league pages, Instagram stories, bar conversations after games. And in doing so, they left no doubt about how they felt. The support showed up visibly, immediately, and warmly.

I would later learn there were probably quiet conversations happening behind the scenes. Corridor reassurances, someone correcting a misconception, someone else shutting down a joke that didn't land right. But none of it ever touched me. What reached me was only the support.

By the end of that week, I could feel it forming around me, subtle but unmistakable. The bubble. Soft and protective, a buffer made of friendship and team spirit and queer community instinct.

Chapter Twenty

The case stopped belonging to me before I fully noticed it had happened.

Ian Wilhite managed the transition with a calm efficiency that felt almost invisible. My calendar filled without ever tipping into chaos. Interviews were spaced just far enough apart that I could reset between them. Calls got routed through him, so nothing arrived unannounced. I didn't decide who spoke to me or when. Someone else had taken custody of the edges.

Lambda Legal invited me to my first fundraiser in that window. Not at the filing, not during the first interview.

Ian was factual.

"They want you there. They'll introduce you. You don't need to do anything. Just stand when they ask."

There was no further guidance. No briefing or explanation of what being there meant. That alone told me this was something new.

The event was a VIP reception at the Newseum, just off Pennsylvania Avenue. I had never been inside.

We arrived on time and immediately realized we didn't know where we were supposed to go.

The front doors were open, but no one was checking names. People moved through the space with confidence, as if the rules were obvious and long settled. We paused, scanning for a sign, a table, or someone who looked like they might be in charge. Instead, we drifted past glass cases and softly lit exhibits, into corridors that felt both public and not.

My phone buzzed.

Are you here yet? We're trying to find you.

I looked around, then back at the screen, unsure how to answer. Here didn't seem specific enough.

We doubled back once, then stopped again near a cluster of people who were mid-conversation. I recognized a few faces. Men I'd seen around the city before, at kickball games, at bars, at community events. Now they were dressed differently, carrying themselves differently. No one was performing. No one was watching anyone else. It was just a context I hadn't seen them in before.

Eventually, someone approached us, relief on their face.

"There you are," they said and ushered us forward, then introduced us to someone else, then someone else again. Each transition was quick, polite, and incomplete. No one explained the entire plan. They didn't seem to have one to explain.

At one point, we were standing near a small side room when another person appeared, apologetic.

"We're going to do photos now," they said.

Inside, Joe Kennedy III and Cory Booker waited, both patient and clearly nearing the end of a long sequence. We took our places as the staff directed us where to stand and where to look. We shook hands and exchanged a few words while cameras flashed. Almost immediately, the staff thanked the congressmen and released them.

The doors of the auditorium opened.

And just like that, there was no one directing us anymore.

We followed the flow of people into the space and found seats among the crowd. Just in the middle, surrounded by everyone else. For a moment, I wondered if we were supposed to be somewhere different, but no one came looking for us.

So we stayed.

When the program began, one of Lambda Legal's leaders stepped forward and spoke about the case, not the filings or the doctrine, but the human cost. Policies frozen in time. People were sidelined despite years of service, hard-won experience, and a record that had already proven itself. The words felt familiar, even if the setting didn't.

Then, they said my name.

It took me a beat to realize I was being asked to stand.

When I did, the response came from all directions at once. Applause rising and spreading. I stood there, aware only of the sudden shift in attention and of Baraq beside me, his hand resting lightly on my back. Just there.

I stayed upright long enough for the moment to pass, then I sat down as the program moved on.

Afterward, people approached us in small, uncoordinated waves. A handshake, a quiet word, someone asking for a photo. We stayed for a bit, letting those moments land without trying to manage them, then slipped out once it felt natural to do so.

Outside, the air hit like a wall, warm and wet, carrying the faint smell of exhaust and river. People spilled onto the sidewalk in twos and threes, talking and smiling, holding their phones out for one last photo as if they could pin the night in place.

We walked until the noise thinned and the blocks stopped feeling like an extension of the event. When we found a place that looked quiet enough, we slid into a booth and sat there with our menus open longer than we needed to.

My phone buzzed again. A leftover thread from one organizer: Thank you for coming. So glad you could be here.

I stared at it for a second, then set it face down.

Baraq watched me without comment, as if he was giving the moment room to pass. When the server came back, he ordered first.

We let the moment sit between us. The booth did what certain places do best, holding us in a pocket of low light and insulation that made silence feel permissible. Applause still lingered in my body, not as pride, but as an unsettled pressure, like a question waiting for language.

What I didn't understand yet was that this wasn't just attention. Baraq did. It was a role you learned by being walked through, or you learned by making mistakes.

He didn't hand me principles. He gave me examples and then told me how they applied to me. Usually later. After the room had cleared, after the adrenaline wore off, when it was just the two of us, and I was still replaying something I'd said or wishing I'd said it differently.

He'd start with a story. Something he'd picked up while handling people at Victory Fund events or Human Rights Campaign dinners. The places where no one was listening closely, and people spoke plainly because they were tired of being careful.

He once told me about Edie Windsor and how, waiting to go onstage, she talked about joy as if it were a political demand. "Never postpone joy. And keep it hot." Then she laughed and said, almost affectionately, "They won't let me say that."

They didn't. By the time she stepped out front, the sex was gone, the heat turned down, the edges smoothed so the audience could applaud without being unsettled.

Baraq didn't leave it there. He looked at me. "That's what they'll do to you, too. Not because they're malicious, but because they think they're helping. Decide in advance what you're willing to let them clean up, and what you're not."

He also told me about Jim Obergefell and how his partner, John Arthur, died before the court reached a decision. The victory carried Jim's name, but not the life it had been for. Backstage, Jim talked about the case as something that had already closed over him. "Winning doesn't always feel like winning," he'd said. "Sometimes it just means you lived long enough to be cited."

Baraq turned that into an instruction. "This is why you don't chase the applause. And why you don't confuse being thanked with being taken care of. The work will move on regardless of whether you do."

He coached me on specifics. Which questions deserved straight answers and which ones needed deflection. When saying less mattered, even if the truth would have sounded better. How to recognize the difference between someone who wanted me and someone who wanted what my name unlocked. Sometimes he stopped me. "Don't commit to that." "That's not your fight." "You don't need to give them that."

None of it came from instinct. It came from proximity. From years of watching people get celebrated, simplified, and constrained by the visibility meant to honor them.

That difference mattered. Becoming a named plaintiff no longer meant guessing my way forward or learning only through error. Someone stood beside me who had already seen how this ends, who cared enough to slow the process down, translate it, and make sure I stayed intact while the story moved ahead of us both.

I didn't recognize it, but that night reshaped everything that followed.

* * *

Not long after the Newseum, Lambda Legal put me on a flight to San Francisco for another event.

They made the arrangements the same way they seemed to do everything in those first months. Last-minute, loosely held together. Spirit Airlines. They forwarded the ticket the night before. No itinerary beyond the address of the venue and a vague assurance that someone would meet me there.

No one did.

San Francisco, though, didn't feel like an extension of the lawsuit the way DC did. I had never really seen it. I wandered between the airport and the event, enjoying the waterfront air, the hills that burned my calves, and the city, which was laid out in bright angles as if designed for viewing. For a few hours, I was just a person in a place, not a name moving through someone else's calendar.

That's how I almost missed the welcome lunch.

Someone forwarded the schedule without explanation, and the event time appeared in Eastern. 3:00 p.m. on my phone, which felt safely distant. I was still out when the voicemail hit.

Nick, where are you? Call me. Now.

Scott's voice wasn't angry. It was frantic, the sound of someone realizing that nobody was responsible for getting me into the room.

I called back, apologized, sprinted, and showed up flushed, trying to pretend it hadn't rattled me. Nobody scolded me. Nobody made it a thing. But the absence was visible: no handler, no point person, no one whose job it was to keep the logistics from swallowing the purpose.

The venue itself was beautiful, a space that tries to dignify the work with light and clean lines. And once I was there, the night moved the way these nights always moved. I found the room, felt that familiar lack of a place to stand or wait, and noticed another plaintiff also walking around the room tentatively. We both kept moving, pausing near conversations, retreating, checking our phones as if instructions might appear.

Eventually, someone pulled me into a conversation. Then another. Nothing went badly. Nothing cohered either. I spent most of the night waiting to be useful.

On the flight home, somewhere over the middle of the country, I opened my notes app and typed what I didn't want to forget. An end to last-minute tickets, time-zone surprises, and showing up alone.

By the time we landed, it had turned into something practical.

*　*　*

Veterans Day at the Congressional Cemetery moves at a different tempo.

It is quieter than Arlington National Cemetery, less ceremonial, less rehearsed. People arrive without instructions. No one needs to be told where to stand or when to lower their voice. People already understood the meaning of the morning. The DC Center held the wreath-laying at Technical Sergeant Leonard Matlovich's grave every year as a ritual. An act of continuity. A way of saying we remember who made this possible.

In the days beforehand, the invitation to speak found its way to me indirectly.

The organizer reached out and explained that David Mariner had suggested it. He had told her I had a story that needed to be told here, on this day, in this place. He didn't present it as a consensus. It carried the unmistakable imprint of David's style. Direct, opinionated, certain. We had disagreed often when I was on the board about tactics, about tone, about how far to push institutions that preferred to creep. But he had also watched me closely enough to know when something mattered beyond strategy.

He hadn't framed it as a case or mentioned coverage at all. He had called it a story.

On the morning of the ceremony, the air was sharp and clean. The cold that keeps you alert without numbing you. The sky was pale and brittle. Baraq walked beside me through the rows of headstones.

Our steps crunched softly on gravel and fallen leaves. His hand brushed mine now and then. Just present.

The crowd gathered loosely. Veterans in dress uniforms stood among civilians in coats and scarves. I noticed small things instinctively. Ribbons out of order, devices placed incorrectly, and insignia misaligned. Details I would normally fix without thinking. The muscle memory of an NCO asserting order where it's needed.

I said nothing.

This wasn't that kind of space. Correction didn't belong here. Memory did.

Matlovich's grave sits among the others.

No monument. No flourish. Just a marker bearing the name of a man who had done something almost unthinkable in his time.

Leonard Matlovich had come out while still on active duty, deliberately forcing the military to confront a truth it had worked hard to avoid. He had earned medals for combat service. He had done everything the institution asked of him and then refused to lie to preserve its comfort. Years later, he would die of AIDS during a period defined by fear, neglect, and moral panic, when government silence was as lethal as the virus itself.

Not far away lay the grave of J. Edgar Hoover.

I noticed it because of how close it was. How little distance separated the resting place of a man who had wielded enormous power while guarding his own truth with secrecy, from a man who had lost nearly everything by refusing to hide his. The proximity felt unintentional and precise at the same time.

When it was my turn to speak, I stepped forward and felt the quiet settle. Attentive.

Veterans stood shoulder to shoulder. Activists who had survived the worst years. Elders who remembered when coming out meant exile. Younger people who had inherited protections without always knowing the cost.

Performance never entered it, and the moment didn't require volume. The truth carried itself.

Service came through as a lived experience. Policy followed as a consequence. Progress in the military revealed itself as something never given and always taken, piece by piece, by people willing to risk their careers, their health, and their futures. Matlovich appeared as a man who had walked alone so others would not have to.

"I'm standing here because people like Leonard Matlovich stood alone when standing alone meant everything."

The words landed without an echo.

Something aligned. Recognition. A sense of stepping into a current that had already been flowing long before me. This wasn't new. It wasn't accidental. It was a continuation.

When I finished, people applauded in a restrained but sustained manner, acknowledging rather than celebrating. People weren't clapping for me. They recognized the name.

As attendees stepped forward to lay the wreath, I spoke briefly with Major General Tammy Smith. The exchange was courteous, almost understated. Beneath it, though, was something unmistakable: proof embodied that the institution could change, even if it resisted every inch of the way.

Walking back through the cemetery afterward, Baraq was quieter than usual.

Finally, he spoke.

"You're different when you speak."

I asked what he meant.

"It's not performative. It's like you step into something that already exists. You don't disappear, but you're not just you, either."

"That matters. If I ever stop feeling that when I watch you, I won't be able to help you anymore."

I didn't answer. I didn't need to.

* * *

We flew into Green Bay on Wednesday afternoon. Baraq's nephew picked us up at the airport in a warm car that felt good against the November cold. The forty-minute drive to Peshtigo took us through farmland and small towns, and we kept conversation light and careful. Everyone knew this weekend mattered. We'd have Thanksgiving with his family, then drive straight to Chicago for the fundraiser on Sunday.

Thanksgiving came first, and it wasn't where they usually held it. Baraq's father had just gone through a divorce, so this was the first year at his girlfriend's house. The new setting added another layer to an already unfamiliar moment. I was meeting parents and siblings, and all the conditions for tension were stacked up and waiting.

Baraq had carried tension in the days leading up to it, even though he tried to hide it. Logistics never worried him. He was concerned about me instead. Would I feel out of place? Would I like them? Would I seem like someone real rather than the version he had to describe when I wasn't in the room?

If anything, the pressure ran in the other direction. They seemed more worried about impressing me than I was about impressing them. They checked details and made sure everything felt right. No one announced anything or set expectations. The room never sharpened.

It was relaxed in a way that felt almost disorienting. Conversation flowed naturally, unforced. My relationship with Baraq had settled into itself the same way, without ceremony or negotiation. No tests. No accounting. People simply moved around one another as if they had already agreed on the shape of the day.

When we arrived, the house was already alive. The kitchen hummed with activity, voices overlapped from room to room, and the smell of food had been cooking long enough to feel inevitable. People moved around one another with the easy choreography of familiarity. Someone reached past another for a serving spoon, someone else refilled a glass without asking, and conversations paused and resumed without explanation.

Attention settled on me without weight or demand. Questions came easily. Where was I from, how did we meet, and what had brought me to Chicago this time? No one asked me to account for myself or tried to triangulate me. No one pressed for the version of my life that had appeared in the news.

I noticed small things anyway. The way teasing stayed kind. The way disagreements didn't sharpen into weapons. The way people listened all the way through before answering. Not because it was some revelation about family, but because it was so different from the posture I'd trained myself to take at home. Watch the temperature, anticipate the turn, brace for the moment a harmless sentence becomes leverage.

Here, nothing tightened when certain subjects came up. No one lowered their voice to avoid punishment for saying the wrong thing.

For a few hours, the room asked nothing of me beyond presence. Hands moved through familiar motions of passing dishes and rinsing plates while I leaned into Baraq's shoulder and listened to a story I recognized by the way the punchline drew the same shared anticipation it always did. Conversation never drifted toward the case, and work stayed uninvited. No one needed a summary or an explanation.

When dessert came out, someone slid a plate toward me without asking what I wanted. Someone else refilled my glass the way you do for family, not guests. I didn't register it at the moment. I noticed it later.

Chicago was already waiting. The organizers had scheduled the Liberty Circle reception and a panel for that weekend. Part of the same stretch of travel, part of the same expectation that I would show up and be present and useful. The details were light, the tone casual, as if the shape of the thing mattered less than the fact that I would be there.

"Small," the message said. "Private home. Major donors."

After the Newseum and San Francisco, small sounded like relief. I said yes, and we made our own travel plans.

The house sat in one of those parts of downtown where the streets feel composed. Tall buildings lined quiet sidewalks with a rhythm that hinted at affluence without announcing it. We climbed a few steps to a front door that opened into a space that was both expansive and warm. The home was meant to be lived in as much as displayed. High ceilings let light spread easily. Art looked chosen rather than acquired.

Inside, the air was warmer than outside. Not just from bodies, but from the way people stood and talked, as if comfort was part of the architecture. Clusters formed and dissolved. People held glasses and carried half-finished thoughts from one conversation to the next.

This wasn't a crowd waiting to be addressed. This was a room that expected you to enter the flow.

At the Newseum, someone had called for everyone's attention. I stood when asked. Someone else managed the choreography.

Here, there was no choreography. There was only movement.

Small talk has never come easily. Careful listening and direct answers feel natural, but stepping into a circle already in motion does not. Instinct has always kept me on the edge, waiting for an explicit invitation before crossing the boundary into the conversation.

Baraq has no edge. Within minutes, he was greeting people with a warmth that wasn't performance. He remembered names, smiled genuinely, and had that easy ease that invited others to lean in. The questions he asked weren't pleasantries. They were invitations. "How did you get involved?" "What brought you to this work?" Questions that made people tell stories instead of reciting resumes.

As he did that, he did something else at the same time. He made me legible. Not as a case. Not as a symbol. As a person standing next to him.

A couple approached who were longtime Lambda Legal supporters, and Baraq greeted them like old friends. Brief embraces, quick laughs, a few shared asides. Then he angled just enough to include me.

"This is Nick," he said casually, like we were just neighbors running into each other. "We live in DC. He's in the Army. We've been together long enough that I get to claim him."

Laughter followed, and the room softened by a degree.

"Tell them what you do," he said.

I reached for the safe version. Facts, credentials, a succinct summary. The words came out too neat, too practiced, like something memorized to avoid saying the wrong thing.

Baraq read it instantly and stepped in. Not to rescue, but to translate.

"He's not here to give you a legal brief. But the way this fight found him. That's worth hearing."

The questions that followed felt different from the ones I'd heard elsewhere. They didn't ask me to justify my presence. They asked where the story actually lived. Someone touched my arm. Not pity, not performance. Just contact.

Baraq stayed close without hovering. A hand on my shoulder at the right moment, a joke that lowered the temperature, a pause that made space for me to speak without scrambling.

Later, a small group of junior attorneys gathered nearby. Associates in sharp suits with eyes bright from the worn focus of people who worked too hard and still cared. Sloppiness never entered it. Intent did.

One of them spoke first, almost sheepishly. "I've read everything. All the filings. Like, all of them."

He said it the way someone admits to staying up too late.

"We do a lot of pro bono. But this one feels different."

I didn't know how to respond without sounding self-important, so I didn't try. I thanked them and asked what they were working on, how they managed their hours, and how they kept their lives from shrinking into billable time. The moment loosened into conversation. Someone laughed, and the little knot of formality broke.

That was when Kevin Jennings arrived. I recognized him. Not just from the resume, but from the way the room subtly shifted toward him. People edged closer, not obsequiously, but with the quiet attention reserved for someone whose presence changes the temperature without demanding it.

This was his first appearance as Lambda Legal's new Executive Director. He spoke not like a fundraiser or a politician, but like an educator. Measured, thoughtful, expansive. He talked about the work being larger than any one case, about shaping belief before harm hardens into policy, about the moral context that makes progress durable.

And then, without dwelling on specifics, he mentioned me. He placed the case and me into a moral frame. A lived example of commitment, consequence, and courage.

"This is what courage looks like."

The applause that followed wasn't loud so much as close. Direct, almost personal.

Afterward, he found me in the flow of conversation, shook my hand, and met my eyes in the way educators do when they want you to feel seen rather than used.

"You're a genuine hero."

I smiled because that's what the moment required. But the word lodged in my chest the way it does when someone names something true without ornament.

Much later, Scott Schoettes told me Kevin had pulled him aside.

"I know they're all important," he'd said. "But this one matters."

It didn't make the evening louder. It made it quieter.

When the night finally thinned, it did so gently. People retrieved coats, shared lingering hugs, and softly closed a door that probably cost more than most people's rent.

Outside, the street was colder. Chicago kept moving, indifferent.

* * *

By the time spring fully settled over Washington, the LGBTQ+ veterans movement was no longer celebrating. It was consolidating.

The repeal of Don't Ask, Don't Tell had been real, historic, and overdue. But it had also stripped the movement of the pressure that once held it together. Organizations built for resistance suddenly navigated a world where people insisted the work was over. Donors shifted their attention. Coalitions thinned. The urgency that had once been existential was now expected to justify itself.

What remained faced a choice between fragmenting or restructuring.

The Capital Hilton hosted the American Military Partner Association's annual gala, where that choice became visible.

On the surface, it was a black-tie dinner. Chandeliers, pressed linens, the familiar cadence of formal advocacy. Underneath, it was a moment of deliberate transition. Andy Blevins had been clear with me ahead of time about what the evening would be, and just as clear about what I was not to do. Talk about it.

The merger announcement wasn't public yet. Trust, I was learning, was a currency of its own.

Baraq and I arrived early. I wore my full-dress uniform because Andy understood how the room would perceive it. When they escorted us to the head table among senior advocates and movement leadership, the message wasn't subtle.

This case wasn't peripheral. It was being placed deliberately at the center of what came next.

The room filled gradually. Old allies greeted one another with familiarity softened by time. New faces took stock quietly, measuring where influence now sat. The energy felt different from other fundraisers I had attended. Less celebratory, more attentive. People weren't there to be inspired. They were there to understand direction.

When Andy stepped up to the podium, he didn't ease into it.

He spoke about contraction, about reality, about the danger of mistaking survival for completion. Then he announced what many in the room suspected, but few had heard stated aloud. OutServe-SLDN and American Military Partner Association would merge. Not as a branding exercise but as a necessity. Duplicative missions would collapse into a single organization with enough scale to apply pressure again. The Modern Military Association of America would continue what they built, not as a monument to past fights, but as a tool for the next ones.

The standing ovation that followed was deliberate.

When Andy spoke about HIV+ servicemembers, about how exclusion hadn't vanished so much as shifted form, I felt the room subtly reorient. Conversations paused. A few heads turned. Recognition.

I wasn't being shown as a guest. I was being positioned in context.

Across from me sat Eric Fanning.

Our previous interaction had been strained. Efficient in a way that leaves no warmth behind. Seeing him there, now occupying a visible place in the movement's public face, stirred something instinctive in me. Not anger exactly. Memory.

Baraq noticed before I said anything.

"You should go say hello," he said. An instruction grounded in experience. "This is one of those moments."

I knew what he meant. This wasn't about resolving the past. It was about whether the future stayed available.

Standing up, I crossed the short distance between tables and greeted Eric as if nothing had ever been wrong. The smile came, the handshake held firm, and the brief exchange stayed open and unguarded.

For a second, he looked surprised. Then relieved.

We spoke the way people do who understand public life. Courteously, efficiently, without rehearsal. No accounting. No defensiveness.

The door wasn't flung open, but it was no longer closed.

Later in the evening, Eric introduced the next speaker: Ray Mabus.

I knew his record in broad strokes, but not personally. As Secretary of the Navy, he had pushed further on HIV policy than other service secretaries. Something those of us watching closely had noticed. His remarks reflected that awareness. Measured, candid, unadorned. He spoke about leadership as something defined not just by action taken, but by action deferred too long.

When he finished, the room rose again. Then, as always happens at events like this, the gravitational pull toward the exits began.

Scott was with me. We waited. Something I had learned to do instinctively. Not rushing or forcing the moment. Letting the line thin.

Scott had hoped to speak with him, but someone pulled him away.

I stayed.

When Mabus turned from his last conversation, I stepped forward.

"I just wanted to say thank you. The Navy was ahead of the other services when it came to HIV policy. That mattered."

He didn't deflect it.

"I wish I could have done more."

"I have a case challenging the military's HIV policies. There's an amicus brief being drafted."

He cut in before I finished.

"Have your people call my people. We'll see what we can do."

That was it. A door left unlatched.

I thanked him, stepped back, and the space closed behind me almost immediately. Another hand reaching him, another face, another brief exchange. The line kept moving the way it always does at these things, like it had its own gravity.

Baraq was there when I turned, already angled toward the exit, not rushing me, and not inquiring about the conversation. We threaded out through the gaps between conversations. Past half-finished drinks, past people leaning in close to be heard, past the bright, practiced smiles that stayed in place even as the night thinned.

Outside the ballroom, the sound dropped a notch. The hallway felt cooler. That strange transition where you can feel yourself becoming anonymous again.

We waited for an elevator with a few other couples, everyone facing forward, shoulders squared, hands occupied with clutching purses, smoothing lapels, checking nothing in particular. The doors opened. We stepped in. We went down.

In the lobby, the hotel had already returned to itself. Marble, quiet light, the muted churn of other people's evenings. We crossed the threshold, and the night air met us cleanly.

* * *

A few weeks later, we were back in Chicago again, this time for a panel at the Pritzker Military Museum & Library. The building carried its own authority. Just history, carefully preserved. Uniforms behind glass. Letters written home. The long record of service was reduced to artifacts that had survived their owners.

It was the right place for this conversation.

Congressman Mike Quigley moderated the panel from the front of the room, standing with a microphone beneath muted lights. A fixed camera recorded the discussion for later broadcast. Scott took the seat to my left, while other panelists extended down the line. A small but serious crowd filled the audience, made up of advocates, staffers, and veterans who understood how quickly military policy stops being theoretical.

When the first question arrived, hesitation never entered it. The response began with identity rather than HIV. I described the decision to become a JAG officer as a way of carrying forward a life already in motion. Enlisted infantry service, deployments, law school between orders, and a deliberate choice to remain in uniform in a different capacity had shaped that life. The process moved forward step by step through the application, interviews, and medical screening I had passed many times before, until everything stopped.

Factually.

I explained how I ran straight into a policy that didn't care what I had done, where I had served, or how effectively I had done it. A policy frozen in time, unmoved by modern treatment or by my actual medical record. A policy that treated my diagnosis as dispositive regardless of service, performance, or readiness.

I talked about the unfairness of it plainly as an imbalance.

"I had deployed. The work was done. Command had already trusted me with responsibility in environments where mistakes mattered. And suddenly, none of that counted."

I let it sit.

Then I explained the impact, not just on me, but on anyone watching the system closely enough to understand the lesson it taught. Honesty carries penalties, service does not insulate you from stigma, and the institution defaults to exclusion long after the science has moved on.

That was my part of the story.

And then I stopped.

"This is where the law comes in." I turned slightly toward Scott. "He can explain how the policy works and why it fails."

The transition was clean. Almost seamless.

Scott continued where I had left off. The regulatory framework, the contradictions, the waivers that weren't really waivers, and the way bureaucratic inertia preserved outdated assumptions. He translated impact into argument, harm into doctrine.

I let it stand without interruption, resisted circling back, and avoided adding color where none belonged.

The moderator noticed. I could see it in the small, appreciative pause. The way he leaned back slightly, tracking the exchange. The design ensured that it worked.

When the panel ended, the questions that followed reflected that structure. People asked me about service, about identity, about what it feels like to be told you are suddenly unfit after years of being relied upon. They asked Scott about remedies, standards, and outcomes.

Later, as we walked out into the afternoon air, Baraq glanced over at me, half-smiling.

"That was different."

"How so?"

"I've seen you talk before. But that was controlled. You knew exactly where to stop."

He paused, amused. "Even the Congressman noticed. You could tell how smoothly you handed it off, which impressed him."

* * *

In the middle of everything else, my thoughts kept circling back to Oklahoma. Not in a general or nostalgic way, but with precision.

I remembered Oklahoma City from fluorescent-lit rooms where voices dropped around the word HIV. Folding chairs set in imperfect circles. Careful pauses before disclosure when everyone silently calculated what telling the truth might cost. That place taught me early that survival sometimes required leaving, and that leaving never meant the place stopped living inside you.

From there, Robin Dorner came back into focus.

I had known Robin through Other Options, Inc., the HIV nonprofit in Oklahoma City. Even then, she was everywhere at events, at meetings, behind a notebook or a camera, making sure stories didn't vanish just because they made people uncomfortable. As editor-in-chief of the *Oklahoma Gayly*, she understood how visibility functioned in places that weren't built to absorb it easily. She knew that sometimes the most radical act wasn't shouting, but naming.

As the case moved forward and my name began appearing in national coverage, it felt wrong to let Oklahoma remain untouched by it. The story could travel everywhere except the place that had shaped it. The people who had taught me how costly honesty could be didn't get to see what had grown out of it.

So I reached out to Robin.

I told her about the lawsuit. About challenging the military's HIV policies. About how the story was already circulating far beyond Oklahoma, and why it mattered that it be told there, by someone who understood how it would land.

Her response came quickly, warm and immediate. She didn't pause or ask what might come of it. The idea of telling the story pleased her. She understood what it would mean, and she knew who would read it and who would need to.

With Lambda Legal's communications team alerted, I sent her the filings, the background, and the shape of the case. Micromanagement never entered it, and worries about framing fell away. I trusted her instincts completely.

Weeks later, the issue came out.

She had put me on the cover.

My face, familiar to people from support groups, fundraisers, and community events, now anchored the story. The headline spoke directly to the case, to HIV, and to the military policy that had stopped me cold. No euphemisms softened it, and no protective language crept in. The truth appeared in print, circulating through the city that had taught me the cost of silence.

Robin had acted deliberately, with a clear understanding of me and the terrain. Familiarity with both made the choice intentional, rooted in what it meant to put a hometown face on something that still carried actual weight and risk there.

Holding the paper, I felt the full gravity of that choice.

In Oklahoma, HIV still moved through lives with a distinct pressure. Disclosure still carried consequences. Many people never got the chance to leave. Never found distance or anonymity or a place where their diagnosis didn't precede them.

For them, this wasn't a national story unfolding somewhere else. It was local. Immediate. Close enough to feel personal.

My life had taken me far from Oklahoma City to deployments, to law school, to Washington, DC, and now into federal court. But seeing the story land back home, deliberately and without apology, made the arc unmistakable.

Chapter Twenty-One

By late 2019, I had picked up another government contract at the Defense Threat Reduction Agency. The agency handled weapons of mass destruction threats, which meant security clearances and strict protocols.

I didn't carry my phone at work.

You couldn't. Not inside.

The building had lockers at the front. Narrow metal doors, a strip of numbers, a thin key that always felt too light to trust. You dropped your phone into an empty slot like you were leaving a piece of yourself behind, shut the door, and walked through security with the slight, background awareness that the rest of the world would have to wait.

Most days, it was a relief. That afternoon felt different.

I stepped out during a break, passed back through the controlled air of the lobby, and went straight to the lockers. The key turned stiffly. The door popped open. My phone lit up the moment it touched my hand. A stack of notifications catching up all at once.

Missed calls. Texts. Two emails from numbers I didn't recognize. And one voicemail flagged with a name I didn't know.

Nadine Shiroma.

I stood there for a second, unsure whether to listen right there in the vestibule with people drifting past, or wait until I was outside.

I listened anyway.

Her voice was careful. The careful you use when you're not sure you've reached the right person.

"Hi, my name is Nadine Shiroma, calling from the Hepatitis B Foundation. I'm calling for Nick Harrison. I'm not entirely certain this is the correct number. If it is, I've been following your case and the coverage surrounding it, and I recently read the article you were in. That piece raised something I believe we should discuss. If this message reached the right person, I'd appreciate a call back."

She left her number twice. Slowly, as if I was taking notes.

I walked out into the dull winter light, found a patch of sidewalk away from the door, and called back before I could overthink it.

It rang once.

"Hello?"

"Hi, Nadine? This is Nick Harrison."

She paused. Not long, but long enough for me to feel her checking for the trick.

"Okay." An exhale. "Okay, hi. I'm sorry. I wasn't sure that was you."

"You weren't sure you had the right number?"

"I wasn't sure you were reachable." A quiet laugh. "It took some digging. Your name surfaced first through the coverage, then through an article, and then through a trail that led further on. Each step brought the same thought back again: this couldn't be the actual person. It had to be a spokesperson or a communications inbox."

"It's me. You got me."

"Okay. Thank you for calling back."

The gratitude came through immediately. Not performative. Just real. Like she'd expected silence, and had prepared herself for it.

"What can I do for you?"

"I'm with the Hepatitis B Foundation. And we've been watching what's happening with your case because the structure of the discrimination is familiar."

I leaned back against the brick of the building and watched people pass as if nothing in my life had changed. Office workers. Someone with a coffee. A couple arguing gently about directions.

"What do you mean?"

She didn't launch into a speech. She started where advocates always start: with the part that never makes it into the headlines.

"There was an amendment. Barbara Lee. NDAA 2014. You probably know it as the HIV piece."

"I do."

"Right. But it wasn't just HIV. It was HIV and Hepatitis B. We paired them deliberately. The idea was to force the Department to stop treating manageable conditions as automatic disqualifiers. To make them justify it. To make them modernize."

Something tightened in my chest. Recognition more than surprise.

"Okay. Go on."

"The problem is that Hepatitis B ended up folded into the same category of stigma, with no one really noticing. Scientific understanding moved forward, while policy stayed frozen in place. That failure carried consequences. It fell hardest on Asian-American communities."

There it was. The sentence that explained why she'd gone looking for me instead of writing a memo to an office that would never respond.

"You're saying the discrimination is doing double duty."

"Yes. Exactly. It's disguised as readiness, but it's really bias preserved as policy."

Behind her words, I could hear the faint office hum. Phones, printers, and people working under sustained pressure.

"I saw the coverage. And I read your piece. And I thought, if there's already a case forcing them to explain themselves, we can't stay next to it. Not if we want anything to change."

I glanced at my watch and saw how little time remained, yet the decision not to hang up had already settled in.

"Have you talked to Lambda Legal?"

"We've tried. Work on Hill relationships came first, followed by the policy route, but seeing your case felt like the first time someone's efforts produced real leverage."

I let that sit for a beat.

"Okay. Here's what I can do. I'm not the strategist on this. I'm not drafting the briefs. But I can connect you to the legal team. Scott Schoettes is my lead counsel at Lambda Legal. If you're willing, I'll send him your information today and tell him this matters."

"You would?"

"Yes. And I'll do more than forward an email. I'll flag it and make sure it doesn't disappear."

Her breath caught. Audible in the pause before she spoke again.

"Thank you. I wasn't sure how this would go."

"Neither was I."

She laughed with relief.

"I'm not trying to ride your case. The goal is to make sure the same machinery doesn't keep harming people in parallel lanes."

"That makes sense. You're not riding anything at all. This is the point. It's exactly why we filed."

She paused.

"Okay. I'll send you what I have. The legislative language, the policy history, and our documentation. And anything you need."

"Send it. I'll connect you to Scott."

I looked back toward the entrance. The controlled air, the lockers, the expectation that you step back inside and neatly compartmentalize the outside world.

"Nick?"

"Yeah?"

"I'm sorry if this is too personal. But… are you okay?"

The question landed harder than I expected. Not because it was dramatic, but because it wasn't.

"I'm okay. I'm… busy."

"Okay. Well. Thank you for picking up. Really."

When the call ended, I stood there a moment longer with the phone in my hand. Nothing about the sidewalk had changed, the building remained unchanged, and the day still looked ordinary.

But the world had widened.

* * *

Peter Perkowski didn't circulate my case. He carried it.

When he brought Winston & Strawn in, it wasn't through an intake process or a pro bono committee. He called someone he trusted and asked them to listen to me, not to the policy.

That's how I ended up sitting in a conference room at Winston & Strawn, with a draft declaration already on the table.

The office looked exactly as you'd expect. Glass, clean lines, the low hum of people moving between rooms with purpose. John Harding met me in the lobby himself. No assistant. No handoff. Just a handshake and a quick, amiable smile.

"Nick. Good to meet you finally."

We sat down with coffee and a draft declaration already printed out. That alone told me something. They hadn't come to hear the story for the first time. They had read the record.

John slid the document toward me and tapped it with his pen. "Let's make sure we've got the timeline right. Start with the application, move to the clearance, and then mark where it stopped."

We went through it carefully. Dates, orders, forms, and checking details. Every so often, he paused with a small, exact question. He asked how it would sound under oath, not how it read in headlines.

"They're going to stall. Make it procedural. Make it administrative."

He didn't need to elaborate.

What he was offering wasn't strategy in the abstract. It was capacity.

When the government responded, it wouldn't be with a tidy production. It would come as volume. Enough paper and data to exhaust a team without the bodies to absorb it.

Winston & Strawn did.

He didn't brag about it. He didn't say it outright. It showed in how he talked about the next steps. Who would review what, how quickly they could turn things around, and how Lambda Legal wouldn't have to divert its lawyers from the core arguments just to manage the flood.

At one point, he looked up from the declaration. "So, JAG was always the plan?"

"Yeah. From the start."

A nod, as if he filed that away.

"This isn't theoretical. Your qualifications stand. You're already serving, and the commission remains your goal."

A faint smile. "That part's pretty straightforward."

They didn't say why this matters. They didn't need to say it.

It was there in how carefully he handled the details. This wasn't a sprawling policy fight to him, but one person, one application, one door that had closed for the wrong reason.

He wasn't there to take on the entire Department of Defense. He was there to help a combat veteran get a commission.

When we wrapped up, John gathered the papers. "We'll coordinate directly with Scott on discovery support. He shouldn't have to fight this battle alone."

Outside, walking back toward the street, I understood something I hadn't fully named before.

Individuals don't fight institutions like the Department of Defense on their own. Even nonprofits with brilliant lawyers can see their efforts stall under the weight of process. The system favors the institution.

What Winston & Strawn brought wasn't ideology or outrage. It was the ability to stand in the blast radius and keep working.

And they were doing it quietly and professionally because this case was concrete enough to hold on to.

A soldier who had done everything right and wanted to keep serving.

* * *

The "Deploy or Get Out" policy didn't arrive as a theory. It arrived as policy directive.

By then, the team at Lambda Legal was already inside my case. Calendars mapped, timelines locked down, drafts circulating. We weren't waiting to see what the government might do next. We were already responding to what it had done.

That's why the Air Force didn't catch us flat-footed.

The first time Roe and Doe came up, it wasn't dramatic. Scott mentioned them in the middle of a working session. He said it like a status update that had already passed an internal test.

"They're Air Force," he said, scrolling. "Active duty. They've started the separation process."

He didn't say we should take them. He said it like a status update.

The documents followed the same shape we were already looking at. Medical clearance on one page, administrative action on the next. Different branch, same logic. The policy shifted from paper to consequence, and the Air Force moved faster than the others to enforce it.

What mattered was that this wasn't landing on an empty desk.

The legal team had already built my case around the premise that the military's HIV policies didn't just limit careers. They rested on assumptions that no longer matched reality. That work was underway before Wilkie's announcement ever made the news. The arguments were already being sharpened. The timeline already mattered.

So when Roe and Doe appeared, the question wasn't Can we respond? It was where do they fit?

Scott slid the files into the stack we were already working through.

"This doesn't change the theory," he said. "It confirms it."

The Air Force forced what the Pentagon preferred to keep abstract into something immediate. Two people, two sets of orders, and two clocks already running.

Lambda Legal didn't have to pivot. It adjusted.

Within days, the filings reflected that shift. Not as a detour, but as the frame expanded. What had started as a challenge to a barrier in my path now included servicemembers being pushed out entirely under the same reasoning.

The same machinery, but louder.

Judge Brinkema saw it immediately. The government's logic connected the cases; no one stitched them together for convenience. Treating them as related expanded nothing. It acknowledged what the government itself had put in place.

There was no sense of escalation in the room. No panic or rush to catch up.

Just the quiet acknowledgment that the policy had finally moved fast enough to expose itself.

* * *

Over the months after Baraq moved in, the neighborhood stopped being incidental. Places with long memories reveal themselves slowly, not all at once, but in layers that only make sense after you've lived among them for a while. It revealed itself that way.

He noticed it before I did.

Baraq would step outside and pause, taking in the block as if it were asking to be read rather than crossed. Next door, the Mount Pleasant Library sat with quiet assurance. A public building in the old sense of the word, solid and dignified, its broad steps worn smooth by generations of people who had come there to read or study, not to be impressed. Inside, light filtered through tall windows and settled into corners where time felt slower, more patient.

Across 16th Street rose the Shrine of the Sacred Heart Catholic Church, massive and unmistakable. Its concrete walls were thick, almost sculptural, the magnificent dome planted firmly against the sky. In the afternoon, sunlight softened the surface, turning something imposing into something luminous. It wasn't ornamental but declarative, one of many churches crowning the ridge of Columbia Heights. Their steeples and domes punctuated the skyline like markers of belief and ambition, climbing uphill.

That pattern repeated itself everywhere you looked. Churches didn't hide here; they announced themselves. The hilltop skyline was a conversation between faith, permanence, and aspiration.

Between those anchors, the street stayed alive. Tennis courts rang with the sharp echo of serves. Baseball diamonds filled with shouts and laughter. A playground churned with movement. Children climbing, falling, running, trying again. Joggers moved steadily along the paths, circling the park as if the city itself were a track meant to be shared. At the corners, statues stood watch. Guglielmo Marconi, Francis Asbury, James Cardinal Gibbons. Figures cast in bronze and stone, reminders that planners designed this street to carry meaning beyond traffic.

A few blocks down, Meridian Hill Park opened suddenly, terraced and formal, its long steps and cascading levels suggesting a vision that had almost reshaped the city.

Mary Foote Henderson had imagined this place differently.

At the turn of the twentieth century, she bought land along this stretch of 16th Street and conceived a grand plan. An "Avenue of the Presidents" leading north to Meridian Hill, where the executive mansion would sit atop a landscaped terrace. A garden modeled after European capitals, where power was elevated, framed by beauty, and set apart. At the crest stood Boundary Castle, her own home, looming above the city like a prototype for what she believed Washington should become.

She commissioned grand residences for foreign embassies. Monumental, symmetrical, dignified buildings. She assumed the city would grow into her vision. Some of those buildings still stood. One directly across from us, beside the Powell Recreation Center, now housing the Department of Parks and Recreation. Others down the street, former embassies repurposed but unmistakable in scale and intent. Even the old Masonic Temple nearby, later converted into apartments, carried the imprint of an era that believed architecture should teach people how to see themselves.

But the city chose otherwise.

Washington did not become a capital of enclosed terraces and aristocratic promenades. The President stayed closer to the center. Power remained visible, reachable. Instead of formal gardens meant to be wandered by elites, the city embraced open spaces. The National Mall, broad and democratic, where people could gather, protest, picnic, play sports, and claim space. It was a decision about values as much as design. This was not a nation meant to be contemplated from above, but lived in from the ground.

Henderson lost the fight, but she didn't lose the neighborhood.

Her ambition shaped everything. The embassies that never housed diplomats, the park designed around her vision, the way this stretch of the city feels ceremonial without being sealed off. The beauty survived even as the purpose shifted.

Living there, you could feel both impulses at once. The pull toward grandeur and the insistence on access. The monumental and the ordinary coexisted. Children played beneath the statues. Runners passed beneath church domes. Public libraries stood shoulder to shoulder with religious sanctuaries.

As autumn settled in, Baraq and I found ourselves ready for more space. Not as an escape, but as an expansion. When a larger one-bedroom became available in the same building, with a wide bow window facing 16th Street, it felt inevitable.

That window changed the apartment entirely. It curved outward, generous and open, drawing the street into the room. From there, the neighborhood unfolded. The recreation grounds alive below, the steady rhythm of daily life, the church anchoring the view like a compass point. Morning light spilled across the floor in long arcs. Evening brought the soft rise of city noise. Voices, footsteps, the distant hum of movement that never fully stopped.

Inside, the apartment felt ready. Hardwood parquet floors caught the light and returned it warmly. The walls seemed to wait, patient, as if they understood this was a place meant to hold stories. The kitchen promised the small rituals that make a life. Meals cooked without hurry, cups left on the counter, conversations that didn't need an endpoint.

Standing at that window, it was impossible not to feel the contrast with where I had started. The cramped spaces of childhood, the instability that made homes feel temporary. Here, history pressed close, not as a weight but as a reassurance. This was a place shaped by ambition, tempered by choice, and ultimately open to everyone.

Amid hearings and filings and the quiet pressure of a case that refused to slow down, this neighborhood offered something rare. Beauty that wasn't exclusionary, history that remained accessible, space that invited you in rather than holding you at a distance.

It wasn't the city Mary Foote Henderson imagined.

But it was exactly the one we chose.

* * *

The courthouse announces itself before you ever step inside.

The red-brick façade rises clean and formal against the street, federal in the old sense of the word, meant to endure, meant to outlast whoever passes through it. From the front of the building, a massive bronze figure leans outward into space. Justice herself, blindfolded, robes pulled taut by motion, scales lifted unevenly in her hands. The statue doesn't stand serenely. It lunges. The title, *Justice Delayed, Justice Denied*, feels less like an inscription than a warning. You can't miss it. You're meant to understand before you enter that time matters here.

Inside, the courtroom amplifies that message.

The ceilings stretch higher than they need to. Dark wood frames everything, polished smooth by decades of use. The room is deliberate more than ornate. The design diminishes the people inside, reminding everyone who speaks that they are temporary and the institution endures. Even empty, it would feel full.

That morning, it wasn't.

The gallery filled early with reporters, advocates, uniformed servicemembers, people who had learned to recognize one another by context rather than introduction. I wore my dress uniform, standing out without trying to. The government's lawyers sat in a tight formation, binders stacked neatly, prepared to argue a narrow case about a single plaintiff and a single set of Army policies.

They were ready for something small.

Judge Brinkema was not.

When she entered, the room recalibrated instantly.

She was a small woman, older than most of the people standing when she took the bench. Her movement was unhurried and precise. There was no flourish, no attempt to fill the space physically. The courtroom bent toward her. When she sat, it was immediately clear that the scale of the room existed for her, not the other way around.

She listened first. Let the government begin. Let them frame the issue the way they wanted to see it.

And then she interrupted.

"I'm not sure the government fully understands what's at stake here."

The sentence landed flatly, without emphasis, which somehow made it sharper. She was diagnosing, not scolding.

The government drew a narrow line. Only the Army's HIV policy counted, they argued, the one that governed my service. Policies from the other branches would impose an undue burden. They fell outside the scope.

Judge Brinkema leaned forward slightly.

She began asking questions. Pointed questions that cut straight to the record. She pulled specific references from the discovery as if she had placed them there herself. Dates, language, inconsistencies. Each time the government tried to retreat into abstraction, she brought them back to the text.

Then she widened the frame.

She referenced the two Air Force cases she had already pulled into hers. The airmen were facing discharge under the new "deploy or get out" policy. She spoke of them not as outliers, but as confirmation. As evidence of a pattern still unfolding.

"And I expect there may be others," she said.

It was the first moment anyone said out loud what the case had already become.

This was not about one branch. Or one policy. Or one plaintiff.

This was about whether the military could continue to enforce exclusion through different rules, different labels, and different timelines while insisting that nothing systemic was happening.

The government tried again to narrow it. To keep it manageable.

Judge Brinkema didn't raise her voice. She simply clarified that she wasn't interested in a version of the case that avoided its consequences.

At one point, she turned her attention briefly to me. Asked where I had gone to law school. Observed dryly that it couldn't have been inexpensive. Then, she said what she clearly believed the record already showed. This was an individual who wanted to serve, who had developed skills the government had paid to cultivate.

The implication hung there, unspoken but unmistakable.

Institutions don't get to discard investments casually, especially not when the justification no longer fits the facts.

Before the hearing ended, she did something else.

She suggested simply that the government consider a settlement. Not as a concession, but as a recognition that individual relief and systemic challenge did not have to move on the same track.

"You have an individual," she said. "And you have a group."

Nothing prevented resolving one while the other continued.

It was a roadmap. And it was intentional.

Walking out of the courtroom afterward, the feeling wasn't triumph. It was orientation. The sense was that the case now sat with a mind capable of holding its full weight. That the fragmentation the government relied on would no longer protect it from scrutiny.

Judge Brinkema hadn't promised an outcome.

What she had done was more important. She had signaled that she understood the shape of the fight and that the government would have to confront it whole.

Chapter Twenty-Two

Scott was already talking when the video connected.

"Okay," he said, smiling, a little breathless, like he'd been mid-thought before I appeared. "Before we talk about tomorrow, I need to say something that's going to sound like I'm complaining about my colleagues, and I want the record to reflect that I love them."

"Duly noted."

"They're very smart. They're doing excellent work. And they are absolutely, one hundred percent, trying to win their cases."

The pivot was coming.

"But?"

"But," he said. "They're leaning hard on Administrative Procedure Act claims."

I didn't stop him.

A finger went up. "Which, to be clear, are not frivolous. Not weak. Not stupid. If they win, the court says: Department of Defense, you did this wrong. Go back. Clean it up. Explain yourselves better."

"And then?"

"And then, the military goes back, rewrites the memo, adds some footnotes, maybe a working group, and reaches the same conclusion."

He leaned back.

"They do this for a living. They lose on process, adjust the process, and never abandon the policy."

"And none of that answers whether the policy itself is lawful."

"Correct. It avoids the question entirely."

A quick, precise grin from someone who knew exactly where the argument was going and enjoyed watching everyone else pretend it might end up somewhere else.

"It's a very elegant avoidance. Judges love it. Everybody gets to feel restrained and institutional and very adult about it."

"But nothing changes."

"But nothing changes. And five years from now, someone else is back in court asking why this is still happening."

He clicked his pen and then stopped himself.

"And this is why I am not leading with the APA."

Not telling me not to argue it or warning me off it. Stating a choice.

"I'm happy for those claims to exist. They can run in parallel. They can protect people in the short term. But they cannot be the engine of this case."

"Because the engine has to be constitutional."

"Yes." He brightened. "Because constitutional law is the only thing that tells the military: you don't get to do this at all."

He leaned forward now, energized.

"The APA tells them how to behave while discriminating. The Constitution tells them to stop."

I nodded.

"And the reason people get nervous," he went on, "is because once you do that, you don't get to hide behind deference anymore. You're asking the court to say: even under rational basis, this makes little sense."

"And that's where deployability comes in."

Scott closed his eyes for half a second, like someone savoring a word they'd been waiting for.

"Yes, that's the monster in the room."

He opened them again.

"Some lawyers don't want to touch it. Which I understand. Messy. Military-sounding. Judge-scaring. And the government loves it, because they think it's a magic phrase."

"Non-deployable."

"Exactly. They say it, and suddenly the analysis stops. Rational basis. End of discussion. Courts don't have to like it. They just have to imagine a reason."

"And if they can imagine one, they never have to decide if it's real."

He pointed at the screen. "So if we don't deal with deployability, we lose — even if we're morally right, medically right, scientifically right."

He shrugged.

"Rational basis is a very low bar. You don't clear it by being correct. You clear it by showing the government's justification is nonsense."

"And deployability is nonsense."

"Yes. But we prove that on the record, with experts, with facts, with your case."

His voice softened.

"And that's why your case matters in this configuration. Not because you're special. Because the facts don't let them wiggle."

I smiled. "I worked hard on that."

"I know. It shows."

He glanced down at his notes.

"Tomorrow's deposition isn't about catching you in something. It's about whether they can manufacture a different reason after the fact. Any reason. Doesn't matter what."

"I've seen that movie."

"I know. And this time, they don't get a sequel."

A pause settled between us.

"So," lightly, "no pressure. We're just trying to dismantle a decades-old military policy under rational basis review."

"Sounds relaxing."

He grinned.

"Get some sleep."

The screen went dark.

Morning brought the deposition.

* * *

It began the way these things always do. Slowly and deliberately, carried forward by people who believe time itself is a tool.

They weren't there to understand the packet. They aimed to shape the record so that it would later treat the packet as irrelevant. The questioning began with the application materials.

"You assembled it yourself."

"Yes."

A pause. Just long enough for the court reporter's fingers to catch up.

"And it was complete when submitted."

"Yes."

Another pause.

"Let me mark this as Exhibit 12."

Paper slid across the table. The exhibit sticker tore softly.

They moved line by line. Physical fitness, passing scores, dates, medical clearance, security clearance, and financial disclosures. Answers stayed short. They already had the documents. Yet each question landed as if it might still produce a surprise.

The billet.

"At the time you applied, the office had already filled the position you sought, correct?"

"No. It was vacant."

He looked down, then up, then down again.

"There was an open slot," I said. "They were interviewing candidates and building an order of merit list."

"And you were where on that list?"

"At the top."

Silence. The reporter stopped typing, waited, then resumed.

"So you were not double-slotted."

"No."

"And you understood that selection to mean what?"

"That the command selected me for the billet. That it was mine pending completion of the administrative process."

He repeated it back differently.

"So you believed it was yours."

"No. I was told it was mine."

Another pause. Longer.

"And later you were told the Commanding General would 'hold' the position for you?"

"Yes."

"As a courtesy?"

"No. Because the selecting authority chose me. He said it would still be mine once the process was complete."

That answer landed. Not well, but cleanly. They moved on.

Rank.

"You were told they would appoint you as a captain?"

"Yes."

"And you didn't ask how that would occur?"

"No, that's what I was told by my commander at the time of selection."

Education. JD-MBA.

"The Army paid for your education using veterans benefits."

"Yes."

"And you intended to use that education in the service of the Army."

"Yes."

Another exhibit. The clock ticked audibly now.

Afghanistan. Kuwait. Iraq. Dates. Units. Evaluations. Awards. Clearance — Top Secret, continuous eligibility. Financial stability. No adverse actions, investigations, or discipline.

Nearly two hours.

Methodical. Repetitive. Exhaustive.

Each answer triggered a pause; each pause summoned a document; each document hinted that something still might be missing.

Nothing was.

A shift in the chair.

"Let's talk about your time in ROTC."

The words hit harder than I expected. Not because I hadn't prepared, but because this was the part I had trained myself not to revisit. Not out of shame, not because the facts were unclear, but because the ending had been wrong.

For years, I'd turned it over and replayed conversations and rewritten outcomes and argued with people who weren't there anymore. Eventually, I stopped. Not because anything changed, but because the anger went nowhere.

So I built past it instead.

Sitting there, the old frustration flared. Sharp, familiar. Not fear. Not embarrassment. The resentment of knowing you were wronged and knowing there would never be a clean remedy.

I grounded myself. The conference room, the microphone clipped to my jacket, the clock on the wall. Short answers. No speeches.

"Yes."

More than a decade ago.

"They disenrolled you from the program."

"Yes."

"You had not yet graduated."

"That's correct."

"You did not yet have a security clearance."

"No."

"You had student debt."

"Yes."

"You failed a physical fitness test."

"I later passed."

"So at that point, you failed a physical fitness test."

"I later passed."

They stacked the facts the way I remembered. Unfinished things, context stripped away.

"So at that point, there were multiple reasons you might not have been suitable for commission."

"No."

A look up.

"No?"

"No. Those were requirements in progress. Not disqualifying factors."

A pause. Another exhibit marked. Nothing new was introduced.

"Then why were you disenrolled?"

I didn't hesitate.

"Because I reported the misuse of student activity fee funds by the Professor of Military Science."

"That's your interpretation."

"No, that's what happened."

Plainly.

"He used the funds without authorization. I raised the issue. The Professor of Military Science told me explicitly that if I told anyone, he would fail me and ensure I did not commission."

"And you're saying this was retaliation."

"Yes."

"You have evidence of that?"

"I took a polygraph examination at my expense. It supported my account of the events."

A single nod. Then on.

They didn't need to resolve ROTC. That wasn't the point.

The point was to suggest there had always been something wrong with me.

I'd seen it before.

When someone challenges authority, the institution looks backward and gathers every unfinished requirement it can find. Things that were never disqualifying suddenly become explanations.

That was the lesson ROTC taught me.

It was why, for the next fifteen years, I left nothing unfinished.

Back to the present.

"So other than your HIV status, is there any reason you believe the Army denied your commission?"

"No."

"You don't believe there were any legitimate concerns?"

"If so, they would have raised them when I applied. They didn't."

A final pause. Longer than the others.

A few more questions. None of them landed.

When it ended, the familiar weight settled in. The way these sessions push you to replay answers, second-guess tone, and wonder whether you should have said less or more.

But I knew exactly what had happened.

They were trying to invent one.

* * *

In the same stretch of weeks, while discovery in my case continued to grind forward, a different clock was running alongside it.

February settled in with the dull persistence of winter in Alexandria. Gray mornings, early dark, the sense that everything was happening indoors and under pressure. Depositions were being scheduled and taken. Briefs were being drafted and revised. And the Air Force plaintiffs were moving on a faster track toward something immediate.

They were asking for a preliminary injunction.

Not a final ruling or a ruling that settled rights. Just an order preventing their discharge while the case moved forward.

Everyone understood how high the bar was.

To grant a preliminary injunction, the court had to believe the plaintiffs were likely to prevail on the merits. Not possibly or someday, but likely. It required the judge to make a provisional judgment about where the law was going.

Judge Brinkema listened the way she always did. No tells. No theatrics. She stayed close to the record, to consequences rather than abstractions. What would happen to these two servicemembers if the court did nothing now and later decided it had been wrong? What damage would time lock in place?

When she ruled, she exercised exactly the restraint required.

She barred the Air Force from discharging the plaintiffs and any other Airmen facing separation specifically due to their HIV status while the court considered the case. Nothing broader. Nothing permanent.

But the implication was unmistakable: to issue that order, she had to conclude that the plaintiffs were likely to succeed. The policy they challenged could not, on the record before her, justify itself.

It wasn't a promise or a commitment, but it was the first clear sign of how she was reading the law.

The government responded immediately. Within days, it appealed and asked for a stay of further proceedings related to the merits. It's the standard move when a case stops going the way it expected. Freeze the moment and push the question upward.

Judge Brinkema granted the stay.

From the outside, it could have looked like hesitation or retreat. Watching it happen in real time, it felt like something else. She had acted decisively enough to protect the plaintiffs in front of her, but she refused to declare the issue settled simply because she believed she was right. She let the question move up to the Fourth Circuit to test her reading of the law. Whether it would hold under scrutiny, whether the appellate court would see what she was seeing, whether it would agree that the ground under this policy was already shifting.

That was what it felt like to watch precedent being made. Not grand declarations, not certainty, but a judge choosing when to act and when to wait, knowing that both decisions mattered.

For us, the stay wasn't a pause so much as a narrowing.

For the moment, the court shielded the Air Force plaintiffs. The injunction question moved upward. But nothing else stopped. In my case, discovery continued. The parties scheduled depositions, took them, and reset them. The government kept building its record. So did we.

What the stay did was fix the frame. Judge Brinkema had made clear how she understood the law without binding herself to the last word. The government tested that understanding immediately rather than waiting.

* * *

After my deposition, the case didn't slow down. It widened.

While discovery continued, Scott was assembling the amicus briefs with the same deliberateness he brought to everything else. This wasn't about signaling support. It was about building a record that didn't depend on trust or sympathy, only credibility.

"This is how you give judges confidence," Scott said. "You show them that everyone who should know better already does."

HIV advocacy organizations filed the first briefs. No one found that surprising. They wrote with the fatigue of people who had explained the same facts for years: HIV was manageable. Undetectable meant non-transmissible. No medical basis supported the categorical exclusion. They didn't express outrage. They stated conclusions they had already settled long ago.

The medical associations followed. Scott was careful here. Different specialties, different institutional voices, all saying the same thing in their own language. These briefs stayed dense and clinical, built from standards of care and professional consensus. They didn't urge the court to break new ground. They asked it not to manufacture doubt where none existed.

The last group took longer.

Retired service secretaries don't move casually, and they don't move without history. Some of them had been in office when people like me were asking for help and not getting it. I hadn't forgotten that.

Two years earlier, at an OutServe-SLDN reception, I had raised the issue directly with Eric Fanning. The conversation wasn't comfortable, and that was intentional. The point wasn't to resolve it on the spot. It was to make the issue memorable, to make sure that the next time it crossed his path, it would register as something unfinished rather than abstract.

A few months ago, at the American Military Partner Association gala, I didn't revisit it. I was polite. Cordial. Professional. The confrontation had already served its purpose.

That night, it was Ray Mabus who connected it.

He spoke with the calm authority of someone who had already pushed as far as he could while in office. Someone who understood both the constraints and the responsibility that came with the position.

"I wish we could have done more," he said. It wasn't an apology, and it wasn't a performance. It was an acknowledgment from someone who had, in fact, done more than most.

Then he said, "Your people should talk to my people."

It wasn't a favor. It was a handoff.

When Scott told me later that Eric Fanning had agreed to join the amicus brief, I didn't feel vindicated. I felt something quieter.

Fanning's participation didn't rewrite his tenure. It didn't excuse what hadn't happened when he had the power to act. But it mattered. A former Secretary of the Army was putting his name to the proposition that HIV status should not bar service, doing so in a case where the facts made that conclusion hard to avoid.

That was growth. Not absolution. Growth.

The same was true of the other retired service secretaries who joined. Their brief didn't praise the plaintiffs or dramatize harm. It spoke in institutional terms: readiness, retention, the waste of trained talent. It said that exclusion based on HIV no longer made sense as a matter of military judgment.

When the amici filed their briefs, the effect was cumulative.

Advocates. Physicians. Former civilian leaders of the services. Different voices, different incentives, the same conclusion. Together, they narrowed the space the government had to maneuver.

Watching it come together, I recognized something experience had already taught me.

Change doesn't always come from the people who get it right the first time. Sometimes it comes from giving someone who got it wrong an obvious opportunity to do better and paying attention to whether they take it.

Eric Fanning did.

That mattered procedurally. A former Secretary of the Army had now said, in writing, that HIV status should not bar service. In a filing, the court would read.

Once that happened, the government's position changed shape. It no longer faced only the plaintiffs. It now faced the expertise of people who had run the institution, written its standards, and lived with the consequences of its decisions.

That pressure didn't resolve the case.

It clarified it.

From that point on, the record forced every deposition, transcript, and evasion to answer a question the military could never resolve: if this policy still made sense, why had no one who led the institution said so?

* * *

Discovery didn't reveal some hidden sophistication in the government's position. It did the opposite. It shrank it.

By the time Scott deposed Colonel Clinton Murray, the Command Surgeon for U.S. Forces Korea, it was clear why the government had put him forward. He was supposed to be the medical authority who could explain why the military was different, why rules that made no sense anywhere else still somehow made sense here.

What never appeared in that deposition was transmission risk. Not as probability, contingency, or even a worst-case hypothetical.

No one argued that I would endanger other soldiers. No one argued I posed a risk in combat, in training, or in the field. The military's record showed no instance of a soldier with an undetectable viral load transmitting HIV. Not in garrison, not in deployment, not even under catastrophic conditions.

They couldn't make that argument. There was nothing to support it.

Colonel Murray didn't dispute the medical consensus. He couldn't. He acknowledged that people living with HIV were otherwise healthy, capable, and able to serve. The problem wasn't the virus, he said. It was the environment.

Austere conditions. Prolonged training. Remote operations. Limited space. Every ounce mattered.

And then eventually we got to it.

The pill bottle.

That was the argument.

In certain training scenarios, soldiers could only carry what fit in their rucksack, Colonel Murray explained. They carefully managed weight. Soldiers cut excess packaging and stripped gear to the essentials. HIV medication posed a problem because of its container. The desiccant, the packaging requirements. You couldn't just toss pills into a plastic bag without deviating from the package insert. That mattered, he implied.

I remember sitting there listening to it and thinking: this is what they've got.

After the deposition, I said it to Scott plainly.

"They're bullshitting you."

He laughed. Not because it was funny, but because once you said it aloud, you could hear how thin it was.

Soldiers carry more snacks than that pill bottle weighs. Extra socks, batteries, protein bars. I'd carried radios, spare parts, ammunition, notebooks, energy gels, whatever the day required. That a few tablets, measured in grams, made someone unfit for service wasn't just weak. It was insulting.

And worse, it matched nothing I'd actually lived.

I'd worked alongside federal law enforcement, intelligence agencies, and contractors operating in forward environments. I'd seen people handle medication in places just as remote and demanding. No one turned a pill bottle into a logistical crisis. They addressed it and moved on.

Listening to Colonel Murray, I understood something clearly.

Medicine, readiness, and deployment didn't drive the fight. The government fought to preserve a rule no one wanted to defend on the merits, so it hid behind hypotheticals and edge cases and the imagined weight of a container no one had ever bothered to measure.

Under oath, that kind of reasoning doesn't expand. It collapses.

And once you hear it collapse, you understand why the government fought so hard to keep the case abstract for as long as it could.

* * *

By September 2019, the case had reached the Fourth Circuit.

The hearing wasn't about the merits in full. It was narrower than that. Whether Judge Brinkema had been right to grant a preliminary injunction protecting the two Air Force servicemembers. Whether, based on the record so far, the plaintiffs were likely to prevail.

But everyone in the room understood what was really being tested.

I sat in the gallery in dress uniform. This was about people who were already serving being told that the same facts that once allowed them to stay now required them to leave.

The government argued first.

They framed the policy as cautious, as measured, as a response to operational realities that courts should not second-guess. The same themes we'd heard for months, now compressed into appellate time.

And then the questions started.

The questions weren't hostile. They didn't need to be.

One judge cut directly to the problem the government had been skirting. He noted that the military had long allowed servicemembers with HIV to continue serving. Senior leaders adopted that policy when the treatment was crude, the prognosis was poor, and the fear outweighed the evidence.

Now, he said, treatment had improved. Knowledge had advanced. Outcomes were dramatically better.

"And now the military decides it can no longer tolerate them?"

The question didn't accuse or editorialize. It set the government's position against time itself and let the contradiction sit there, exposed.

Another judge followed the same thread. If deployability was the concern, how had servicemembers been deployable for years under worse conditions, but not now? If readiness was the justification, why did every medical advance seem to make exclusion easier rather than harder to defend?

The government tried to answer. It talked about caution, standards, and deference.

None of it landed.

What the judges kept returning to was the same problem: the explanation ran in the wrong direction. The government was offering progress as a reason for exclusion and knowledge as a reason for fear.

There was no way to make that logic move forward in time.

Sitting there after months of depositions and expert testimony and carefully constructed hypotheticals, I realized the case had shifted. The court was no longer being asked whether the policy was wrong. It was trying to understand how it could be right.

That was new.

The hearing ended without a ruling. It was supposed to. But the last thing left hanging in the room was the judge's observation that the military had once said we don't know enough yet, and now, knowing more than ever, said that's why you must go.

The government offered no explanation for why the future required less tolerance than the past.

Chapter Twenty-Three

The decision came back with the force of forty pages and the weight of precedent. Not quietly, but with the methodical thoroughness of an appellate court that had taken the time to dismantle the government's arguments piece by piece.

The Fourth Circuit delivered a sweeping affirmation of Judge Brinkema's injunction. Judge James Wynn's opinion dismantled the military's logic systematically, detailing the modern science of HIV transmission and rejecting the military's claim to special deference. The court cited former Secretaries like Eric Fanning and Ray Mabus, who had filed briefs showing that even the military's own experts disagreed with the policy. It wasn't just an injunction. It was a roadmap that boxed in the government for everything that would follow.

Not long after, word came from another courtroom entirely. The federal district court in Baltimore denied the government's motion to dismiss in Deese. Different plaintiffs. Different judge. Same result.

The pattern was impossible to ignore now.

Across jurisdictions, across judges, the government was losing the same arguments in the same ways. The case was no longer about disputed facts. It hadn't been for a while. It was about whether the law could tolerate a policy that no longer matched reality.

By then, everyone knew how this would end.

The next step was obvious: summary judgment.

There was something almost anticlimactic about it. Years of litigation, discovery battles, injunctions, appeals, and now the case was being reduced to paper. The parties filed cross-motions and exchanged briefs. The question presented cleanly: whether, as a matter of law, the military's HIV policy could stand.

When the day for oral argument arrived, I sat in the courtroom and watched Scott step to the lectern with the calm focus of someone who knew exactly how narrow the path had become.

He argued what we had always believed. Policies singling out people living with HIV deserved more than reflexive deference. They warranted intermediate scrutiny. History, stigma, and animus mattered.

But he didn't linger there.

Because he didn't need to.

He pivoted to the simpler truth. Even under rational basis, the most forgiving standard the law allows, the policy failed. Decision-makers ignored medical reality. They dismissed evidence. They kept the policy alive through inertia rather than necessity.

As the argument unfolded, Judge Brinkema leaned forward and asked a question that made the air in the room shift almost imperceptibly.

Wasn't rational basis, she asked, functionally the same as asking whether the policy was arbitrary or capricious?

The question hung there. Not as a challenge, but as a synthesis.

Two doctrines converging on the same point. Constitutional law and administrative law both required that the government explain itself, and that explanation still had to make sense.

Both counsels answered. They took notes. The argument moved on.

And then it was over.

No ruling from the bench. No indication of timing. The court had taken the matter under submission.

We stood, gathered our things, and filed out of the courtroom.

Everyone had said what needed to be said.

***

By then, the court held the case, and there was nothing left to do but wait. Life, however, refused to remain paused. At home, in the ordinary rhythms of living together, something small and unexpected took shape.

Baraq already had a cat.

Yuki was his. She followed him from room to room, stationed herself beside him on the couch, and slept curled against the crook of his arm at night. They understood each other instinctively. Even when he admitted, with a small smile, that I sometimes seemed better at interpreting what she wanted, there was no question who she belonged to.

One evening, he said that he thought I needed a cat of my own.

That was how we ended up at a local rescue shelter a few days later, walking past rows of cages and small laminated cards, until a volunteer stopped and asked, "Have you ever had a nervous cat?"

In the last cage, tucked against the back, was a tiny black-and-white kitten. She wasn't pacing or crying like the others. She stayed inside the nylon tube the shelter had placed in the cage, leaving only the faintest suggestion of fur in the shadows.

The volunteer explained that someone had called about a litter of feral kittens living outside. They'd set traps. This one was the only kitten curious enough to wander in.

I remember thinking about the moment after the trap closed. About a small cat family scattering back into the dark, leaving one behind.

When the volunteer reached in and gently picked her up, the kitten froze and then saw me.

She climbed.

Straight up my chest, over my shoulder, clinging there. She pressed her face against my neck and stayed. The volunteer laughed, a little surprised. Baraq just smiled and said that it looked like she'd decided.

We named her Socks.

From the start, any sudden movement or unfamiliar sound sent her skittering across the floor, vanishing behind furniture with astonishing speed. Curiosity followed close behind. Lift a cushion, open a drawer, or crack a box, and she had to know what lay underneath. Fear and curiosity both lived in her, neither quite winning.

Yuki did not approve.

When we brought the kitten home, Yuki hissed once, then fixed Baraq with a look of pure betrayal before retreating to a corner and refusing to acknowledge him for the rest of the evening. He followed her around apologetically, offering treats, trying to coax her back into her usual places. She was unmoved. She had enjoyed being an only child, and she would not forgive this.

Socks, meanwhile, was already exploring.

The moment we let her into the living room, she vanished.

It took us a few panicked seconds to realize she'd found a narrow tear in the couch and crawled straight inside. She wouldn't come out. We tipped the couch over, cut away the fabric from the bottom, and reached in carefully until I felt the small, tense weight of her body in my hands.

After that, we confined her to the bathroom.

For weeks, she hid behind the hollow pillar beneath the sink. Every few hours, I would come in and gently pull her free. She'd cling to the pillar with surprising strength, tiny paws gripping porcelain as if the sink itself might protect her. I'd set her in the litter box, and she'd decide reluctantly that yes, she needed to go. Then, the food, which she always accepted. Then I'd hold her, burp her like a baby, and finally return her to her hiding place.

It became our routine.

When we eventually brought her into the bedroom, she disappeared again. This time under the covers. It took patience, bribery, and eventually an empty soda box. If she could hide inside a box, peering out through a small opening, she felt safe enough to be present. I'd carry her into the living room so she could sit with us, believing she was invisible.

Over time, she relaxed. Not completely. She was always going to be a nervous cat. But she became mine the way Yuki belonged to Baraq.

At night, when we finished in the living room and started toward the bedroom, she would stop in the middle of the floor and cry. She didn't chase after us. She waited.

I learned that the routine mattered. I had to go back for her. In the living room, I'd crouch down and tell her it was time, that we were going to bed. Only then would she answer with a relieved sound and trot after me down the hallway, happy once she knew she wasn't being forgotten.

It felt like a ritual, one she needed us to keep. Proof offered nightly that we would come back for her.

As the case entered a long period of waiting, Socks filled the quiet spaces, needing reassurance, consistency, and the certainty that someone would return.

* * *

The first sign that something was coming wasn't an announcement. It was a rumor that someone mentioned about sending us home. Not for a day or two, but for a while. We were told to start the paperwork for telework agreements, to make sure our training was current, and to clean off our desks just in case. There was no urgency in the instructions, but there was a tone beneath them that didn't invite questions.

Then one afternoon, we were told to go home.

At first, it felt temporary. We grabbed our laptops and left monitors glowing on our desks, exchanging casual goodbyes with little thought. But the stay-at-home orders followed quickly, and soon the city emptied in a way I had never seen.

Washington, DC, went quiet. The streets weren't just less busy because people had vanished. Restaurants closed, gyms locked their doors, and movie theaters went dark. Some never reopened. Offices emptied almost overnight while people disappeared from neighborhoods without explanation, leaving behind darkened windows and For Rent signs taped hastily to doors.

Baraq had already left the Human Rights Campaign by then. He was enrolled in a graduate program in emergency management and studied disasters as one unfolded in real time. I worked at a job that I could do remotely. We stayed home with each other and our two cats for company.

We ordered groceries and waited. The deliveries became their own minor event with bags left at the door and then wiped down on the kitchen counter. We made quiet calculations of what might last if the supply chains failed. Rumors spread faster than facts while stories of overwhelmed hospitals circulated constantly, especially out of New York. Sirens seemed louder at night, sharper against the emptiness.

Walking outside felt like stepping into a world people had abandoned mid-sentence. No traffic, no crowds, just the echo of your own footsteps and the sense that something vast had closed its doors all at once.

People adapted quickly as meetings moved onto screens and collaboration software became essential overnight. Movies stopped arriving in theaters and began appearing on streaming services in living rooms instead. Entire industries rearranged themselves in a matter of weeks, though some people weathered it better than others.

For a long stretch of time, the world felt suspended. Not broken exactly, but paused, as if waiting for permission to move again. Inside our apartment, with our routines narrowed to rooms and screens and delivery windows, it felt less like living through a crisis than surviving an extended, uneasy stillness.

The case was still pending.

* * *

The video of George Floyd's death spread faster than anything I had seen before. Eight minutes of a knee pressed against a man's neck while he said I can't breathe until he couldn't say anything at all. There was no ambiguity to argue over, no competing narrative to retreat into. The footage landed like a blunt instrument and stayed there, impossible to look away from.

And then, despite the pandemic, the stay-at-home orders, the empty streets, and the fear, people went outside.

Washington changed almost overnight. Protests formed around the White House and spilled outward, filling spaces that had been silent for weeks. The city felt awake again, but not in relief, in anger. Sirens returned while helicopters circled constantly. Something sharper and more volatile took the place of the quiet that had defined the early months of COVID.

I wasn't called up. At that point, I worked full-time as a contractor at the Department of Defense. My National Guard status still existed on paper, but no one treated me as essential. The system triggered no automatic mobilization and made no assumption that it needed me.

If the National Guard had activated me, I would have left my civilian job, taken a pay cut, and absorbed a financial hit when uncertainty already hung over everything.

That mattered practically, not abstractly.

There was also the question of visibility. I was a named plaintiff in active litigation against the military. I had learned painfully that once a narrative attaches to you, it rarely lets go. Being seen, photographed, quoted, or framed as part of a moment could follow me into filings, hearings, and decisions that were still very much unresolved.

So I stayed inside. I understood the protests and felt connected to what people were demanding, but my role at that moment was narrow and constrained. I was watching events unfold from the position the system had placed me in. Present, informed, but deliberately kept at a distance. Useful when quiet, inconvenient when visible.

Then they cleared Lafayette Square. I watched it happen on a livestream. Tear gas and shields scattered the crowd while helicopters pressed low overhead. A public space emptied by force so quickly it felt rehearsed. The justification shifted by the hour. The effect didn't.

That was when the protests crossed into something else entirely.

Soon after, National Guard troops appeared on the National Mall. Not to police demonstrators, but to protect statues and monuments from being defaced. The symbolism wasn't subtle. Stone was being guarded more carefully than people had been.

What disturbed me most wasn't the National Guard's presence. I understood that mission. What disturbed me was who they were standing next to.

The lines were mixed. Uniformed soldiers stood shoulder to shoulder with unidentified personnel who wore no name tapes and no clear insignia. People pulled from a scatter of federal agencies who had never trained as soldiers, who lacked preparation for crowd control, and who didn't understand unit discipline. Some of them looked thrilled to be there, wearing tactical gear and carrying assault rifles, finally getting a chance to play a role they had no business inhabiting.

That is not how military operations work. You do not interweave your troops with anonymous, unaccountable actors and expect command and control to hold. You do not dilute unit integrity and pretend it won't matter. Any competent military commander would have pulled those people out of the line immediately. Not as punishment, but as a necessity. You maintain control by knowing who answers to whom.

Instead, they mingled freely, breaking formation, darting behind soldiers, acting independently. To the public, it was impossible to tell who was military. To anyone trained in operations, it was a nightmare.

Then came the helicopters. I didn't care about the rotor wash. The breathless commentary comparing it to combat tactics was nonsense. Anyone who had spent time around aircraft knew better.

What mattered was the red cross painted on the sides. Pilots flew clearly marked medical helicopters low over civilian crowds. That symbol isn't decoration. The law protects it. The military teaches this early. You do not misuse it for intimidation, for convenience, or because someone in Washington tells you to.

They crossed a line no one should cross. The crew chief should have refused. Not dramatically or with insubordination, but plainly. We're not flying this mission with these markings visible. I didn't care if the order came from the Secretary of the Army. If you want an aircraft used that way, you land it and paint over the symbol first.

That refusal is not defiance. It's professionalism.

Watching it unfold, I wasn't uncertain about what I was seeing. I was watching basic rules get ignored. Unit integrity, command and control, and the inviolability of protected symbols all thrown aside.

* * *

By the time the election arrived, nothing about it felt normal.

Voting had become a logistical exercise instead of a civic ritual. Absentee ballots were no longer a convenience reserved for the elderly or the infirm but a necessity for everyone. Ballots arrived in the mail, and everyone read the instructions carefully before signing and double-checking the envelopes, then sealing and handing them over like something fragile. People voted weeks in advance because waiting until Election Day felt reckless.

The campaign itself moved in a strange, almost disembodied way. Candidates appeared on screens more often than on stages while rallies shrank or vanished entirely. Press conferences, virtual town halls, and carefully staged moments replaced the familiar rhythms of retail politics meant to reassure a country that was no longer gathering in public.

Leaders made promises during this time, and one stayed with me. The military would accept anyone capable of serving. It was a statement that felt both obvious and quietly radical.

The President's relationship with the machinery of governance appeared increasingly strained. Public health briefings blurred into political theater while disputes with experts played out in real time. COVID deaths climbed while explanations grew thinner, and then police killed George Floyd, so the streets filled anyway.

It didn't feel like a referendum on ideology. It felt heavier.

Joe Biden didn't win because people thought he was extraordinary. He won because he was there and because the country had reached a point where it wanted the noise to stop. There was no sweeping mandate or wave of enthusiasm, just enough votes in enough places to bring an exhausting chapter to a close.

Presidents run during crises, as Lincoln ran during the Civil War. A pandemic didn't invalidate an election but demanded one. Absentee ballots weren't fraudulent but were an adaptation. Courts said so, state officials said so, and recounts said so. The results followed the same patterns elections always do.

But acceptance of those results did not. There was no concession, no quiet packing, and no acknowledgment that the process had functioned as designed. Instead, they repeated claims that could not withstand even minimal scrutiny, amplifying them until they hardened into belief. Watching it unfold, the actual damage wasn't in the margins of the vote but in the refusal to accept the outcome.

When the results were finally called, relief came, but it never rose very far. People felt release, not celebration, and the sense that someone had interrupted something dangerous but not resolved it.

For those of us watching closely, especially on issues that had lived in obscurity for years, the election felt like an opening rather than a victory. Biden hadn't promised transformation but had promised competence, stability, and the space for unfinished business to be addressed.

*　*　*

By January, the year had already taught us to expect the unimaginable. COVID had emptied the city, George Floyd's murder had brought it roaring back to life, and the election had ended while the President refused to accept it. None of that felt resolved but suspended, like a system running on momentum alone.

I was at home when it started. The livestream was already on when the first barriers fell and people began climbing walls. Windows broke as crowds poured into a building that was never meant to be defended from within. Members of Congress were rushed out of chambers and into secure locations, disappearing from view as the footage kept rolling.

This wasn't a protest or even a riot in the ordinary sense but an insurrection. For hours, I watched the Capitol being overrun while the National Guard did not move, and that absence mattered deeply.

Anyone who understands the American system understands this much: you cannot lawfully order the U.S. military to carry out a coup. The obligation to disobey illegal orders is not a loophole but foundational. Anyone expecting tanks in the streets or soldiers clearing a path for power would have misunderstood how the system works.

But there is another way a system can fail. You can withhold direction, delay decisions, and leave the machinery that normally responds automatically idle long enough for damage to occur, and that is what the public could see that day.

There were no orders for deployment, no clear authorization from the President, and no unambiguous civilian direction to act. In the hours after people breached the building, rumors spread about who asked for help, who declined it, and who hesitated. But the simpler, more troubling reality was that the National Guard was not moving because they had not yet received an explicit order.

Our system assumes that when the Secretary of Defense acts, he does so with the President's authority, but that assumption did not hold. The chain of command did not break dramatically but stalled, and in a crisis measured in minutes, that stall was consequential.

The military eventually moved because the Vice President called the Secretary of Defense and emphasized that the Department had to stop the situation. That is a remarkable sentence to write since the military does not give itself orders but responds to civilian authority. On January 6, that authority did not come, at least initially, from where the system expects it to come.

There was a moment when the Speaker of the House asked who was in charge of the nuclear arsenal. People later joked about it, but they shouldn't have because it was a rational question when the normal assurances of control were visibly fraying.

When the National Guard finally arrived, the response was massive, deliberate, and unmistakable as units flowed in from across the country to restore order. But by that point, they had already delivered the lesson, not about force but about how fragile restraint becomes when leaders defer responsibility.

It may be true that it was better that the military was not there at the start. The Capitol Police performed as trained, focusing on protecting people, moving elected officials out of harm's way, and yielding ground because the building was not the nation.

The military trains soldiers differently. We train to hold ground and defend positions. A military unit does not withdraw because a crowd presses forward but only when someone orders it to do so or when the unit is overrun, and not before it exhausts every available means. If uniformed soldiers had taken positions between that mob and the chambers of Congress, the day would have ended differently in bloodshed.

That reality does not lessen the failure of January 6 but clarifies it. The danger was not that the military acted improperly but that the system, under extreme stress, depended on restraint by the military while civilian authority failed to mount an effective response to an attack on the constitutional order.

People eventually cleared the building, Congress reconvened, and officials certified the election as the system continued to function, battered and exposed. After a year of watching institutions strain, adapt, and sometimes fail, I watched from my apartment and couldn't ignore how narrow the margin had become.

Chapter Twenty-Four

The phone rang in the middle of the night with a real ring that was sharp and insistent, cutting through sleep. I reached for it without thinking, then stopped when I saw the number on the screen.

My mother.

It was so late that, for a second, I considered letting it go to voicemail. Nothing good comes from a call like that at that hour. But it kept ringing, and the part of my brain that still believed in ordinary explanations lost its argument.

I slid out of bed and took the phone with me into the living room, closing the bedroom door behind me. The apartment was dark and silent with the kind of quiet that only exists in the middle of the night. I sat down on the edge of the couch and answered.

She said my name first. Her voice didn't sound panicked but careful, as if she were trying to hold the words in place long enough to hand them to me intact. I knew something was wrong before she said anything else.

She told me that a truck had hit my brother while he was riding his bike in a hit and run accident. The driver hadn't stopped, and my brother was gone.

The sentence landed all at once, without unfolding. It sounded absurdly like something you heard on the news, something that happened to other families. I felt oddly detached from the sound of my voice, listening and responding when it seemed appropriate.

When the call ended, I sat there for a moment with the phone still in my hand, staring at the dark screen. The apartment felt unfamiliar, like I had stepped into the wrong place by mistake.

I walked back into the bedroom and told Baraq. He was already awake by the time I spoke, resting on one elbow with concern crossing his face before I finished the first sentence. I said the words quickly, as if speed might keep them from settling. My brother had been in an accident. He listened without interrupting while his expression tightened as the shape of it became clear.

I don't remember what he said in response. I remember the weight of exhaustion hitting me all at once, sudden and overwhelming. It felt physical, like my body had simply decided it was done. I told him I was tired and needed to sleep.

I lay back down and closed my eyes. Sleep came quickly.

*　*　*

Morning came quietly, and I woke up without the jolt I had expected. For a moment, there was only the familiar weight of the bed, the low light in the room, and the ordinary sense of having slept too long or not enough. Then the memory surfaced, fully formed, and I knew it hadn't been a dream.

I reached for my phone, and the screen lit up immediately. Notifications stacked on top of each other with messages arriving faster than I could register them. Texts, missed calls, and direct messages from platforms I rarely check filled the screen. Names that I recognized instantly appeared alongside names that I hadn't seen in years. People told me how sorry they were, asked if I was okay, and asked if there was anything they could do.

I opened a few of them and then stopped because the words blurred together. Sympathy, concern, and offers of help were all well-intentioned but impossible to absorb. I felt nothing in response, no comfort or irritation, just distance. I knew with surprising clarity that I was in no condition to reply.

I set the phone down and stared at the ceiling for a while, understanding that people who cared were trying to reach me. They were doing what you do when something terrible happens, extending themselves toward the person at the center. That made sense intellectually, but meeting them there wasn't possible yet.

So I turned to Baraq and told him I couldn't handle it. He was already awake, watching me carefully, waiting for the moment I opened my eyes. I asked if he could respond to people for me, just enough to acknowledge them and let them know I wasn't ignoring them. He said yes immediately without hesitation or questions about what I wanted to say. He took the phone and started working through the messages one by one while I felt an enormous sense of relief.

There were a few things I knew I had to do. I needed to let work know I would be taking time off and book a flight home. When everything else felt suspended, I couldn't postpone the logistics, so I focused on those tasks because they were concrete and finite. They didn't require feeling anything but only action.

Baraq stayed close, asking occasionally if there was anything else he could take off my hands. What he could handle, he did, and when I said no, he didn't push. The quiet stayed intact with no reassurances or advice, just steady presence, attentive, letting me move at the pace I could move. I was deeply grateful for that.

* * *

I grew up learning that home was not a place you could relax into because every problem was a catastrophe. Not an inconvenience or something to be handled, but the end of the world. A flat tire meant chaos, a broken appliance brought panic, and an unexpected bill created a crisis. Each

323

one arrived fully formed, already swollen with panic and accusation, demanding immediate attention and absolute emotional commitment. There was no such thing as proportion because everything was urgent and everything was overwhelming.

The house itself was barely habitable since things broke and stayed broken. We didn't have friends over because you learned quickly that it was easier to keep people at a distance than to explain why the floor sagged here, why that door didn't close, or why certain rooms were off limits. There was abuse there, too, not always loud or visible, but constant enough that you learned to read the room the way other kids learned multiplication tables.

Carrying that level of worry everywhere wasn't possible, so school became the focus, along with activities and the work of building a life that existed somewhere else. Everything from home went into a sealed mental room, and I tried not to open the door unless it was necessary. It was a survival mechanism that worked.

In that house, in that environment, there was my brother. It was just the two of us most of the time, sitting on the floor with board games spread out between us, rules half-argued and half-invented. We played endless Dungeons & Dragons campaigns and strategy games that took hours. We had movie marathons where we laughed at the same scenes every time, finishing each other's quotes without thinking. We shared a language that didn't require explanation and understood pacing, tone, when to disengage, and when to lean in.

He was the sane one in my family and the steady one who thought the way I did.

When I left home, I kept that distance intact because I couldn't afford to carry the stress with me everywhere I went. I told Baraq that once, early on, explaining that I had learned to keep things at arm's length because I couldn't live in a constant state of alarm. He understood it had been necessary, but he also saw what it cost.

My parents and I were never especially close, but my brother was the constant thread. He managed them, buffered them, and translated. He carried that emotional load quietly and competently, without ever making a show of it. I assumed that he always would.

He followed me to the University of Central Oklahoma, but not along the same path. I served as student senate president, residence hall association president, and a fraternity chapter founder while his path took a different shape. He became chief justice of the student court and president of the Gay Alliance for Tolerance and Equality. He came out before I did, with a calm certainty I admired.

After graduation, he stayed at the university, working in the office that helped students from disadvantaged backgrounds find a way into college. The work amounted to social work in practice. He returned to get a master's degree and completed it in May.

Baraq was the one who nudged the reconnection from something assumed to something intentional, so we did. We split holidays with Thanksgiving at his family and Christmas back in Oklahoma. We catered Christmas dinner because my family didn't really cook. David would pick it up before we arrived to have everything ready. He said we should do it more often because there wouldn't be many chances like this left with our parents.

I met his boyfriend and their cats. He was living in our grandmother's old house, paying the mortgage and holding things together in ways I had never explicitly acknowledged but had always relied on.

He and his boyfriend were the only members of my family who ever came to visit us in DC. We showed him the city, took him to dinner, and walked the monuments. He wanted to see everything.

During COVID, we started playing games online with full campaigns and long sessions, voices coming through headsets late into the night. He was the Dungeon Master for his gaming group in Oklahoma. Baraq sat next to me, running characters alongside me, and it felt effortless, familiar, and solid.

I had assumed that once David finished his graduate degree, he would leave Oklahoma and find something better and bigger. I imagined he would always be the one handling things back there, the level head and fixer, the person who sorted out the chaos so I didn't have to reopen that sealed room.

Then, he was gone.

* * *

We coordinated first with his boyfriend, Jaime, whose entire family came into town to support him. Together we worked through the immediate decisions and planned to cremate my brother. There would be no burial plot or graveside service, just something simple like a memorial.

When I asked my parents what they wanted to do, there wasn't really an answer because they weren't sure. There was no community outside the family, no obvious sense of who would come or what a service like this was supposed to look like. The instinct was to keep it small, private, and manageable, but it didn't feel right to let it end there.

My brother's gaming group wanted to help and asked what they could do and how they could be part of it. I reached out to people I remembered from my time at the University of Central Oklahoma and asked a simple question: could we hold a memorial service on campus, was there a space, and would they be willing to help put something together?

The answer came back quickly with a yes and of course, and they said they would take care of it. They opened the Y Chapel for us and put together an entire service. A professor who had served as the advisor for the Gay Alliance for Tolerance and Equality agreed to conduct the memorial service. Students my brother had helped, students he had walked through applications and paperwork and second chances, volunteered to speak. His gaming friends brought items that had mattered to him, small artifacts of the life he had built outside work, and even the university president came to pay her respects.

People kept arriving throughout the day. Old friends, former students, and colleagues showed up, including people I hadn't seen in years. Some of them knew me from my time at the University of Central Oklahoma and knew my brother from his, but had never connected the two. When someone mentioned it to me, I said I wanted it that way because I wanted him to be known on his own terms, not as my younger brother, since he had forged his own path there.

As the service unfolded, it became clear just how many lives he had touched. My parents sat quietly, taking it in, because they hadn't known and I hadn't known. The scale of it surprised all of us, along with the breadth of the stories, the depth of the gratitude, and the way people spoke about him as someone who had steadied them when they might otherwise have slipped through the cracks. My mother held herself together, and at one point, she leaned over and said that this was good and right.

The university announced that they were establishing the Second Chance Scholarship in his name for students who hadn't had a straightforward path to college, who had struggled or dropped out, and who needed another opportunity to finish what they had started. It was exactly the work he had devoted himself to, helping people finish and helping people stay.

After the service, there was a reception at Old North, one of the stately buildings on campus where the university provided the refreshments and had university shirts for us. People lingered, talked, and shared stories in what felt like a gathering where you belonged.

This was where I had finished my bachelor's degree and where he had come after me and made his own way. This was where he had worked and built a life and mattered deeply to people. When he died, the university didn't treat us like outsiders or guests, and for me, it felt like coming home to an extended family.

* * *

After the memorial service, I flew home and let a month pass while the shape of the loss didn't change. I knew it never would because the death of a younger sibling isn't something you get over. You learn how to carry it, build a life around the absence, and keep going.

I was back at work and functioning while the days moved forward, even if I didn't feel as though I had. My mother reached out to the police several times, and each call followed the same pattern. The detective said he would get back to her, that he would pull the traffic camera footage, look for video of the vehicle that hit my brother, and follow up once he had more. He was working on it, but nothing happened.

I waited and gave them room because experience taught me what would happen if I moved too quickly. People would reframe the concern as impatience, and the tone would overshadow the substance. So I let the silence stretch and let the delay speak for itself until the delay itself became the story, but still nothing happened.

I watched the police department's social media posts scroll by with announcements about community contests, photos from potluck lunches, and updates about package thefts and minor arrests. Ordinary policing content stayed steady and upbeat, but there was nothing about my brother.

I called and left messages that no one returned, while my mother grew furious in a way I had rarely seen. She was brittle and worn thin as answers never came, and no one disclosed what they had found or said whether they had reviewed the cameras.

I kept thinking about what my brother had done with his life, the people he had helped, and the students who had stayed in school because he had taken the time to walk them through one more form and one more conversation. None of that seemed to matter here.

In Oklahoma, hit-and-run accidents were commonplace as motorists struck people in the street at night, and the deaths hardly registered. They passed without scandal or crisis because this was how some people died. In Washington, DC, it would have been unthinkable. Someone killed in the street and left there? There would have been outrage, demands, and press conferences. In Oklahoma, it passed without comment.

I thought about my brother and his last moments riding his bike with the lights on, doing everything right, and how little interest the department, the city, or anyone in authority showed afterward. That made me angry.

My brother had seen that version of me before, back in Oklahoma, when I decided that patience wasn't working and politeness wasn't enough. He had watched me stir things up and understood why. At a certain point, patience stops being a virtue and starts being complicity.

So I made it uncomfortable by posting on Facebook after a month with no action, no released footage, no request for public help, and no explanation for why silence surrounded the hit-and-run killing.

The response was immediate with messages, calls, and shares flooding in. Someone I had gone to school with, who was now a city councilman, reached out directly while a local newscaster contacted me and said they were going to the police department to ask questions.

They called me back later that afternoon to tell me that the police were releasing the video and asking for the public's help. The police chief called me after that, and I imagined my brother would have found it funny, the way nothing mattered until it did, the way people who had been going about their days now found themselves very uncomfortable.

* * *

The newscaster warned me before she sent the video, saying it was a little graphic and stayed with you in a way that wasn't typical. She told me it came from the ATM camera across the street and that you could see my brother clearly because he was very visible with lights on his bike.

She wasn't exaggerating about what I would see. When I watched the video, the first thing I saw was him riding past the camera, lit up like a Christmas tree with flashing lights on his tires and lights in front and behind. He was impossible to miss and doing everything right, exactly what you're supposed to do when you ride at night.

A couple of minutes later, you hear the sound of a truck spinning out in the street with an engine revving too hard and tires losing traction. Someone was showing off and driving the way people drive when they think the road belongs to them. The truck passed the camera and went offscreen, and then there was the impact.

You don't expect an ATM camera to have sound, but this one did, and the reporter told me it made her jump when she first heard it. I understood why because it was sudden, loud, and final. Immediately after, without hesitation or pause, the engine revved again, and the truck sped away. There was no delay or confusion and no pause to see what had happened because the driver fled.

I watched it all the way through, and the station asked if I would give an interview. I said yes, and they put me on camera and asked me about my brother, about who he was and what he did. I knew what they were doing because they were waiting for when my voice would break and when I would cry on camera since that's part of the job.

I held it together and talked about my brother's work, the people he helped, and the students who finished school because of him. I asked for the public's help in finding the person who had hit him and left him there while I held it together because there was nothing to be gained by falling apart.

Later, the police told me that someone might eventually come forward because usually they hear nothing at first. Then someone has a falling out with a friend, someone gets arrested and wants to make a deal, and the truth comes out sideways.

I try to imagine how I'd respond if that happened, though I don't know that it would help my brother since he's dead. What stays with me is the knowledge that the police could have done something sooner. If they had released the video that first week or asked for help while the night was still fresh, someone might have remembered a loud white truck because someone was coming home late and something was out of place. A month later, whatever anyone might have noticed was gone.

Chapter Twenty-Five

Trump left office in January.

Nothing about it carried lasting drama, at least not the kind that clings. The inauguration passed quietly, flags gave way to new colors, and the tone of public life shifted almost imperceptibly. Press secretaries returned to speaking in complete sentences. People across the country exhaled with care, as if a deeper breath might tempt something fragile to fracture.

The candidates made promises during the campaign. They were specific enough to remember and broad enough to leave room for interpretation. The administration would review the policy, respect the science, and address discrimination. People said it would happen.

And then nothing.

The case stalled without resolution, and the policy remained fixed in place. Yet, the calls kept coming.

Weeks passed. Then months. The docket remained silent.

At first, I assumed the delay came from procedure. Courts move slowly by design, and our case had reached a point where we had nothing left to submit. The court had already held oral argument, both parties had fully briefed the motion for summary judgment, and the filings closed the record. All that remained was for the court to decide.

But as the administration settled in, it became harder to ignore it.

Judge Brinkema wasn't hesitating. She was waiting.

She was exercising restraint. Courts avoid deciding constitutional questions when they can. They give the political branches space to act first, to fix what they broke without being ordered to do so. It is not deference so much as discipline: a recognition that some changes are better made voluntarily, and that a judicial ruling should be the last step, not the first.

That space was being given quietly and deliberately.

The military refused to take it up. The Department of Defense remained still, the services left their standards untouched, and nothing followed. No outreach, no request for time, not even the pretense of engagement. They opened the door. The system did nothing.

From the outside, it looked calm. Inside the case, it felt like suspension, a pause without relief, a silence that carried weight. The court was waiting for the other branches of government to fulfill their promises.

* * *

There were many stories during that period. Articles, background calls, and quick interviews were folded into other people's narratives. Most of them blurred together. I stopped keeping track of where things ran or how long they lasted.

The Vice documentary stayed with me because of how much of it never made it on screen.

Most of an afternoon passed with the apartment in Columbia Heights turned into a set. Cameras arrived first, followed by lights, then a steady stream of people moving quietly around the furniture, adjusting angles, asking for one more take. Sit here, stand there, cross the room again. They filmed emails answered at the kitchen table, phone calls placed, and even the moments when I said nothing at all.

At one point, they asked me to put on my uniform.

Then to take it off.

Then to put it on again.

They filmed the process from different angles. Hands on fabric, boots on the floor, the slow, familiar sequence broken into pieces to be reassembled later. I remember realizing that the editors would cut what felt like a single moment in real life into fragments. This shot layered under that sentence, my voice carried over something else entirely. The editors never intended most of it for direct viewing. It was what they called B-roll, the filler, the connective tissue, the quiet visuals that made everything else flow.

Later, we went to the National Mall.

We learned quickly why people don't film interviews there. Planes roared overhead constantly, lining up to land at Reagan. We'd start an answer, stop, wait, try again. Sometimes we'd get a few clean seconds before another engine cut across the sound. It took forever.

Tourists stopped constantly. Some wanted to thank me for my service. Others asked for pictures. A few just hovered, unsure whether they were interrupting something important. I smiled, nodded, and tried to stay focused. My beret wouldn't sit right. I was aware of it in a way that felt absurdly distracting.

By the time the crew packed up, they had logged hours of footage. In the edit, they would discard some sequences, cut other conversations into fragments, and compress a long afternoon into minutes.

When they left, the apartment slipped back into its usual rhythm. Cameras disappeared, the lights came down, and ordinary silence returned. The case remained pending, and the policy stayed unchanged. Yet, the court offered nothing in response.

Months later, the documentary finally aired. After it aired, people started finding me.

* * *

The calls didn't wait for convenient moments.

They came while I was at work, mid-meeting, halfway through conversations meant to matter. A glance at my phone, an unfamiliar number, and the meaning landed before the call connected. Explanations fell away. I rose, gave a single nod, and slipped into a hallway or stairwell, letting the door close behind me.

Most of the time, that was enough.

"Hi, is this Nick?"

His voice sounded younger than I expected. Careful, like he wasn't sure he should be calling.

"Yeah. What's up?"

"Oh. Okay." A pause. "I saw the documentary. I looked you up. I didn't really know who else to reach out to."

"That's fine. I'm glad you did."

A nervous laugh. "I'm sitting in my car. I didn't want anyone to hear."

"Take your time."

Another pause. The engine idled in the background.

"I got diagnosed. Last week. And everything feels off. Like I'm walking around in someone else's life."

"Yeah. That part's familiar."

"They put me on meds already. One pill a day." He hesitated. "Everyone keeps saying that's good news."

"It is. It just takes a minute to feel like it."

"I don't feel dangerous. I just feel smaller. Like I lost something."

I leaned against the wall. "Most people feel that way at first. Like you have to make up for something. Prove something. Fix yourself."

"That's exactly it. I already signed up for a gym. Immediately."

A smile crept in. "Yeah. That's a thing."

"It is?"

"Oh yeah. A lot of guys do that. You pay closer attention to your health. At first, it's about coping. Or proving you still have value. But after a while, it just becomes taking care of yourself."

Silence, then: "I keep thinking no one's going to want me now."

I shook my head. "You're going to be surprised."

"By what?"

"By how many really attractive, confident, put-together guys are HIV+. Guys you never would have guessed, men you already know, the ones you assumed wouldn't be interested."

A soft laugh. "That seems unlikely."

"It's not. Sometimes they just didn't want to bring it up. Or they didn't know how. Or they weren't out about it yet. Then later you find out through someone else, or it comes up casually, and suddenly things make more sense."

"So it's not like the end of the dating pool."

"No. If anything, it makes things clearer. More direct. Less guessing."

He let out a breath. "That actually sounds kind of nice."

"It is. And at some point, you stop measuring yourself against how other people react. You just know your worth. And if someone can't deal with reality, you don't spiral. You just think, okay, that's not my problem."

"So you don't take it personally?"

"Eventually? No, you realize it saved you time. And energy. And a lot of unnecessary bullshit."

A laugh. "I would really like to get there."

"You will. Not because you forced yourself to be confident, but because you stopped letting other people define you."

The pause that followed wasn't tight this time, just space.

"Okay. I think I can breathe again."

"That's usually how it starts."

Another soft laugh. "I'm really glad I called."

"Me too."

"Seriously. Thank you."

"Anytime. You're going to figure this out."

When the call ended, I stayed where I was for a moment before heading back inside. The case was still pending.

But one more person wasn't alone anymore.

* * *

By the time Scott told me Lambda Legal had fired him, it hadn't come out of nowhere.

I just hadn't known it was coming.

There had been things brewing for a while. Internal tensions and disagreements that I only learned about later. None of it touched the substance of the case, and no one shared anything with me. Scott had said nothing while he was navigating whatever was unfolding behind the scenes. That was his choice, and I understood it. Until they decided, it wasn't my business.

Now that they had, it was.

He called me in the spring and told me plainly that Lambda Legal had fired him. An employment decision. An internal dispute. Nothing that went to the merits of the case, but enough to end his role at the organization. I was stunned. Scott had led this case from the beginning, not just in title, but in fact. He knew the record cold, shaped the strategy, and carried it through every inflection point. I trusted him completely.

"I'm really sorry," I said. And I meant it.

That first call wasn't about the case. It was personal. We talked about what it feels like when something you've poured years into decides it can move on without you. About anger and disappointment and the particular insult of being cut loose after you've done the work. I didn't offer advice. I didn't talk strategy. This wasn't a legal conversation yet.

A few days later, he sent me a draft memo.

Scott wrote it the way he wrote everything. Clean, efficient, confident. It formally ended Lambda Legal's involvement in the case and continued representation under his leadership. At the bottom was a signature line.

Mine.

By then, he had already spoken with the other plaintiffs. They were going with him. From his perspective, this was the natural next step. He was still lead counsel. He had earned that. The case would continue, just without the institution that had fired him.

That was where I had to intervene.

The memo went unsigned. After a careful read, it went back onto the desk, and the call followed.

"I want to be very clear about something. You remain lead counsel on this case. That isn't changing."

He didn't argue.

"But I'm not signing this. Lambda Legal is not out."

A long pause.

"I'm not weighing in on what happened internally. That's not my place, and it isn't my fight. This case didn't reach this point without them. They committed real resources, took risks, and amplified my story when it mattered. And if we win, they deserve to be part of it."

The pushback was practical, not emotional. How do you work with an institution after something like this? How do you manage continuity after they've broken trust?

"That part's on you. But the institution stays."

What Scott hadn't fully appreciated was that this fight couldn't belong to one person, no matter how capable. Institutions matter because they outlast individuals. They replenish the resources that make the work possible. They turn individual victories into precedent, into training, into infrastructure for people without the same visibility or support.

I supported Scott fully as lead counsel. He had earned that role, and I trusted him to keep carrying the case. But I wasn't willing to strip it of the institution that could make a victory matter beyond me.

"I'm thinking about the people who come after. They need an organization that can carry this forward after I'm gone."

I knew I was an outlier. The other plaintiffs had already made their choice. This was the first time I said no to Scott, not out of disloyalty, but out of responsibility.

"You're lead counsel. But Lambda Legal stays involved. You'll have to work with them."

After the call ended, I stayed where I was longer than usual. There had been no argument, no raised voices. Just a refusal to sign.

The case would continue to move forward, but not in the way it would have without me.

* * *

After Scott left Lambda Legal, the plaintiffs stayed in touch.

Not constantly, not dramatically, just enough to know we were all carrying the same unresolved weight. We talked about what had happened with Scott, about how strange it felt to watch something so central to the case unfold without us being part of it. We talked about work, about relationships, about the way this case sat in the background of everything else.

Mostly, we talked about the waiting.

Every so often, one of us would check in with Scott to ask if anything had moved.

Nothing had moved.

Each time, he answered with care and restraint.

"Opinions are split. Some see the delay as a bad sign. Others take it as a good one. Almost everyone agrees that pressing a judge to move is a bad idea."

"So they're stalled."

"Yeah. They don't want to be the ones who poke her."

We waited longer. Then checked again.

Same result.

By then, whatever the delay meant, it carried actual costs. Procedurally, the case had reached the end of the road. The record stood closed, the court had already heard oral argument, and both sides had fully briefed summary judgment. From a legal standpoint, nothing remained.

And yet, nothing was happening.

That was when I told Scott the plaintiffs wanted to meet with the legal team as a group.

A pause on the line.

"That's not typical."

"I know. But we're not asking to run the case. We're asking for help in bringing it to a close."

So he set it up.

When the call started, the tone stayed careful but respectful. Plaintiffs and lawyers on the line at once for the first time.

I opened by thanking them.

"For everything you've done. The years of work. The care you've taken with this case. We know how much discipline is required not to overreact to every delay or stray signal."

Murmurs of agreement.

"We appreciate that," one attorney said. "And we understand how hard the waiting is. But judges really don't like to be rushed."

"We're not asking you to rush her. We're asking whether the waiting is still doing any work."

That shifted the mood.

"Just to be clear, we've explored settlement," Scott said. "More than once. There's been no interest."

Another voice cut in. "But going back to the court can be risky. Sometimes a delay means the judge is struggling with something."

"And sometimes it means she's waiting for someone else to act."

A pause.

"What we think is happening," I said, "is that Judge Brinkema is giving the system every opportunity to fix this without the court stepping in. The administration changed. They had made promises publicly during the campaign. We've tried to see whether that translated into any willingness to resolve this without a ruling."

"It hasn't."

"That's true."

"So what we're asking is whether there's a way to let the court know that the political branches declined to act, that we offered discussions and they refused them, and that the harm the case addresses continues."

Silence.

"If we do that," one of the senior attorneys finally said, "it has to be framed carefully."

"Of course. We trust you on that."

"And before we update the court, we'd need to try to reopen discussions. Formally. Even if we expect the answer to be no."

"That makes sense."

"We'd have to say we made one last good-faith effort after the change in administration. Otherwise, it looks like we skipped a step."

"We can do that," Scott said. "It'll take some time."

"That's fine. We're not asking for speed. We're asking for closure."

The tone shifted then, still cautious, but aligned.

"I think we can do this."

"Carefully."

"Yes, carefully."

Over the next few weeks, that's exactly what happened.

The legal team reached out. They offered discussions and waited.

The answers, when they came, changed nothing.

Once that process had run its course, they went back to the court and provided an update. Not a demand, not a complaint, just an update of where things stood.

Chapter Twenty-Six

The decision came down cleanly a few weeks later.

Judge Brinkema granted summary judgment and struck the policy down in full. The government lost on every justification it offered. The court didn't hedge, didn't defer, didn't suggest revisions or remand for further study. It ruled that the military's restrictions on asymptomatic, undetectable servicemembers were arbitrary and capricious. They were unsupported by science, cost, or readiness.

There was no credible risk or rational basis. No lawful excuse.

I found out a few hours later, shaken awake by Baraq.

"Scott's been trying to reach you. A lot."

My phone lay dead on the coffee table. When it powered back on, notifications flooded in — missed calls, texts, a voicemail marked urgent. All from Scott.

I called him immediately.

"We won."

No qualifiers. No legal caveats. Just the words.

"She granted summary judgment. She rejected everything the government argued."

A pause, then more deliberately: "She found the policy irrational. Arbitrary and capricious."

That phrase cut through the haze. Not outdated. Not mistaken. Unreasonable. Indefensible.

Scott walked me through the opinion, but certain lines lodged immediately. Judge Brinkema rejected the idea that courts should stand aside simply because the policy involved the military. She pointed to the amicus brief filed by former Secretaries of the Army, Air Force, and Navy. These leaders had spent their careers inside the institution and still concluded there was no legitimate reason to bar people living with HIV from service.

Not hypothetical risk, she wrote. Credible risk grounded in current medical evidence.

The government had none.

When the call ended, the apartment was quiet again.

We had won.

Validation, relief, and confirmation arrived all at once. No one had imagined, exaggerated, or misread anything. A federal judge had said plainly that the policy was unlawful. That what the military had been doing could not stand.

* * *

This is usually where the story ends.

In every version I'd ever absorbed, this was the moment of resolution. Movies, articles, and the way people talked about landmark cases after the fact all followed the same pattern. The ruling comes down. Someone senior appears. There's a handshake, maybe a carefully worded acknowledgment. The institution accepts the outcome, signals compliance, and the screen fades to white.

I had never questioned that assumption. Of course, someone would be waiting. That's how the military handles things that matter. A general officer. A senior executive servicemember. Someone high enough to stand in for the institution itself. The military rarely apologized, but it would acknowledge the ruling, explain the process, and clarify that it would carry out what the court ordered.

I didn't expect warmth. I expected process.

So I went to the DC Armory the following weekend, believing that the story would pick up where it was supposed to.

Nothing did.

Nothing about the place had changed. Cracked pavement, flags snapping in the wind, soldiers filtering inside with coffee cups and garment bags, complaining about traffic and schedules. I walked through the doors, waiting for someone to pull me aside.

Hang back for a second. Legal wants a word. The commander needs to see you.

That was how it worked when something significant happened. Promotions. Investigations. Changes in status. No one ever announced it. They handled it.

They slotted me straight back into the routine.

Within minutes of walking in, I was being directed the same way I always had been. Brief, transactional instructions delivered without eye contact. Move this. Check that. Stand here. Wait.

Nothing slowed or shifted. No one pulled me aside, asked a question, or acknowledged my presence at all. The institution handled me exactly as it handles someone whose status it does not recognize.

Just days earlier, a federal judge had ruled that the policy barring my commission was unlawful. Standing there in uniform, it was clear that the ruling hadn't even registered as something requiring awareness.

This wasn't neglect. It was normalization, the quiet reassertion of hierarchy, a reminder of where I still sat and how little the law had disturbed that arrangement.

The silence wasn't confrontational. No one warned me to keep my head down. It was seamless. The system absorbed the ruling without friction and carried on as if nothing had happened.

I followed orders and finished the work, and my bearing never slipped. From the outside, nothing had changed. That was the point.

This was the part the movies never show. Not resistance or defiance, but the quiet decision to do nothing at all.

By the end of the day, it was clear that no one planned to show up. No senior official, no acknowledgment, no sign that the ruling had altered my status.

My teachers hadn't taught me to expect the story to end that way.

The screen didn't fade to white.

* * *

Nothing happened.

Days passed, then weeks. The ruling sat there.

Unchanged and undeniable.

My enlistment ended in July. I had already reenlisted once to keep the case intact, to make sure no one could say I had walked away before the court ruled. I had carried the burden while the outcome was uncertain.

Now the ruling was in. The obligation had shifted.

I wasn't supposed to be deciding whether to reenlist again. I was supposed to be commissioning. That was the point. Whether I stayed after that was a separate question, one most people don't face once they've received their twenty-year letter. Very few choose to remain. Watching the institution do nothing after a binding order made the idea of staying feel increasingly absurd.

What they seemed to expect instead was that I would keep signing extensions and keep absorbing their delay as if nothing had changed. As if the burden were still mine.

My legal team asked what would happen next. How the military would implement the ruling. What steps the Army intended to take to remedy the injury the court had identified. The responses were deliberate and consistent. The government declined to discuss an individual remedy. Declined to engage on implementation as it applied to me. Declined to say how or when anything would move.

Before the ruling, that posture would have been unremarkable. While litigation is ongoing, the government does not discuss remedies for named plaintiffs.

But the litigation was over.

There was an order. No stay. No request for one. The ruling was in effect immediately. The obligation was not abstract or future-facing. It was present. And they were refusing to acknowledge it.

The realization landed as a betrayal.

For more than a decade, I had followed the rules. Respected the chain of command. Deferred when told to. Trusted processes that demanded patience and offered little in return. I had genuinely believed that obedience meant something, that discipline rested on more than convenience.

And now, the institution that demanded absolute compliance from everyone below it was treating a federal court as optional.

What I couldn't get past wasn't just the delay. It was the posture. The quiet certainty that nothing would happen unless someone forced it. They thought they could wait out, absorb, and set aside the law because it was inconvenient, not because it was unclear.

That was the hypocrisy. Not the failing of one office or one person, but a system that enforced obedience downward while treating civilian authority as conditional when it applied upward.

The chain of command only works if it rests on something real. Obedience for legitimacy. Authority grounded in law. The understanding that everyone eventually answers to something higher than themselves.

Watching the institution sidestep a binding order made the bargain feel hollow. If the law only mattered when it was useful, then the discipline it demanded was habit, not principle.

As the weeks stretched on, the delay felt corrosive. A grinding sense that something fundamental had given way.

What surfaced wasn't new. It was everything I had been postponing.

For years, I had lived in a kind of suspension. I functioned, testified, and showed up while keeping everything else sealed off. I didn't process what was happening to me. I deferred it. Compartmentalized it. Addressed my interior life later, once there was space to breathe.

There never was.

The case filled every available space. Anything that threatened to slow me down, blur the record, or complicate the narrative, I pushed aside. I told myself I would address it afterward. I always told myself that.

By the time the ruling came down, I wasn't just tired. I felt completely drained. The structures I had built to keep moving had done their job and then collapsed all at once.

The fight hadn't broken me. Its end did. I held myself frozen in time, afraid that any change would cause the case to collapse with it, and packed everything else away under the promise that I'd return to it later.

The lawsuit. Becoming public about my HIV status. Being in DC during 2020. The constant tension. The death of my brother.

I had held it together because I had to. Because there were two thousand other people who couldn't fight for themselves. Because the case required me to remain steady.

And then the ruling came.

There was nothing left to hold on to.

The thought kept returning, uninvited and persistent: It's like I lost — even though I supposedly won.

One afternoon, I stood in my apartment staring at a pile of military gear in the corner. Uniforms, boots, and the ruck all waited for something that wasn't coming.

I couldn't look at it anymore. I couldn't put it on again and pretend none of this mattered.

So, I packed it up.

I folded everything, sealed the box, and carried it to the DC Armory.

I left it there with a note.

Call me when you're ready to follow the court's order.

Then I walked out.

* * *

The First Sergeant called two days after I left my gear at the DC Armory.

"Sergeant, we need to discuss how you handled this."

I said I understood and asked when she wanted me to come in.

When I sat down in her office, she didn't waste time.

"Normally, if someone stops coming to drill and leaves their equipment, we'd be looking at adverse action."

I nodded. "That's fair."

"But that's not what we're doing. You have over twenty years. You're coming up on your ETS. They're letting you ETS quietly and retire."

After a breath: "I'm not trying to create a problem."

"That's not how this reads to us."

A pause.

"But we're confused."

"About what?"

"Why you haven't extended."

The question landed harder than I expected.

"No one's asked me to extend. No one's told me anything at all."

"The understanding was that you would."

"Based on what?"

She stood abruptly. "Give me a minute."

She stepped out, closing the door behind her. Her voice carried through the wall, calm and professional, then growing sharper. When she came back, she lowered herself into the chair.

"We don't have guidance. Nothing has come down from the National Guard Bureau or the Big Army."

"So this is just an assumption?"

"That you would extend while this gets worked out."

The edge crept into my voice. "I've been waiting eight years. A court ruled in my favor. No one has told me what happens next. And I'm supposed to just stay?"

She met my eyes. "I get why you're frustrated."

I shook my head. "This isn't frustration. It's anger. A court ordered them to reconsider my application, and they did nothing. No reconsideration, no acknowledgment, nothing at all."

She nodded once.

Then she surprised me.

She picked up the phone and dialed the Commanding General's office herself.

I watched her face as she laid it out. The lack of guidance, the ETS date, and the court ruling. She listened, thanked whoever was on the other end, and hung up.

"They have nothing either. No instructions. No timeline."

"So what happens now?"

"They're treating this as if it's unresolved. And unresolved means they expect you to stay put."

I leaned back. "That's not a plan."

We sat there for a moment.

"I can't fix what's happening above us," she said finally. "But I don't want you to think we're ignoring this."

When I left the office, I hadn't agreed to extend. But I understood the shape of the problem now.

No one was going to tell me to stay. They were just going to wait to see if I did.

* * *

The calls came one after another.

Different voices with the same message.

"You can't ETS."

"I don't want to reenlist. I did everything they asked. A court ruled in my favor. They're pretending it didn't happen."

"I understand. But if you leave the service, the court loses leverage. You lose any meaningful remedy."

"So I'm being forced to stay?"

A pause. "I wouldn't put it that way."

"I would. They're ignoring the order, and the only reason they can do that is they know I'm trapped."

Another call came later that day, and the pleasantries didn't last.

"I can't keep showing up. I can't walk around as a sergeant while everyone asks when I'm commissioning."

"If you ETS, there's no mechanism left to force compliance."

"So what's the option?"

"An extension."

"That's not an option," I said. "That's surrender."

"It's temporary. Six months."

"And then?"

"We reassess."

A hand went to my temples. "Drills won't work. I'll say something I can't take back."

No argument.

"What about inactive status? ING. I stay in on paper, but I don't come in until they actually comply."

"Let me make some calls."

That evening, the phone rang again.

"The Department of Justice will excuse you from drill."

"For how long?"

"For the duration of the extension."

"And the extension is?"

"Six months."

I stared at the wall.

"So I stay in. I don't drill. And they keep pretending this is normal."

"Yes."

"And if I don't sign?"

"You ETS. And whatever happens next happens without you."

Silence stretched.

"Send me the paperwork."

When the call ended, relief never came. The moment closed in instead. Reenlistment didn't come from faith. It came from a system that had made exit indistinguishable from surrender.

* * *

The call with the legal team felt different from the others.

Less urgent. More choreographed.

"The Department of Justice is going to file a notice of appeal."

I closed my eyes. "So they're appealing."

"No. They won't follow through."

"Then why file it?"

"They need time to get comfortable with the ruling."

A short laugh escaped. "So this is about managing feelings."

"They also need to notify Congress that they're no longer defending the policy."

"And what reason are they giving?"

A pause.

"They're saying the military was already planning to change it."

"That's not true. For eight years, the policy drew an active defense through litigation, in court, and even after they lost."

"I know."

"So the court just disappears from the story."

"Yes, publicly."

"They're holding the policy announcement."

"Why?"

"Because the Senate hasn't confirmed the nominee for Under Secretary of the Air Force. They don't want to muddy the waters."

"With what? The truth?"

"They don't want the confirmation to turn into a discussion about the litigation. About HIV. About why the Air Force fought this so long."

Silence again.

"Gina Ortiz Jones. A historic appointment they can point to."

353

"Yes."

"And meanwhile, over two thousand HIV+ servicemembers are still living under the policy a court just struck down."

No interruption.

"So accountability waits. Because it competes with the story they want to tell about themselves."

"That's the concern."

"And once she's confirmed, they roll out the change stripped of context. No admission they were wrong, no acknowledgment the court ordered them to stop."

"That's the framing."

I leaned back.

"This isn't defiance. It's erasure."

A slow shake of the head. "From their perspective, compliance exists in substance."

"Without acknowledging authority."

"Yes."

When the call ended, I understood something I hadn't before.

They weren't challenging the ruling. They were simply refusing to acknowledge it.

* * *

They told me they needed a new packet.

Not because the original had been deficient. Not because anything about my qualifications at the time I applied had changed.

Because they no longer had it.

During the litigation, someone had destroyed my original application.

"So you'll need to rebuild it. They want a complete submission."

"A reconsideration. That's what the court ordered."

A pause.

"They're treating it as a new application. Under the revised policy."

I understood immediately what that meant.

There would be no reconsideration. No retroactivity. No acknowledgment that they had ever denied or delayed anything. The years between 2014 and now would simply disappear, absorbed into a narrative where nothing improper had occurred.

They sent me the checklist.

Medical records. Security clearance. Fitness assessments. Everything required of someone just beginning a career.

A blind packet, they called it. Neutral and objective.

It wasn't.

Someone at the starting line gets assessed by this system. Someone young enough to pretend momentum was endless. Someone whose body hadn't yet begun keeping its own account.

Mine had.

Over twenty years of service were showing, quietly and relentlessly. Nothing dramatic. Just enough to matter on a form designed to ask a single question about whether this person would last an entire career.

I already had.

At the start of a military career, you minimize every ache and pain to avoid giving them reasons to reject you. At the end, you document everything that happened during your service because you never know what might develop later. They had me minimizing problems like I was starting a twenty-year career when I should have been documenting everything in preparation for retirement, and they were doing so to apply for a career that they had already effectively taken from me through delay and indifference.

As I worked through the packet, the absurdities multiplied.

They wanted a full security clearance questionnaire. I already held a current Top Secret.

They wanted explanations of the gaps created by the litigation itself. Forms that assumed a clean, linear arc where none existed.

Everything on the paperwork expected simplicity, so I had to annotate. Clarify. Correct.

By the time I finished, I could feel it physically. The familiar warning signs meant I was pushing too hard, again. I maintained the same professional tone I always had. The same restraint. The same compliance.

Each memo felt like a concession.

By rebuilding the packet, I was taking part in the fiction they needed.

A fiction that treated the case as just another application, erasing the denial, the order, and even the federal court's intervention.

An inventory, not an application.

Not to declare the body unfit, but to document what the waiting had used and what it had taken.

They hadn't just misplaced my packet.

The moment of refusal vanished, along with any obligation to repair it. Forcing me under the new policy carried a message of its own. No error, no wrongdoing, no court order. Just a quiet claim that they had changed their minds.

*　*　*

In the end, I didn't submit the packet the way they wanted.

I submitted it the way the system should have handled it from the start, as a reconsideration of the application I submitted years earlier, evaluated as of the moment they wrongfully denied it. Along with it,

I included a request for a Special Selection Board to consider the retroactive appointments and time-in-grade promotions I would have received had the military not frozen my career with an unlawful policy.

I wasn't asking for something extraordinary.

I was asking to be made whole.

As part of the packet, they asked for a personal statement.

Normally, this is where an applicant explains who they hope to become and why they want to serve, what they plan to accomplish, and where they see themselves going. It's aspirational by design. Forward-looking, optimistic. That frame no longer fits.

I wasn't writing toward a future. I was writing against erasure.

Alone at my desk, I opened a blank document and stared at it for a long time. Eventually, I wrote about the career I actually had. Twenty-two years enlisted, stepping into leadership roles meant for people senior to me. Taking responsibility that was never assigned, believing that if you did the work and followed the rules, the system would eventually meet you halfway.

And then I wrote the part that no application is supposed to contain.

I explained that the packet in front of them was the wrong one. They had never considered the original application. They destroyed it during litigation, and the court had ordered reconsideration, not a fresh assessment untethered from time, context, or consequence.

I explained I wasn't asking them to imagine who I might become.

I was asking them to account for who I had already been and for the career that should have followed.

When I finished, I didn't feel relief.

I felt something closer to recognition.

I saved the document, attached it to the packet, and sent it off.

That was all I could do.

Chapter Twenty-Seven

Jordan Gonsalves first reached out by email, introducing himself as a graduate student at Columbia's journalism school working on a capstone project about HIV policy in the military. He had been following my case and asked whether I would talk.

I assumed it would be a single interview. An hour, maybe two. Something focused on the litigation: the ruling, the language, the arc of the case. The conversation reporters usually want once the decision is already public.

Instead, Jordan called me.

Then he called again. And again.

The conversations stretched over weeks. Two hours at a time, sometimes longer. He wasn't rushing toward a headline. He kept circling back, asking me to explain things I thought I had already explained — not because he didn't understand, but because he wanted to understand them precisely.

"What actually changed after the ruling?" He asked early on.

"On paper?" Enough to say it changed.

"And in practice?"

"Almost nothing."

I started with the waivers. The court stripped away discretion; the military reintroduced it under a different name. The system looks neutral, but it hands the same decision-making power back to the same people who abused it before.

"So they're complying," he said, "but in a way that keeps the outcome the same."

"Just enough to survive review."

How did we know?

I told him what I'd been hearing about servicemembers reaching out cautiously. When they asked their HIV program managers whether the policy had changed, the answer came back yes — followed by confirmation that nothing substantive had.

"They changed the language, not the result. Non-deployable tags remain. Restrictions stay in place. Press for an explanation, and HIV never appears. Just timing, manning, readiness, 'command discretion.'"

"Would those reasons apply to someone else?"

"No, that's how you know."

He let the silence stretch long enough that I kept going.

I explained how delay works. How postponement replaces denial. Careers don't end with a decision. They erode. Missed schools. Missed deployments. Records that never quite fill out the way they should.

"Time does the work. No one has to say no."

Was that happening to me?

"Not anymore. Not openly."

The pause lingered.

"But it's happening to everyone else," I went on. "Quietly enough that people can convince themselves this is just how the system works."

At some point, the interviews stopped being about the case and started being about the cost. Jordan asked about my career before the lawsuit. About my expectations. About how long I had thought this would take.

He asked about Baraq.

I handed the phone over without thinking about it.

Baraq spoke to him the way he speaks when honesty becomes the only useful option. He dramatized and sanitized nothing. He described the constant low-grade vigilance, how every development carried both hope and dread, how my name slipped into the public domain.

Later, Jordan asked if he could talk to him again. And again.

Only later did I realize how much time Baraq spent on those calls.

Jordan eventually mentioned another servicemember he was speaking with. Someone younger, earlier in his career. Someone who was considering becoming a named plaintiff in the next round of litigation.

Isaiah Wilkins.

At first, Isaiah was peripheral. A contrast. Another data point.

Then Baraq started getting calls from him.

I caught fragments of those conversations without listening. Familiar warnings surfaced — once given to us, now repeated automatically.

The guidance followed a predictable pattern: stay out of the comments, skip online arguments, avoid unrelated positions, and treat every word as something others will pull loose from its context.

One night after a long call, Baraq sat for a while.

"He asked me if it was worth it."

"What did you tell him?"

"That it was."

He didn't sound certain.

I made nothing of it.

I focused on the interview. Getting the details right, explaining what was happening now, and documenting the evasions clearly enough to prevent anyone from misunderstanding them later.

Whatever that conversation had meant to him, or to Baraq, didn't register yet. It passed through the room and out again, unexamined.

* * *

In the weeks that followed, messages started arriving from people I had never met. Some were congratulatory. Some were cautious. Most were brief notes from servicemembers and veterans who had been watching and wanted to say that it mattered.

Most of those messages passed through me the same way everything else did. I acknowledged them, replied when I could, and kept moving.

One didn't.

The call came in the afternoon, from a number I didn't recognize.

I let it ring once before answering.

"Nick Harrison."

A pause on the other end. The brief hesitation of someone deciding whether they'd reached the right person.

"Hi. I got your number through the Modern Military Association of America. I hope that's okay."

"It's fine. What's going on?"

He took a breath and plunged in.

"I'm a lawyer, active duty. A few years ago, I got the diagnosis. Since then, I finished law school, passed the bar, and kept JAG in my sights for as long as I can remember." A pause. "I've been following your case."

I waited.

"There's no stay, so the order's in effect. But when I talked to the specialty branch recruiter, they said there's no guidance yet. They told me to wait until something official comes out."

"And?"

"I talked to a couple of people on your legal team. Same answer. Guidance is probably coming. It just takes time."

Careful. Not naïve, but cautious. Someone is trying very hard not to get this wrong.

"I don't know what I'm supposed to do now."

I leaned back in my chair.

"Where are you?"

"California."

"And you're already serving?"

"Yes."

"Good. That matters."

He waited.

"Here's the thing. If you sit and wait for guidance, you're going to be sitting for a long time."

He exhaled, almost in relief. "That's what I was worried about."

"They're not in a hurry. They don't need to be. As long as recruiters can say they don't know what to do, the system stays comfortable."

"So what am I supposed to do?"

"You don't wait. You insist politely."

A pause.

"I'm not trying to be difficult."

"I know. And you don't have to be."

I said it the way it works, not the way people pretend it does.

"You go back to the recruiter. You acknowledge there's no guidance yet. And then you insist they send the question up."

"What question?"

"That they have an HIV+ servicemember who meets the requirements, wants to apply for JAG, and has been told there's no guidance — but there's also no stay and a court order in effect."

Silence.

"They won't want to do that."

"No. They won't."

"So why would they?"

"Because once they ask, someone above them has to answer. And once someone answers, they can't pretend the order doesn't exist."

He didn't respond immediately.

"They're not ignoring the ruling out of spite. Silence works. Most people hear 'wait,' and they do."

"And if I don't?"

"Then, eventually, someone tells the recruiter what to do. And whatever they say has to comply with the law."

A slow breath.

"So it's not about forcing them."

"No, it's about making them choose."

We sat with that.

"Is this what it's like? Does it always take this much pushing?"

I thought about it.

"Yes. If you want something that disrupts the status quo."

"And if I don't push?"

"Then nothing happens. And no one gets blamed for it."

He paused.

"I wish someone would just tell people this."

I let that pass.

"Okay. I'll do it."

"Good."

"Thank you," he said. "For being honest."

When the call ended, I sat there for a while, phone still in my hand. I realized how little had changed.

The ruling stood. Clarity in the law left no room for doubt.

* * *

After that call, I could no longer pretend the problem was uncertainty. If the ruling was going to matter, it would not be because the military implemented it on its own. It would be because someone with authority insisted that it do so.

That narrowed the field to Congress.

We began talking to staff on the Hill. Language and drafts circulated. There were calls and follow-ups, careful questions about scope and sequencing, polite expressions of interest. This was not improvisation or brinkmanship. It was the ordinary work of seeing whether a judicial win translated into something durable, something that would bind implementation, not just acknowledge principle.

Congresswoman Barbara Lee's office made it clear that they considered this their issue. Her staff knew the history. They had followed the litigation and understood the policy failures. But when we discussed enforcement, the conversation shifted toward committee structure and internal dynamics.

"She's not on the Armed Services Committee. If this is going to stick, it needs to come from committee leadership."

The implication didn't need saying. Within the Democratic caucus, Armed Services functioned as its own ecosystem. Deference mattered. Relationships mattered. If anyone forced implementation, it had to be someone the Department of Defense already recognized as authoritative.

That pointed to Jackie Speier.

"She's senior. And she's trusted."

The logic held. Jurisdiction mattered. Committee leadership mattered. Institutional trust mattered. We drafted the bill accordingly and routed it through her office.

A few weeks later, the draft came back.

A defense fellow in the office had reviewed it. Someone with Pentagon experience, fluent in the language of defense policy and the constraints that shape it. That fluency showed on the page.

What remained barely resembled the original substance.

The enforcement language was gone. So was the timeline. In its place sat a familiar structure: the Department of Defense would conduct a study, report its findings, and issue recommendations afterward.

I read the redlines carefully.

"This does nothing."

A pause on the call. Measured, not defensive.

"It's what they're comfortable with."

"But that's the problem. They're not complying already. A study doesn't change that."

No one disagreed. The silence confirmed that everyone understood the shortcomings and had expected them.

"We can't support this. If it's just a study, it gives them cover without requiring action."

They accepted that without protest. The conversation shifted from substance to logistics.

"We should elevate this to Congresswoman Speier. She should see what her staff sent back. If this is her bill, she should know someone reduced it to something that won't compel compliance."

The response came quickly.

"She will not override her staff."

Reality, not judgment.

"So she never even sees it?"

"There's no point. This is how it works."

I sat with that, letting the implications settle.

"Then you're giving her an out. If implementation stalls and if nothing changes, she can say no one ever brought it to her. That it never reached her desk."

Another pause.

No one contradicted me.

"And if we don't raise it," I went on, "that becomes true. She won't have been involved."

The conversation moved on. There was nothing left to resolve. The bill would not advance. The relationship would remain intact. They would burn no bridges and embarrass no one.

What stayed with me wasn't the decision itself. It was how easily responsibility diffused. Leaders delegated authority downward just far enough that no one at the top had to decide.

* * *

The Modern Military Association of America's Gala took place in the ballroom of the Army–Navy Club in Arlington, a room that signaled seriousness before anyone spoke. High ceilings rose overhead. Warm but restrained lighting settled across the space. Chandeliers hung heavy and symmetrical. Along the walls, flags stood in precise formation. Thick carpeting swallowed sound, muting footsteps and giving even a crowded room the feel of control. Almost everyone was in dress uniform.

Blues and greens dominated the room, rows of ribbons and medals arranged with meticulous care. Senior officers stood easily among political appointees and civilian advocates. Rank softened by the formality of the evening but was never fully erased. Civilians in dark suits and evening dresses moved between tables, careful not to disrupt the visual order. This was not a space built for spontaneity, but reassurance.

Someone guided Baraq and me to our table near the center of the room. The staff had already set place cards. Programs rested at each seat, the evening's agenda printed on heavy paper stock that suggested permanence. Around us, the conversations were low and practiced.

"How long have you been with the organization?"

"Since Andy's tenure."

"Still at the Pentagon?"

"No. I rotated out last year."

Everyone seemed to know where everyone else fit, not just socially, but institutionally.

Jennifer Dane moved through the room with the ease of someone who understood its geometry. The organization's Executive Director stopped at tables, leaned in, touched shoulders lightly, exchanged brief words that sounded personal without ever becoming unguarded. She was doing actual work, sustaining relationships, maintaining trust, and keeping the room aligned.

When she reached our table, she smiled at me.

"I'm really glad you're here. Tonight matters."

"Thank you."

She nodded, then said, almost conversationally, "Change doesn't always come in time to benefit the people who fight for it. That's something we don't say out loud enough."

"I've noticed."

A small, knowing smile. Not defensive, not apologetic. Her hand rested on the back of my chair.

"What you've done is important, regardless of timing."

She did not offer it as consolation. The recognition acknowledged the cost and refused to pretend anyone could recover it. Before I could respond, someone else caught her attention. She excused herself smoothly and moved on, repeating the same pattern at the next table.

Around us, waitstaff moved in quiet synchronization, filling water glasses, placing bread baskets, adjusting silverware that was already perfectly aligned. The room was full now, every table occupied, the hum of conversation steady but contained.

At the table behind us, someone leaned forward and said, "This is a good crowd tonight."

Another voice said, "It always is. You don't get this many uniforms in one room unless everyone's comfortable being here."

That seemed right.

There was no tension in the air. No sense of urgency. They temporarily set aside whatever conflicts existed outside the room. This was a place designed to affirm shared values and to show alignment, requiring no one to test how much those values might cost.

As the lights dimmed slightly and the program prepared to begin, I looked around the ballroom once more. The order, the polish, the careful balance between advocacy and authority. It all felt settled.

Nothing here suggested a demand.

The lights dimmed further, and the murmur of conversation tapered off as the program began. Chairs turned toward the stage. The room adopted the attentive posture it knew well.

Someone introduced Shawn Skelly as the keynote speaker. She walked to the podium carrying notes and clearly reluctant to be there. She wasn't someone who was naturally suited to public appearances, but when she spoke, her voice carried the weight of someone doing what needed to be done.

"Readiness is about people. Talent. Capability. Commitment."

Heads nodded around the ballroom.

"We cannot afford to exclude people who are otherwise fully capable of serving. Not strategically. Not morally."

Applause came reflexively.

"The military should accept anyone capable and willing to serve."

More applause. Louder this time.

I listened to what went unsaid. The remarks avoided implementation, sidestepped the court orders, and left the administrative machinery untouched. The systems that decide who deploys, who advances, and who stalls out. The language stayed elevated, broad enough to unify and abstract enough to avoid friction.

She framed inclusion as a principle. Progress as a trajectory. The military as an institution capable of correcting itself.

"We are stronger when we draw from the full measure of talent willing to step forward."

The room approved. This was the sentence people remembered, repeated, cited.

As she finished, people stood to applaud. The moment was clean and complete. Agreement expressed without obligation incurred.

When the room settled back into its seats, the program moved on.

Someone announced the last award of the evening.

Congresswoman Jackie Speier.

They read her name with care, summarized her career, and praised her advocacy on military issues. The room responded with another round of respectful applause.

The chair beside the podium remained empty.

No one offered an explanation. None was required. She was retiring. Her formal authority was already receding, even if her reputation remained intact. Someone accepted the award on her behalf.

I did not applaud.

Around me, hands came together politely. Acknowledgment without enthusiasm. Applause faded, the program ended, and the lights rose.

Standing there, I felt the convergence of what I had already seen on the Hill. Earlier, her office had declined to press for enforcement. They offered us study language instead. No escalation. No insistence. Now, in a room full of uniforms with people whose careers she once had the power to influence, her presence was no longer necessary.

The recognition proceeded anyway.

It wasn't indifference. It was insulation. The outcome no longer depended on action, only on alignment.

The room accepted this without comment.

Conversations resumed. Chairs scraped softly. People stood, turned, and began moving toward the exits or the next conversation.

I stayed where I was.

Skelly had stepped away from the stage and was now moving through the room, stopping for brief exchanges, accepting thanks, nodding as people repeated lines from her speech back to her.

"Great remarks."

"Really powerful."

"We needed to hear that."

I waited until the space around her thinned.

When I stepped forward and introduced myself, she studied me for a moment, then nodded.

"Yes. I know who you are."

"I wanted to follow up on something you said."

She turned toward me, attentive, already oriented to what came next.

"You said the military should accept anyone capable of serving. That isn't how HIV is being handled right now."

She remained silent.

"The policy language may have changed, but the implementation hasn't. The non-deployable tags are still there. Waivers still get required. Discretion still does the work."

Her expression remained neutral.

"Implementation takes time."

"Time is the mechanism. Delay lets the decision happen with no one having to say no."

A brief silence. One nod.

"Email me. I'll look into it."

She handed me her card, thanked me for coming, and turned as someone else stepped in. The exchange had already closed.

Baraq and I walked toward the exit, past the coat check, and into the cold. Light from the ballroom spilled onto the steps behind us before the doors shut.

"That was disappointing."

No hesitation.

"That's what these dinners do. They're not about forcing change."

I glanced back at the building, flags visible through the glass.

"If the award convinced anyone in that room that the organization has influence," he went on, "and if someone wrote a check because of it, then the night worked exactly as intended."

I stayed quiet.

We walked on in silence.

* * *

The months after the ruling passed without change. Deadlines came and went. Implementation did not begin.

By November, delay had settled into place as a habit. I directly asked Shawn Skelly why nothing was happening and whether I should elevate the issue to Congress.

Her response was brief. She cited "the recently filed lawsuit regarding HIV+ policy" and declined to address the issue.

That was all.

The response contained no reference to the court order, no acknowledgment of the Secretary of Defense's directive, and no distinction between a policy dispute still under debate and an obligation to comply with civilian authority.

A reply went out the same day.

I described the answer as "unfortunate" and noted that versions of it had circulated for the past eight years. Expectations had been higher this time that military leaders might finally respond when specific orders arrived from the Court and the Secretary of Defense, rather than defaulting once again to delay and deferral.

As clearly as possible, I drew the line.

Whether the military intended "to obey the law and respect civilian authority" was one question. Whether it planned to keep fighting over the future accession policy was another matter. Treating those questions as interchangeable was how delay became policy.

What made her response harder to accept was its contrast with what had come before.

Just weeks earlier, standing at the Modern Military Association of America's Gala, she had said that "the military should accept anyone capable and willing to serve." She had spoken about readiness, about talent, about commitment. She said the military "cannot afford to exclude people who are otherwise fully capable of serving."

Those were unambiguous words. The person who ran the office delivered them.

I wrote back that if the military was intent on committing to a fight over accession policy and if the Administration would let that happen, then she and others might need to "reconsider their messaging to certain audiences." Because the gap between what was being said publicly and what was being tolerated privately was growing harder to ignore.

She did not respond.

The silence did what no explanation could. It clarified where restraint had settled among the people with authority to insist.

This was not opposition. It was a decision to say nothing, knowing that silence would be enough.

She spoke as the institution rather than as someone who understood what delay did to the people beneath it. The language stayed careful, the posture professional, and the result was paralysis.

It was easier to sound like everyone else.

And in doing so, the lived experience that justified her presence in that role stopped guiding leadership.

* * *

The article came out in the middle of the day.

I didn't get a heads-up. No "it's live" text, no advance link. I found out the way everyone else did through a notification that landed in my inbox and then started multiplying across my phone.

TIME.

I opened it expecting to see myself. Not out of vanity, just out of momentum. I had spent hours on the phone with Jordan. Long calls that wandered through my childhood, my service, the case, the years of delay, the toll it had taken on my career and my relationship. I had explained things I hadn't explained to anyone else. I had assumed without ever quite articulating it that this was my story being written.

The cover loaded.

Isaiah Wilkins.

For a moment, I thought I had clicked the wrong link.

I scrolled back up. Read the headline again. Looked for my name. It was there, but not where I expected it to be. Context, background, precedent. The case that made this possible.

Not the center.

I sat with that longer than I expected to.

The reporting was solid. Careful. Serious. Isaiah was compelling. He was younger, earlier in his career, still exposed in ways I no longer was. The piece framed him as the present tense of the fight, not its history.

The article moved cleanly on the page.

It just wasn't what I had pictured.

A few minutes later, Jordan messaged me.

He apologized quickly, almost nervously. He said the editor had gone in a different direction. There wasn't as much room for me as he'd thought there would be. He hoped I understood.

I stared at the message for a second before replying.

I told him it was fine. And I meant it mostly.

The irritation was there, faint but real. Not anger or betrayal. Just the strange feeling of having prepared yourself to be seen in one way, only to realize the room has already rearranged itself.

Baraq read the article from the other side of the room. When he looked up, he didn't ask me how I felt.

"They got the story right," he said.

I nodded.

That night, I logged onto Facebook and opened the Modern Military Association of America's Positive Service group. The post took me longer than it should have to write. After pasting the link, I erased what I'd written twice before settling on something simple.

The message made the stakes clear. This mattered, support for Isaiah mattered, and this was how change moved through people willing to step forward while it was still uncomfortable.

I hit post and watched the reactions roll in.

Likes. Comments. Messages of support.

It felt deliberate. Not performative, but intentional.

Later, lying in bed, I thought about how much of myself I had poured into those interviews. How naturally I had assumed that effort translated into ownership. And how quietly that assumption had slipped away.

This, I realized, was what letting go felt like.

Not loss or erasure.

Just when the story no longer needed me to stand in front of it.

*　*　*

By the time my first six-month extension was nearing its end, something had gone unmistakably wrong.

The legal team had been asking for time. More time to decide what to file, more time to coordinate, more time to get it right. I agreed to the extension because it seemed reasonable, and everyone assured me they would use it productively.

But as the deadline approached, nothing moved. No motion, no strategy, no final draft.

When I asked what was happening, I was told Scott had circulated something months earlier. A draft that never became a filing. He admitted other tasks had drawn his focus away. He mentioned a cause he'd been involved in for decades, something about LGBTQ+ people being allowed to donate blood.

I didn't know what to say to that.

The concern wasn't his commitment to the community. It was the fact that, six months after a federal court order, action remained optional and that another extension, rather than a motion, had somehow become the default.

I sent a pointed but not hostile email that asked why no one had filed anything and what they were waiting for.

Then I reached out to several of the lawyers individually. I asked if I could speak with them one-on-one. Quietly. Privately. Client to counsel.

Every one of them refused.

Each response was polite, identical in substance. They would only speak with me together, as a group.

I wasn't being advised anymore. I was being managed.

A few hours later, Scott texted me.

He asked whether I was "trying to single-handedly alienate everyone on my legal team."

It wasn't profane. It wasn't cruel. It might even have been understandable under other circumstances, between friends who had been through years of litigation together.

But he wasn't texting me as a friend.

He was texting me as my lawyer.

I showed the message to Baraq.

He didn't react right away. He read it, then looked up at me.

"That text should answer the question for you."

I didn't respond.

"An attorney has to be detached. That's the value they offer. Once they're emotionally inside it, once they're reacting instead of advising, they've stopped being useful, no matter how much they care."

He was right. And that made it worse.

Scott had been with me through everything. From the earliest filings, through the setbacks, through the ruling. I had always assumed that we would finish this together. That whatever the ending looked like, he would stand next to me when we reached it.

But he was lead counsel.

Six months had passed, and nobody had filed anything. If there was no consensus on what to file, no plan to enforce the judgment, and I was being asked to shoulder another extension, that responsibility was his.

When Scott later told me he wouldn't speak with me privately, that we could address everything on the group call, I felt something settle into place.

I typed a reply telling him he didn't need to be on that call, then stared at the screen for a long time before finally sending it.

It was one of the hardest messages I've ever written.

I wasn't angry when I sent it. I felt utterly drained.

I sat with the phone in my hand after I sent it.

Nothing dramatic followed. No argument or exchange. Just the sudden absence of someone who had been there for years.

Chapter Twenty-Eight

The screen filled in slowly, one square at a time.

Lambda Legal's attorneys appeared together, already mid-thought, as if the meeting had started before I arrived. Peter logged on next, calm and composed the way he always was when things were uncertain. Winston & Strawn followed, a little more staggered, a little less synchronized.

One square never appeared. Scott's.

"Thanks for joining. This meeting follows a change. Last week, I asked Scott to step away from the case. I thanked him for his work and told him that directly, and I won't revisit the decision here."

No one objected or rushed to fill the space.

Scott's absence lingered anyway. It was like a missing note in a chord everyone recognized but no one named.

Peter broke the silence.

"There are two paths forward. The first is a motion to compel compliance with the court's order — not just with the appointment, but with the continued use of waivers, deployability tags, and related practices. It would force the issue."

He chose each word carefully, but the subtext was unmistakable. This was the same fight Scott had always pushed toward. The systemic one. The consequential one.

"This filing wouldn't be modest. It addresses the system."

A few heads nodded. No one interrupted.

John Harding leaned forward.

"I want to describe the other option."

It wasn't the first time he'd spoken on one of these calls. It was the first time no one talked over him.

"This would be a narrower motion. A motion to clarify. We ask the court a specific question: what does compliance with the order require, and when does it occur — specifically regarding Nick?"

He kept his voice level. No posturing or salesmanship. Just the argument laid out cleanly.

"It avoids broader policy adjudication. It doesn't ask the court to supervise Department practices beyond what's necessary to resolve the appointment issue."

The pause that followed stretched longer than the last.

I spoke before anyone else could.

"Let me be clear about something. The issues you're raising matter, Peter. The reason the motion exists makes sense. It always has."

Peter nodded, waiting.

"But that's not a decision I should make anymore."

The room went still.

"I don't know what my future in the military looks like. I don't know what role I'll have. And I don't think it makes sense for me to be the person allowing a broader institutional confrontation at this point."

I didn't apologize or hedge.

"That fight doesn't belong to me now."

The silence that followed wasn't polite.

It was the kind that settles in when a role changes and everyone feels it, but no one knows what replaces it.

Peter looked down, then back up.

"Understood. We'll continue developing the broader filing. We'll keep you informed."

He didn't argue or try to persuade. He just accepted it.

John didn't move right away. When he did, he slid a legal pad closer to the camera, his handwriting already crowding the page.

"For the clarification motion, we can frame it tightly around the appointment language. No policy findings. No supervisory relief. The question is whether the order requires action now."

One of the Winston & Strawn attorneys nodded. Another unmuted.

"That's workable. We can have a draft early next week."

Peter stayed quiet.

John continued, steadier now. Less tentative.

"We'd ask for a defined timeline—or an explicit statement that continued delay is noncompliance. Nothing beyond that."

Someone from Lambda Legal opened their mouth, then closed it again. The moment passed.

I said nothing.

John glanced at me once. Not for permission, just acknowledgment. Then, he kept going.

"If the court wants to go further, it can. We're not asking it to."

I could hear typing, calendar alerts, and people muting and unmuting.

"Alright," someone said. "Next steps?"

John took over the discussion.

* * *

Over the next few weeks, Winston & Strawn went to work.

Drafts circulated. Questions came in about timing, posture, and scope. John flagged the deadline more than once. Not as a threat or leverage, just as a fact that shaped everything else.

The one-year mark mattered.

They treated it that way.

John called again, direct as ever.

"If we're filing anything, it has to be before the one-year mark."

I leaned back in my chair. "April."

"Yes. The judgment came down in April. After a year, the court's ability to do anything meaningful tightens fast. Not impossible, but risky. And unnecessary."

"So this isn't about appeal."

"No. This is about finality. The case hardens if no one files anything. Judges don't like reopening closed matters unless they have to."

"And the extension I signed in July?"

"It bought time. The clock kept running; the extension only delayed the pressure."

I remained silent.

"Moving to clarify before the year is up keeps the court engaged. That step doesn't change the judgment or reopen the case. It asks the judge to say what compliance actually looks like."

"And if we wait?"

No hedging. "Then we're trusting that something else gets filed in time. And if it doesn't, you're the one who bears the risk."

Scott had always talked about the case. John talked about me.

"When can you file?"

"We're ready. I'd prefer not to wait."

"Don't. File it before the window closes."

A brief pause. Not hesitation, just confirmation.

"Alright. We'll move."

Peter called a day or two later.

I took it because I always had.

"Hey. I wanted to check in after the call."

"Sure."

"I want to say this first. I really understand where you are. You've been clear that you need this resolved for your own peace of mind. Staying in this fight keeps you angry. I hear that."

He did. That wasn't performative. Peter had always noticed the toll this was taking.

"I appreciate that."

"There's just one thing I wanted to flag. Scott's concerned that if Winston & Strawn files now, it could distract from the broader submission we're working on."

There it was.

"The thinking is that overlapping filings could split the court's attention. It might be better to sequence them."

He framed it as strategy, not advice, and left the timing unstated.

I held back, avoided argument, resisted pressing for timelines, and let the unanswered questions stand. What drafts existed, and why, after nearly a year, no one had filed anything.

"I hear you."

"That's all I wanted to raise. I felt like I needed to."

"I understand." And I meant it.

We talked for a few minutes longer. About nothing important. We hung up on good terms.

But I didn't pass the message along.

I kept it to myself. Winston & Strawn did not pause. No discussion followed about sequencing or optics.

That conversation hadn't been about my interests.

The email from Winston & Strawn came that night.

Attached: the motion to clarify. Tight. Spare. Focused on the order and the delay.

The body was brief:

"We intend to file before the one-year mark unless you'd like to hold."

I didn't hesitate.

"Please proceed as soon as practicable."

I knew they would notify the rest of the team. Professional courtesy demanded it. There would be no ambush.

But there would also be no more waiting.

Scott had chosen his fight. Peter was carrying it forward.

I wasn't stopping them.

I was just no longer willing to let my future hinge on whether someone else was ready to move.

* * *

The letter was brief. No call preceded it, no email followed, no warning softened it. Only an envelope in the mail.

The letter said that Lambda Legal was withdrawing from the case. It stopped there, offering neither explanation nor rationale, and acknowledging nothing about where things stood. I stood there holding it, the feeling uncomfortably familiar.

The military had written to me like this once before.

Different institution. Same indifference.

Not at the beginning, when the fight was uncertain. Not when the risk was highest or the outcome unclear. But now, when the only thing left unresolved was whether I would ever actually receive relief.

Whether the person whose name had carried the case this far would ever reach the other side of it.

I had fought Scott to keep them involved.

After Lambda Legal fired him, I had insisted they get to stay involved. I believed they should share in what came next. That they had earned a place in whatever resolution followed. That it mattered for them to see it through. Not because I needed them to do more work.

The letter reflected none of that. It asked nothing about where things stood, nothing about what I needed, and offered no acknowledgment that anything remained unresolved for me personally.

What cut deepest wasn't that they were leaving. It was that they were leaving without staying to see what happened to me.

As if the system could declare the case complete while ignoring whether the human being at its center ever received a remedy. As if the victory could exist independently of the person who had carried it.

I had believed that part mattered.

The letter clarified that, for them, it didn't.

I folded it carefully and set it down.

* * *

Winston & Strawn moved to clarify without ceremony.

No press. Just the routine notification lawyers send to others as a matter of professional courtesy.

Just a filing on the docket. Plain, restrained, exactly what John had said it would be. A request for the court to say what compliance meant, and when.

Nothing more.

I checked the docket once.

Then I stopped.

There was nothing to do now but wait.

Less than forty-eight hours later, the email came.

It was late, well past normal business hours. The hour when government buildings are dark, and most inboxes have gone quiet. I almost missed it.

The subject line was short. Administrative. Easy to skim past.

I opened it anyway.

The Army had accessed me for a JAG position at the rank of First Lieutenant.

They had acted on the application. But they had not considered appointing me as captain as promised in 2014, nor had they responded to my request for a Special Selection Board.

I read it again.

Slower this time.

There it was, clear and unqualified. No ambiguity, no conditional language. Only confirmation that they had finally officially accessed me for a commission. This was what I had been waiting for. Everyone said it took time. It arrived almost immediately after someone finally put a question on the record.

Recognition came first. I sat with it for a moment and let the timing speak for itself.

Years, patience, and faith in the process never moved it. A single filing that made continued inaction harder to justify did.

I forwarded the email.

First to John.

Then to Peter.

I hesitated before closing the window. One name was missing. Scott should have been part of this.

But that wasn't where things were anymore.

My phone buzzed with quick messages, congratulations, exclamation points. I acknowledged a few. I ignored most.

385

Pressure mattered. Filing mattered. Doing anything mattered.

John called not long after.

He didn't bother to hide the satisfaction. "That answers our question."

"It does."

"With that development, the motion's moot. I can withdraw it if you're comfortable."

"Yes, go ahead."

"I'll file something short. Just noting that the Army has acted to resolve the issue."

"Thank you."

After we hung up, I sat back and traced the distance behind me. Months of pushing for someone to force a decision, months where nothing moved, energy poured into patience and process and inevitability. I had been told to wait so often that it blurred together. Then, once waiting disappeared as an option, everything ended almost at once.

Not after some sweeping resolution or years of additional litigation.

But after a narrow filing that made it harder to keep doing nothing.

* * *

Scott texted me a few days after the accessions email.

"I heard the Army accessed you. I'm honestly sad you didn't tell me. Congratulations, Nick."

I stared at the message longer than I should have.

The text omitted the months I had spent asking him to file something just to force a decision. It ignored the fact that the Army moved less than forty-eight hours after Winston & Strawn finally put a motion on the docket.

No acknowledgment of the delay. No concession that waiting had been a mistake.

Only the grievance that I hadn't shared the news.

A little later, another message came through with an attachment.

"We've moved to compel. The court set the argument for next week. Here's the brief."

I opened the document and read it carefully. The work was solid, as it always had been. It was written in Scott's familiar style, ambitious and systemic, aimed at the right injustice, even if it came too late to change what mattered for me.

I knew exactly what awaited on the other side and went anyway. In full dress uniform, I sat in the gallery while Scott and Peter stood at the counsel table. Judge Brinkema took the bench, already reading. She was flipping pages, pen in hand.

Scott began.

"Your Honor, despite the Court's ruling, servicemembers living with HIV are still being required to get waivers. Those waivers are discretionary, and they're still being denied. People are still being excluded."

The judge looked up.

"The Secretary of Defense has issued guidance implementing this Court's order."

"Yes, Your Honor. But what we're seeing is uneven implementation across the services and individual commands."

Peter stepped in.

"The policy has changed on paper. But it is not being implemented."

The judge turned to the government.

"Is that accurate?"

The Department of Justice attorney rose.

"Your Honor, the Department of Defense is complying with the order. The Secretary issued guidance. Waivers are being used in an individualized process."

A pause.

"So the guidance exists," the judge said, "but not all commands are following it yet."

"That's correct. Implementation takes time."

She nodded once, then leaned forward slightly.

"What concerns me is whether some commanders are treating this as optional."

The room remained quiet.

"I've seen reports. A mail handler was removed from a school. Individuals were delayed or sidelined. That troubles me."

Her gaze was fixed on the government table.

"This Court's order was not a suggestion."

"Understood, Your Honor."

She turned back to Scott and Peter.

"I am not prepared to rule that reliance on waivers alone amounts to noncompliance. The Secretary has issued the guidance I ordered."

Scott remained silent.

"But, I am very concerned that the military is not falling into line."

She let the silence do its work.

"I expect that concern to be addressed. And I expect this message to be carried back."

Then, quietly.

"I deny the motion."

That was it.

Scott gathered his papers. Peter nodded once. The government attorneys packed up without expression.

I stayed seated for a moment longer.

Because I knew what they hadn't said.

No one had explained what a waiver was. That it's permission, that the Army could deny without explanation, that discretion is the point.

The court had ruled that the military may no longer exclude someone solely for being HIV+ and undetectable.

The waiver system put that discretion right back, quietly enough to look like compliance.

* * *

They had accessed me, but the rest of the machinery stayed frozen. No Special Selection Board followed, and no one acknowledged the request submitted with the application.

The Army had asked me to repackage the packet. They wanted me to change the rank I was applying for, to strip it of anything that made it unusual, to make it look like every other submission moving through the system. A clean, "blind" review.

I understood what they were doing.

They wanted to say that this wasn't a reconsideration. That the court did not compel them. That the policy had simply changed, and I was applying under a framework they had always intended to adopt.

I also understood something else.

The moment I submitted the request for a Special Selection Board, the clock started.

So, I marked the date and waited.

Ninety days passed, and the system answered with silence. No response, no denial, not even an acknowledgment that it existed.

That silence mattered. It meant the issue was ripe, not because I was impatient, but because the system had done what it always does when it hopes something will simply fade.

It was time to raise it.

So I called Peter.

"I'm going to file on the Special Selection Board issue. In court."

A pause on the line. Calculation, not hesitation.

"So this is the part where you don't want me to withdraw, but you need me to, anyway."

"That's exactly it."

"If you file, everyone has to be out of the way."

"I know."

He offered no argument, did not dissuade me, and gave no warning about risk.

"Alright. I'll make it clean. No fuss."

"Thank you."

"You started this alone. It makes sense you'd have to finish it alone."

Peter stayed until the rules required him to step aside.

And then the field cleared.

One by one, the lawyers called. Polite, professional, brief. Each letting me know they were filing their withdrawals at my request. No drama. No commentary. Just the mechanics of clearing the docket.

When it was done, I looked once.

No counsel listed. No buffer. Just my name.

I had begun this fight on my own, before anyone believed it would go anywhere.

Now I was bringing it to a close in the same way.

***

I walked into the courtroom alone.

I wasn't nervous or rushed, just quiet in a way I hadn't been in years.

I took my seat at the counsel table and set my papers down. A moment later, Judge Brinkema entered, glanced up at the room, then back down at the tables in front of her.

Her eyes paused.

She looked at me. Then at the man seated a few chairs away.

"Who is this sitting with you?"

Peter stood, along with the attorney he had affiliated with locally.

"Your Honor, we represent the Modern Military Association of America. We're not here as counsel for Lieutenant Harrison. We're present only in case the Court has questions."

Judge Brinkema studied them for a beat, then nodded once.

"Alright. Let's proceed."

She didn't wait for me to speak.

Her attention shifted immediately to the government.

"When you were here last time, I strongly urged you to resolve this case. You didn't, and I'm extremely disappointed."

Her tone sharpened.

"I need an explanation for why it took over a year to reach a commissioning decision after this Court made it crystal clear that the government was required to reevaluate his original application. That specific one."

The government attorney shifted.

She didn't give him time to settle.

"I'm frankly shocked that during the pendency of this litigation, there wasn't some form of litigation hold. The Army lost his application, and yet the Army held everything against him."

She paused.

"That delay was not reasonable. And the argument that he suffered no damage from it is simply not accurate."

The government tried to speak.

She cut him off.

"And let's talk about timing. As I understand the record, it was approximately forty-eight hours after his counsel moved for clarification that the Army notified him of his commission."

Her gaze was fixed on the government table.

"I wonder whether that would have happened if he had not filed the motion. Because it does not look good."

Then she turned to me.

She asked me to walk through what had happened since her last order. The delay, the accession, and what had not moved.

I answered plainly.

"I know you can't order a retroactive commission. And I know you can't order a promotion."

She nodded.

"But I'm going before administrative boards. The Army Board for Correction of Military Records. Possibly a Special Selection Board."

I paused.

"Those are rooms full of soldiers. They swear the same oath I do."

Then I spoke the words I had come to deliver.

"If you can say on the record what you've already found, that the policy was unconstitutional, that I deserve redress even if it's not your role to grant it. That matters. Because when a JAG officer stands up in those rooms and says this order doesn't mean that, it matters for you to say it really does."

She listened closely.

When the government responded, she stopped them mid-sentence.

"You understand how devastating it is to the Army's position that you did commission him."

She leaned forward.

"But for the improper use of his HIV status, the Army would have commissioned him years ago. The evidence now shows he was qualified. That creates a real problem when we ask what his career would have looked like absent that unconstitutional policy."

The government hesitated.

She noticed.

"You're struggling. And that tells me something."

Then she asked what no one else in the room had been willing to ask.

"If I were to enjoin the Army from instituting any proceeding that would involuntarily separate him so that he has time to pursue the relief he's now eligible to seek. Do you see a problem with that?"

The government tried to hedge. Regulations. Processes.

She stopped him again.

"I'm going to put the injunction in place. Out of an abundance of caution. Because, frankly, there is an unfortunate aroma here of a reluctance to comply aggressively with the Court's order."

She turned back to me.

"I can't give you a Special Selection Board. I looked it up, and you must have a federally recognized commission before you can apply for that. The military is right about that. But you can go back to the Army Board for Correction of Military Records, and then you can apply for one. And I can protect you while you seek it."

Then she did what I had asked, placing the truth on the record. Finding the policy unconstitutional, recognizing my outstanding record, acknowledging that the use of my HIV status had held me back, and urging the Army to give serious consideration to making me whole.

She denied part of my motion and granted the rest.

And she enjoined the Army from taking any action against me while I pursued relief through the administrative process.

"That's my ruling. We'll recess."

I stayed seated as the room emptied.

A few days later, the written order was issued.

This time, the language mattered.

She urged the Army to give very serious consideration to any request I refiled for retroactive appointment and promotion. She noted I had been fully qualified and denied advancement for years.

And then she said it, not as praise or consolation, but as a finding.

"This officer has provided a great service to the Army, not just through his years of military service, which included two tours overseas, but by courageously fighting in court to correct an outdated, unconstitutional policy that needed to be abandoned."

She could not order a promotion, and she could not convene a Special Selection Board.

But she did what she could.

Chapter Twenty-Nine

The federal recognition board convened only a few days after the hearing. Close enough that I still felt like I was carrying everything with me: the courtroom, the waiting, the years of holding my tongue while the system ground forward inch by inch. I put on my full dress uniform the same way I always had, slow and deliberate and exact. Not out of nerves, but because this was how I had learned to show respect, even when the institution hadn't always returned it.

Three officers sat behind the table, all men. A colonel in the center, with a major and a lieutenant colonel on either side. I recognized one of them as a Judge Advocate at the National Guard Bureau. The room held no ceremony, no audience. Just a table, a packet, and a record.

"State your full name and rank for the record."

I came to attention. "Nick Harrison, Sergeant."

They worked through my service history first, where I'd served, what I'd done, and the roles I'd held. The process felt straightforward, almost routine. Then the major shifted the focus.

"Why do you want to be a Judge Advocate?"

I paused.

"When I first thought about becoming a JAG officer, it grew out of what I'd seen as an enlisted soldier. I'd served under good officers and bad ones, but what stayed with me was the role JAG officers played when the chain of command failed. They were the only place soldiers could turn when the system stopped working the way it was supposed to."

The colonel nodded slightly.

"I've spent most of my career stepping into gaps, taking responsibility for things that weren't technically mine because someone had to. That's what leadership does. It absorbs pressure so it doesn't roll downhill."

I paused long enough to let the thought settle.

"I learned that lesson from an NCO I didn't particularly like. He wasn't easy or warm, but he understood something important. When the new uniforms came in, he made sure every soldier had theirs before he took one for himself. He wore an old, worn set long after he didn't have to."

I kept my eyes forward.

"He didn't do it for recognition. He did it because he could afford to wait, and others couldn't. That stuck with me."

"That instinct of taking the weight when you're able, that's why I wanted to be a JAG officer. It's the same responsibility, just expressed through the law instead of rank."

The lieutenant colonel glanced down at my packet.

"And the litigation?"

"I didn't go looking for a fight. But once it became clear the system would not correct itself, I could carry it. Other people couldn't. They were just trying to stay invisible."

"I stayed because I could. And because walking away would have left the burden exactly where it already was."

The major's eyes moved to my ribbon rack.

"You're wearing an Air Force Achievement Medal. Can you tell us about that?"

"Yes, sir. That came from a joint July Fourth mission with Air National Guard personnel."

I described the work plainly: coordination, long hours, doing what needed doing without drawing attention to yourself. The award had come as a surprise; I learned about it later.

The colonel nodded.

"That usually means you were doing the right thing when you didn't realize anyone was watching."

"Yes, sir. That's how I've always understood it. You hold the standard regardless of whether anyone sees it."

The JAG officer held my gaze for a moment.

The remaining questions stayed procedural: expectations, obligations, nothing adversarial, nothing performative.

When it ended, the colonel closed the folder.

"Thank you, Sergeant. The board will notify you of its decision."

"Yes, sir."

I saluted. They returned it.

A few days later, the notification came by email. Brief and administrative. The federal recognition board had approved my appointment.

After that, the system caught up. Orders appeared in my iPERMS. My status was updated.

* * *

A few days after the orders quietly populated into the system, I found myself with space again, just enough to look outward instead of down. I reached out to Kevin Jennings to ask if we could talk. Not confrontational. Not accusatory. Just unfinished business. We put something on the calendar.

Around the same time, Isaiah Wilkins texted. He was coming into town and asked if we wanted to grab brunch. The casualness struck me, how something that felt momentous to me could arrive wrapped in something ordinary.

We met at a restaurant in Foggy Bottom. Late morning, busy but not frantic. Conversations blended into the background noise unless you were paying attention.

Isaiah was already there with his partner when Baraq and I arrived. Introductions were brief and familiar. We slid into the booth, menus half-ignored.

"How are you holding up?"

Isaiah shrugged. "Some days are better than others."

"That's honest," Baraq said.

A small smile, then a glance toward his partner. "They're managing me pretty tightly. The legal team."

"In what way?"

"What I say. When I say it. Who I talk to. When I don't." A pause. "It's strange being the center of something with so little control over it."

His partner leaned in slightly. "You're the face. Someone else decides the angles."

Baraq nodded. "That tracks."

"It was different for me," I said. "I didn't come to them quietly. I was already out there with Congress, the media. They weren't shaping me so much as trying to keep up."

Isaiah considered that. "Yeah. I can see that."

His partner looked over. "How did you handle it?"

I glanced at Baraq. "I didn't do it alone."

"Someone has to be the bad guy. The plaintiff can't afford to be."

"That's exactly it," Isaiah said. "He's the one who pushes back. I get to stay presentable."

"That's not nothing," Baraq said. "It protects you."

We talked for a while about logistics, media requests, timelines, and the odd experience of becoming symbolic before you feel ready for it. Then Isaiah went quiet. Not withdrawn, but deciding.

"There's something else. Something I've never explained before."

He took a sip of his coffee and set the mug down carefully.

"When I was at West Point, after they gave me my diagnosis, everything moved quickly. Quietly. I was told I was being separated."

His partner's hand rested flat on the table.

"Before I left, they asked if I wanted to talk to the Commanding General. I assumed it was courtesy. Or procedure. Some kind of exit interview conversation."

A shake of the head.

"It wasn't."

He described the meeting without embellishment, the office, the setting, and the General's manner. No anger or defensiveness. Just certainty.

"He told me the courts could say whatever they wanted, and that they were the military."

Silence settled.

"And that they would do whatever they believed protecting the nation required."

No one interrupted him.

"He didn't say it like a threat. He said it as a fact. Like this was the natural order of things."

The table went quiet in the way it does when everyone understands exactly what was just said.

That line about the courts saying whatever they want didn't sound abstract coming from Isaiah. It sounded institutional. The belief that requires no defense because the institution has already absorbed it.

Not about a single lawsuit or policy, but about where civilian authority stops, and military judgment takes over.

I had heard versions of it before, softened and indirect. Institutions dress deference up as professionalism. Leaders sell delay as prudence. Silence becomes respect for the chain of command. What Isaiah described stripped those justifications away.

This was the end state of deference. A separate moral universe. A system so accustomed to being trusted that it no longer recognized limits, so insulated that it mistook independence for immunity.

When an institution comes to believe that compliance with civilian authority is optional rather than foundational, it stops being accountable. It becomes self-justifying. When that belief hardens, it doesn't just endanger the people caught inside it. It endangers the democracy that depends on it remaining subordinate.

"And after that?"

"I left West Point. Not long after."

No one rushed to fill the silence.

"That's the part people don't say out loud. Because once you do, you can't pretend the delays, the deference, and the silence are accidental. They're structural. Protective. Deliberate."

A nod from Isaiah. "That's why I wanted you to hear it."

His partner asked. "What do you do with something like that?"

I waited.

"You name it. You carry it into rooms where it was never supposed to be spoken. And you make it harder for the next person to be told that civilian authority stops at the gate."

A slow breath from Isaiah. "That's what this feels like. Passing something forward."

We finished brunch without ceremony. No conclusions or resolution..

* * *

We scheduled the call a few days later. Kevin Jennings and Lambda Legal's legal director. No formal agenda. Just a conversation we hadn't quite finished yet.

Kevin opened warmly. Familiar. Careful, but not guarded.

"I'm really glad we're talking. I know things got awkward at the end."

"They did." Not sharp. Just factual.

The legal director came in next. "I want to say up front that we didn't step away because we stopped believing in the case."

"I know. That part was never in question."

A brief pause, then Kevin again. "So tell us how it landed."

I took a moment.

"It felt abrupt. Especially after the ruling, when the work shifted from winning to making sure the decision actually meant something."

"That's fair."

"The staffing issues make sense. Scott wasn't easy to work with. None of that is in dispute. What landed harder was the lack of a real handoff. It felt like the relationship simply stopped."

"We could have handled that better."

The moment stretched.

"I want to be clear about something. None of this changes the fact that this commission would never have happened without Lambda Legal. The Army had already said no. Every administrative path had closed. Litigation was the only door left."

Neither disagreed.

"And whatever friction there was at the end doesn't erase that."

Kevin exhaled. "I appreciate you saying that."

I shifted slightly in my chair.

401

"There's one more thing. When the commissioning ceremony happens, I'd like you to be there."

"Of course. I'd be happy to attend."

"I was also hoping you'd take part in the pinning at the ceremony."

A brief pause. Not awkward, just unexpected.

"Oh. I didn't realize that was part of it."

"It is."

"Well, yes. I'd be happy to do that."

The legal director spoke up. "That's very kind of you."

"It's appropriate. Lambda Legal has been more instrumental in making this happen than anyone."

A light laugh from Kevin. "You'll need to tell me what to do."

That was enough to break the remaining tension.

When it ended, no one demanded apologies or tallied grievances.

The ceremony was coming.

And I knew who needed to be there.

* * *

Once I figured out when JAG school actually began, the timeline snapped into focus. I had only a handful of drills left before I would have to leave. If the commissioning was going to happen, it couldn't be someday. It had to be soon.

"Three weeks," I said out loud, scrolling through the dates again. "Maybe four, if everything lines up."

From the other side of the table, Baraq looked over. "So this isn't a slow roll."

"No. This is a now-or-never problem."

The Chief of the National Guard planned to be at the DC Armory around the same time. Staff had already claimed spaces. Rooms vanished from the calendar. Assumptions had no place here, so I started making calls.

"I need the Ceremonial Room." More than once. "Yes, I know it's a busy week. No, there isn't flexibility on the date."

After a mix of polite insistence and careful persistence, everything locked in. I checked with the Commanding General's office to confirm protocol and ensure no one could claim the event lacked coordination.

With the logistics taking shape, the harder question emerged about who would stand with me.

This wasn't about tradition but about the truth.

For the oath, I called Donald Cravins, who was now a major and had recently been appointed as an Under Secretary of Commerce in the Biden Administration.

"I know this is a big request, but I'd like you to administer the oath."

No hesitation. Years earlier, he had facilitated the meeting with the Human Rights Campaign that marked the turning point, making me a named plaintiff at all. Without that moment, none of this would have followed. He understood exactly why I was asking.

For the Master of Ceremonies, I reached out to Joshua Fontanez, Chair of the Board for the Modern Military Association of America.

"The organization stood with us when many people wouldn't. I want that visible."

Kevin Jennings would pin my rank, and we were coordinating through his staff about timing, press, and logistics. Kevin agreed without hesitation.

It wasn't until later, when his staff walked him through how the ceremony actually worked, that the significance of the role landed for him.

Typically, the person who pins a new officer's rank is someone who has had the most impact, been the most supportive, someone you couldn't have done it without. Most of the time, it's a parent or a spouse. For me, that meant Lambda Legal and Baraq.

When Kevin realized that, the invitation took on a different weight. I hadn't framed it that way when I asked. I hadn't needed to.

After that, the remaining pieces fell into place quickly.

Friends from the community stepped in to cater the event. A photographer volunteered to document the ceremony, and I worked with the *Washington Blade*, an LGBTQ+ news outlet, to make sure the moment wouldn't disappear unnoticed.

My phone barely stopped ringing. Emails stacked up. Calendars shifted. Each decision was small on its own, but together they formed something unmistakable.

This wasn't just the first thing I would plan as an officer. I shaped how people understood change for the first time, and I did it deliberately.

The Army still hadn't implemented the court order. There was no guidance. No announcement. No outward acknowledgment that anything had shifted. From the outside, the ruling could still look theoretical, something that existed on paper but hadn't altered reality.

Silence was doing a lot of work.

By then, I understood the dynamic well enough. When no one spoke, and no one acted in the open, the institution could assume nothing had really changed, that it had absorbed the loss and carried on as before. So the ceremony couldn't be private.

This wasn't about celebration but about normalization.

Once people saw it, an HIV+ servicemember standing in uniform, being sworn in, being pinned, the question stopped being whether it could happen and became how it would happen next. Commanders wouldn't wait for guidance that hadn't arrived. Servicemembers wouldn't accept that the answer was still no.

That was why the advocacy organizations had to stand at the center, not symbolically, but openly. They carried the case after every other door closed. If the military refused to acknowledge the pressure that compelled change, the ceremony would do it instead.

Once the change became visible, no one could reverse it.

* * *

By the morning of the ceremony, I was already running late. I'd been up too late the night before, changing the script, reprinting briefing packets, checking and rechecking details. I dressed quickly, loaded myself down with binders and folders, and called an Uber to the DC Armory. Baraq and his mother would follow later with the rest.

When I walked through the front doors, Major Lejuan Strickland was waiting. He was my commander at Joint Force Headquarters, and he had served with me years ago when I was in the military police company. He smiled a smile that instantly lowers your blood pressure.

"Relax. We've got this."

Downstairs, in the Ceremonial Room, I handed him the VIP briefing packet. The color-coded tabbed binder contained a full nine-page operations order, a five-page run of show script, maps and satellite imagery, and detailed logistics coordination. He flipped through it, nodding as he went, clearly impressed by the level of organization.

"This is the most organized commissioning ceremony that I've ever been part of."

That didn't mean everything went smoothly.

Building security never responded about guest access or parking. The Public Affairs Office insisted on routing all communications through its office. At one point, Major Strickland returned with a careful message outlining concerns others had flagged about logos, materials, and visibility. The resistance was unmistakable. Some people would have preferred this to stay smaller, quieter, and easier to pass over.

He relayed the concerns, then paused.

"You should do what you think is right. And tell me how I can help."

That was enough.

While we waited to rehearse, I wrote thank-you notes, one for each person taking part in the ceremony.

Outside the room, I set up the visual display I'd planned with posters showing short profiles of the people involved, bordered with words like Justice, Service, and Honor. It took about thirty minutes. When I stepped away briefly to greet Baraq and his mother, I came back to find the wall bare. Someone had taken it down, muttering something about building policy.

I was furious, but there was no time.

Baraq looked at the empty wall, then at me.

"Let's use the tables. Inside."

If the wall was off-limits, we'd make the display inside the room.

So we moved everything into the room.

By then, the guests were arriving. Familiar faces. Supportive faces. People who understood what this moment represented, even if the institution still treated it like any other ceremony. The room filled, the noise softened, and when Captain Fontanez called everyone to their seats, a calm settled in.

Major Strickland and I entered as the official party. We stood during the National Anthem. For the invocation. The weight of it hit me then, not as drama, but as gravity.

Major Strickland welcomed everyone. Captain Fontanez walked through the customs and traditions, explaining what a commissioning ceremony signifies and why it matters. Then it was time.

Major Cravins stepped forward to administer the Oath of Office. I repeated the words, feeling their weight in a way I hadn't expected, not as aspiration, but as obligation.

Then Baraq and Kevin Jennings joined me on stage. Captain Fontanez read the appointment orders. They reached for the rank insignia. Baraq fumbled slightly, his hands uncooperative in the moment. Kevin leaned in and said with perfect timing, "It's harder than it looks."

The room laughed. The tension broke. Then the insignia was in place.

An NCO stepped forward and rendered the first salute. I returned it.

Just like that, I was First Lieutenant Harrison.

When I stepped up to the podium, I kept the prepared remarks in front of me. I had written them out because so many parties were involved in making this happen, and I wanted to get the words exactly right. I never read from a script, but this time I did. I spoke to the room, to the people who had carried this with me.

The remarks focused on why the ceremony didn't center on me, but on honoring the network that made it possible. The people standing beside me represented entire communities of effort and persistence. I acknowledged the case as well, not as a victory lap, but as a turning point forced into existence by advocacy and resolve.

Eventually, the moment arrived when there was nothing more to say.

Rather than summarize the journey or catalogue what it had taken to get there, I asked the only question that mattered.

"So, what comes next? We continue to strive, to learn, to adapt. We respectfully challenge what we know to be wrong, and we do so with dignity and grace. We work tirelessly towards becoming a military institution that fully represents the diverse nation we serve. And, we never cease in our quest to ensure that the institution we are part of is one that is truly accepting of us all."

Afterword

I did not set out to write this book. I also did not set out to occupy the place in which I wrote it.

Over the course of these events, I found myself at an unusual intersection. I was at once a servicemember and a lawyer, a named plaintiff and an advocate, an insider within military institutions and an outsider challenging their assumptions. I moved through spaces that rarely overlap. Courtrooms and command offices. Policy discussions and personal consequences. Public scrutiny and private doubt.

Most people encounter these systems from one side at a time. Activists see the pressure points but not the internal logic. Lawyers see the record but not the lived cost. Officers see the mission but not always the machinery behind the policy. Public figures see the headlines while lobbyists see the leverage. Rarely do those perspectives converge in a single moment, within a single unfolding conflict.

I was there when they did.

My experience isn't universal, and my perspective isn't definitive. I simply stood close enough to watch institutions under strain. How leaders defer decisions. How organizations fragment responsibility. How process obscures consequence. How individuals inside large systems choose whether to act with clarity.

What struck me was not malice, but how easily systems avoid correction once they govern themselves.

This book does not tell you what to think about any of this. It does not aim to instruct, persuade, or resolve. Instead, it records what it felt like to stand at the center of that, to experience the collision between principle and procedure, between stated values and lived reality.

What I hope stays with you after reading is not a conclusion, but what it feels like to go through these systems as they operate, not as people describe them.

I leave what comes next to you.

www.ingramcontent.com/pod-product-compliance
Lightning Source LLC
LaVergne TN
LVHW010146070526
838199LV00062B/4276